This book is to be returned on or before
the last date stamped below.

12. MAR. 1987

30. APR. 1987

28 5 87

16 NOV 89

20 FEB 1990

- 4 MAY 1990

17 JAN 1992

11 DEC 1992

18 SEP 1998 A

25 JAN 1999 A

16 NOV 2001

28 OCT 2004

11 NOV 2004

25 NOV 2004

301. 54 SHA

The
HOMES
and
HOMELESS
of
POST-WAR BRITAIN

The
HOMES
and
HOMELESS
of
POST-WAR BRITAIN

by

Frederick Shaw MA FIEHO

The Parthenon Press

Published by The Parthenon Press Ltd.,
Casterton Hall,
Carnforth, Lancashire, UK.

ISBN 1 85070 104 0

Printed in Great Britain

CONTENTS

FOREWORD

After clean water and an adequate supply of wholesome food, a satisfactory house is man's most vital need. How one nation tackled the problem of providing for that need is lucidly illustrated in Mr. Shaw's book. The successes, the failures; the advances, the reverses; the well designed homes and the constructional disasters are reported upon with equal clarity in what I am sure will be regarded increasingly as an important social history of this aspect of life in Britain in the post-war period. There is no ideal house any more than there is an ideal housing policy; every county and every local authority district is different; there are expanding towns and contracting towns, new towns and old towns, congested towns and very rural districts; districts with a preponderance of the elderly, the unemployed, the rich or the young.

These variations together with changing economic conditions, social factors and public expectations make it necessary to review policies frequently. Since the end of the war there has been in Britain a Housing Act of one sort or another about every second year as governments have tried to meet the challenge of providing a satisfactory home for everyone. As an environmental health officer Frederick Shaw has not only had to implement those statutes but has had the opportunity to visit very many homes to see for himself the conditions under which people live. As an adviser to various organisations and committees he has been able to draw on many interesting reports.

Anyone remotely concerned in housing policy, construction or the history of post-war Britain will find this comprehensive volume a source of interest, information and pleasure. Anyone involved in planning the future will find it a remarkable commentary from which to learn the lessons of the past.

Roy Emerson, F.I.E.H., F.R.S.H., F.I.H.
President, The Institution of Environmental Health Officers

PREFACE

During World War II the British people were united in two resolves: to win the war and thereafter to build a new society in which there would never again in Britain be the mass unemployment and the absolute poverty which had existed during the 1930s. The end of the war seemed to be a splendid time for a new beginning, a new birth.

In the General Election held in July 1945 the Labour Party, which never before had won a working majority in the House of Commons, was swept on a flood tide into power, winning 392 of the 620 seats. The Labour Party itself was surprised and unprepared for the victory. The Conservatives had ruled Britain for almost the whole of the inter-war period and therefore were associated in the minds of the electorate with mass unemployment and social injustice, and in consequence, it seemed, were unlikely to make the social changes so earnestly desired by the mass of the people. This was in spite of the reconstruction programme prepared by the wartime coalition Government in which the Conservatives were in the majority.

The new Government was faced with two main sets of problems: getting Britain back to a leading industrial and commercial role in the world, and creating a new comprehensive system of social services. The first set of problems was economic, and unless solved it would be difficult, or even impossible, to achieve the set of social aims. However, the Government decided to tackle both sets of problems simultaneously.

The social aims included the creation of comprehensive health and social services, improved provisions for secondary and higher education which had been included in the Education Act 1944 passed by the wartime coalition Government, and the provision of a satisfactory home for everyone who wanted one. This book is concerned exclusively with the last aim – the provision of satisfactory homes. However, it is not restricted to the provision of homes for families but deals also with, for example, homes for the elderly who are unable to look after themselves, homes for the physically handicapped and children who are in the care of the community, the housing problems of ethnic minorities and finally with those who are homeless.

The first chapter deals with matters which at first sight might seem to be irrelevant to the rest of the book but they are included to explain some of the economic and social conditions which existed in Britain after six years of war, and the foundations on which the country had to begin to build a new social structure. For example, during the war families and whole neighbourhoods had been dispersed, the number of households and potential households had increased, but virtually no new houses had been built and very little maintenance had been carried out to the existing stock of houses. In the country as a whole three and a half million houses had received war damage of varying degrees. Britain's industry had been run down and much of the plant was obsolete. There was an acute shortage of many kinds of materials and Britain had lost much of her overseas investments and was heavily in debt. But all that was thirty-five years ago and since then much has happened in Britain, including several changes in Government. However, the conditions which existed in 1945 make a good beginning for an examination of the changes which have occurred in British housing since the end of World War II.

This book does not attempt to analyse complicated statistical data about housing shortages, etc., but it does give a great deal of statistical information, obtained from many sources, about, for example, the numbers of dwellings built, the numbers improved, and the numbers of slums during the period. It is not a text book on housing law but it does explain the changes that have been made in the laws relating to housing since 1945, sometimes quoting the law itself, and, what is more important, in many cases it gives the reasons for the changes. It attempts to present a general picture of how housing needs and the measures designed to deal with them have changed during the period.

In writing the book I have to a great extent drawn on experience gained during many years in local government, but perhaps the illustrations speak more clearly than the printed word.

Chapter 1

IMPACT AND AFTERMATH OF THE WAR

The housing standards of any society, at any point in time are a product of economic, technological, social, political and historical factors. They reflect the stage of economic, social and political development of the society. Each epoch can be characterised by its social problems and the way it sets about solving them, but it cannot be viewed in isolation because the present is in a degree dependent on the past. For example, in 1953 out of a stock of about thirteen million houses in Great Britain two and a quarter million were a hundred years old or more, a further one and three-quarter million were about 75 years old and there were three-quarter million which were about 65 years old. These four and three-quarter million homes, 35 per cent of the total housing stock, had been built to meet the needs of bygone ages and not those which existed at the end of the Second World War.

When in 1938-39 war seemed imminent many people anticipated that it would mean an immediate aerial bombardment of London and other big towns, with hundreds of thousands of casualties and vast uncontrollable mobs fleeing in terror. This did not happen, though there was a movement of population away from the big towns, a movement which was partly planned and partly unplanned. The first dispersal of the population came with the outbreak of war. Reservists of various kinds were called up to the Armed Services, mothers and children were evacuated and so were many offices of different kinds with their staffs. By the middle of 1940 the Armed Forces had enlisted two and a quarter million men, nearly 15 per cent of the male working population. By the middle of 1944, the figure had been doubled; that is four and a half million men, or 30 per cent of the male working population, were in the Armed Services. Very few of these men were stationed near enough to their homes to be able to pay frequent visits and thus give help in times of trouble. The men serving abroad were especially inaccessible to their families, often for long periods. By the end of 1945 at least a quarter of a million Army men had served abroad during the war for continuous periods of five years or more. The mobilisation of the Armed Services was an important factor in the dispersal of families.

Many civilian families were also separated from their homes. Munition workers had to move to areas where big new factories had been established and some office workers were evacuated from London and a few other big towns. Although during the war the Government built a small number of houses near the munition factories, only an unknown proportion of the married male civilian workers who had to move found temporary homes for their families near their work; the others had to leave their families behind.

The operation of the Government evacuation scheme for mothers and young children coincided with the outbreak of war in September 1939. One and a half million children and many mothers were evacuated from danger areas to safer places, e.g. to rural areas and small towns some distance from the large industrial centres. Within a few months most of the evacuees had returned to their homes because the expected bombing had not taken place. However, in the late summer of 1940 the long-expected air attacks began and large numbers of mothers and children again left the danger zones for safer areas. Some made their own arrangements, others used the official scheme. The householders with whom the evacuees stayed were paid by the Government five shillings (25p) per week for the mother, and three shillings (15p) for each child. A great many people left London, including many who had returned after the first departure in 1939; and thousands of Londoners slept in the Underground stations. From some provincial towns, those who could moved into the country each night, sometimes, when the weather permitted, sleeping in tents or caravans.

In 1944 the Germans launched V1 flying bombs, pilotless planes which fell when their engines cut out, and V2 rockets which gave no warning whatever of their approach. These two weapons caused great damage in London and south-east England, killed almost 10,000 people, and brought about a renewed evacuation of London.

The war broke up not only families but also neighbourhoods. This happened in varying degrees all over the country but especially in the bombed areas. There is no doubt about the magnitude of the movements among the civil population. In anticipation of the outbreak of war in 1939 every inhabitant of Great Britain was registered on a National Register and given an identification number. The Register was kept up to date, e.g. by the addition of births and the deletion of the names of people who died. It has been calculated from the National Register that between the outbreak of war in September 1939 and the end of 1945 there were sixty million changes of address in a civilian population of about thirty-eight millions.

1

The dispersal of families and neighbourhoods removed many of the possible sources of self-help among families and friends. The Ministry of Labour estimated that at the peak of mobilisation in mid 1943 80 per cent of all single women aged between 14 and 59, 41 per cent of wives and widows of these ages without children under 14, and 13 per cent of those with children under 14, were in the Forces, industry or Civil Defence. For the age groups 18 to 40, the percentages were 90, 81 and 12, respectively. At the peak of war-time mobilisation in 1943, over twenty-two million men and women out of a population of thirty-three million between the ages of 14 and 64 were serving in the Armed Forces or Civil Defence, or were employed in industry. This situation called for an expansion of the social services. What the family and the neighbourhood could no longer do for themselves the State had to help them to do. New services had to be built up and old ones expanded to deal with some of the problems associated with evacuation, the dispersal of families, the mobilisation of women, and the housing difficulties which war had brought in its train. It was important that the war-time social needs should be met, if only for the morale of the soldiers, sailors and airmen.

Many of the pre-war assistance services were based on the old Poor Law and the Workhouse tradition. Most of the people who needed help during the war regarded the Workhouse and the Poor Law with dread and horror and would not have accepted help with these labels attached. War, therefore, brought great changes in Government policy to meet social needs, many of which had been aggravated by the war. There was an unprecedented interest in the needs of the weak, e.g. the old and deprived children, when it came to the allocation of scarce physical resources. Public interest in social justice increased and a demand arose for higher standards of social services, with no discrimination in the choice of beneficiaries. There was a widespread determination that out of the horrors of war there should emerge a better society, with equal opportunities for all and more provision for social security.

In spite of the fact that about 400,000 British people were killed in the Second World War, including 60,000 civilians killed in air-raids on British soil and 30,000 merchant seamen, the population of Great Britain rose from 47,762,000 in 1939 to 49,182,000 in 1945. Both the number of marriages and the marriage rate per thousand of the population rose sharply in 1939 and in 1940 under the stimulus of war. The marriage rate then fell and reached a very low level in 1943, after which it proceeded to rise. The popularity of marriage was matched by the popularity of having babies. At first the birth rate fell and in 1941 it reached the lowest point ever recorded in registration history, i.e. 13.9 per thousand of the population. In 1942 it climbed to 15.6, which was then the highest point reached since 1931. In 1943 the figure rose to 16.2 and in 1944 it was 17.5. The rate fell again in 1945 to 16.2, but rose again to reach a new maximum of 20.6 in 1947. This increase in the war-time birth rate was unexpected.

Because of the sharp rise in the marriage rate during the war it is reasonable to assume that any housing shortage there might have been in 1939 must have been aggravated by the end of the war and the situation was made worse by the fact that many of the new families had children. Although in the first year of the war permission was given for the completion of houses then in an advanced stage of construction, other house building to meet the general need was brought to a halt in September 1939. The yearly average of the number of houses built between 1935 and 1938 was 334,405, whereas the total number completed during the six years of war for all purposes, i.e. the completion of houses in course of erection in 1939 and the small number built for special purposes, was only 44,860, but the number completed during the last two years of the war was only 5,500.

In the course of the war 222,000 houses were destroyed or damaged beyond repair, and a total of about three and a half million different houses received damage of varying degrees, some of the damage rendering the houses unfit for occupation. On an average, therefore, two houses in every seven were affected in some way by enemy action, but in the areas heavily attacked the proportion of houses damaged was much higher.

As the war continued so the housing problems increased. Many hotels and boarding-houses were requisitioned for billeting members of the Armed Forces or evacuees, and the food rationing arrangements often made it a disadvantage for the remaining hotels to accommodate people for more than short stays. Hotel and nursing-home charges rose considerably, with the result that some middle-class people on fixed incomes and who would probably otherwise have lived in this type of accommodation had to seek other places to live, e.g. furnished rooms in the relatively safe areas of the country. The general shortage of housing outside the vulnerable areas gave rise to problems and danger to the stability of family life. Many families lived in conditions that were unfavourable to a happy and ordered life, and many young couples started their married life in their parents' already cramped homes, or had great difficulty in finding a room, either furnished or unfurnished. The law relating to the prevention of overcrowding in houses could not be enforced, nor could the bye-laws with respect to the condition and equipment of houses in multi-occupation, when so many families had to share houses.

These threats to the stability of family life came at a time when the dependent members of family circles were increasing in number. For example, the number of persons in England and Wales who were under 5 or were 75 years of age or over rose during the war out of all proportion to the increase in the total population. The total increase in the population was about 1,400,000, and the very young and the very old together accounted for over half a million of this increase.

House rents in Britain have been subject to varying degrees of legal restrictions since 1915, so it followed naturally for the Government to restrict the rents to be charged for privately owned houses to their 1939 level. This had consequences for the repair of houses, but the greatest problems in this respect were caused by the shortages of building labour and materials.

By the end of 1943 manpower in Britain had been mobilised to a degree that no other country emulated. The pre-war building labour force of a million men had been reduced to less than a third of this number. By 1945 most of this labour force was concentrated in south-east England, which had suffered the flying bomb and rocket attacks. Supplies of all building materials were very limited. Most of the three and a half million houses damaged by air attacks required repairs to make them wind and weatherproof. The cost of repairs, demolition and debris clearance following enemy attacks rose from M£6 in 1940 to M£113 in 1945. The result was that all other building work, including necessary repair to houses, was either prohibited or strictly restricted by a system of authorisation and licencing. Work of construction or alteration for local authorities and other public bodies required approval by the appropriate Government department. Repair and maintenance work and new work for these bodies under £100 in value did not need Government approval. All constructional work for private firms and individuals etc. required a licence from the local authority, unless it was of a value of less than £100. However, the exemption limit of £100 was lowered in stages until in 1945 it was £10. In the meanwhile the weekly wages of building workers had risen by stages from sixty-six shillings (£3.30) in 1938 to one hundred and eleven shillings and four pence (£5.56½) in 1945. The result was that by 1945 even a small repair required a licence before it could be carried out, but the licence was not a guarantee that the necessary materials and labour were available.

Britain's survival in the war depended predominantly on her capacity to produce and maintain the means to wage war, e.g. the manufacture of guns, aircraft and ships. This meant that a large part of her manufacturing capacity, from which she was able to pay for necessary imports, had to be transferred to the production of armaments. Evidence collected after the war and recently published indicates that in 1940, although her total economic capacity was some 30 per cent smaller than that of Germany, Britain produced more military aircraft than Germany, nearly as many tanks, and many more of other kinds of armoured vehicles. In 1941 British war production far surpassed that of Germany in almost all categories, and this meant a considerable drop in civilian consumption, which the people of this country freely accepted as a price to be paid for freedom. British civilian industry was starved of the capital necessary to keep it competitive and much of the existing machinery and plant deteriorated from the lack of maintenance. A high proportion of the skilled labour not mobilised into the fighting forces was transferred to armament production. Unlike Germany, Britain did not use slave-labour to help man her armament factories. The training of skilled workers for normal peacetime industries was stopped or curtailed. However, the war did result in technical advances in some industries, for example in electronics and certain branches of engineering, and some factories were re-equipped for war production which was found to be helpful for peacetime production.

In spite of the nation's problems, some of which at times seemed to be insuperable, the Government boldly made plans for sweeping social changes for the post-war period. A Minister of Reconstruction was appointed. A plan for a new comprehensive system of social security – The Beveridge Report – was published. In 1943 the Ministry of Town and Country Planning was established; and the Education Act of 1944 made provision for the raising of the school-leaving age from 14 to 15, the abolition of fees for secondary education in state-maintained and state-aided schools and better provision for higher education. In March 1945 the Government appointed a committee to inquire into the methods existing for providing for children, who because of loss of parents or for any other reason were deprived of a normal home life with their own parents or with relatives and were in the care of the Poor Law authorities.

There was great relief and elation amongst the British people when, in 1945, the war ended with Britain and her allies victorious. Six years of war had united the British people as little else could have done, and there was a common hope and determination to create a new social structure and to ensure a higher standard of living for the mass of people than they had had in 1939. With the rejoicings there were high expectations and aspirations, but now, looking back, it would seem that insufficient thought was given to the availability of resources necessary to achieve these aims within the hoped-for time span.

Britain emerged from the war economically much poorer than she had been in 1939. Many of her overseas investments (worth more than one billion pounds) had been sold to pay for war materials. Her external liabilities had increased by about three billion pounds. She had spent two-thirds of the gold reserve held in 1939, worth M£150, and the sterling balancies, i.e. credits held by many countries in blocked accounts in Britain, had increased by about three billion pounds. Exports, by which Britain earns its living, had fallen to about one-third of their pre-1939 volume and some of her former markets were lost for ever. Less than 2 per cent of British workers were employed on producing goods for export, by contrast to nearly 10 per cent before the war. In 1945 Britain was spending abroad more than M£2000 and earning abroad about M£350. Lend-Lease, a device introduced in 1941 which allowed Britain to go on ordering goods from America and to pay later for them, was brought to an end in August 1945. The balance between what she was spending and what she was earning had to be acquired on credit if the basic food ration was to be maintained and her industry retooled and restocked.

A Dollar loan agreement in 1946 provided M£930, which at the time was assumed would be sufficient to set the nation's economy on its feet. However, the value of the loan was quickly reduced by inflation in America and a big rise in the British share of the cost of feeding Germany and the cost of stationing an army there. As a result the loan was quickly used up and there followed a series of financial crises.

Post-war Britain faced many problems as a direct result of the war, and amongst the most important of these was the serious shortage of houses. With millions of men returning from war service and millions of people homeless, in some towns empty houses and other buildings were occupied by squatters. Even in the prevailing circumstances local authorities were unable to accept this way of dealing with the situation. Various measures were used, e.g. the law of trespass, the disconnection of gas and electricity supplies, and the intervention of the police. In some cases the houses were so vandalised that the owners were willing to sell them to the local authority for a nominal sum. For a time squatting became a permanent feature of urban life, acquiring in time its own organisations and rules of conduct. Had it continued and spread it might well have led to serious political instability and a breakdown in law and order. Fortunately, the measures taken before the war ended and immediately afterwards were sufficient to stave off serious unrest on a national scale. However, public expectations for higher standards of living and for the expansion of the social services increased faster than the growth of resources, with the result that there was a series of financial crises.

With the outbreak of war in 1939 not only was house building stopped but also slum clearance was brought to a halt. This meant that many thousands of houses judged in the early and middle nineteen-thirties to be unfit to live in because they were a danger to the health of the inhabitants, had to remain occupied, and by the end of the war their condition must have further deteriorated. Because of the lack of repair many more houses must have become unfit during the war period. The situation was aggravated by the three and half million houses damaged by enemy action. Local authorities had requisitioned for evacuees 71,000 houses which one day would have to be returned to their owners.

The population of the country had increased by about 3 per cent during the war period, but more significant from the housing point of view was the much larger increase in the number of households and potential households, e.g. married children living with their parents because they were unable to obtain a house or flat of their own. There were also the families who had been dispersed, or had moved from their homes because of the war and wanted to return to their old neighbourhoods, even though, as was sometimes the case, their old homes had been demolished. The amount of rebuilding required in the bomb-damaged towns was to a degree evident from the rubble-covered sites.

In a White Paper presented to Parliament in March 1945 the Government set out three housing objectives: the building of 750,000 dwellings, to enable each family which desired to have a separate dwelling to have one, the building of a further half a million houses for the completion of the pre-war slum clearance and overcrowding programmes, and, over the longer term, the progressive improvement in the condition of the older houses in respect of both the standards of accommodation and the equipment. It was recognised that to achieve the last objective a continuous programme of new building would be required.

At the General Election in July 1945 the Labour Party was swept into power by an electorate eager for and determined to obtain social changes which could be obtained only from new leaders not connected in government with the economic depression and social policies of the 1930s. The new Government's housing policy, based partially on that of the wartime Government, had three main elements: the continuation of rent control, subsidies, and the concentration of all house building resources in the hands of local authorities. The last meant the prohibition of building for private individuals.

The first aim of the Government was to provide as many additional housing units as possible. This was achieved by the repair of war-damaged houses, requisitioning of empty houses, the adaptation of suitable buildings, the use of huts and service camps no longer needed for troops and war workers, the production of temporary pre-fabricated bungalows and the building of new permanent houses.

The 'pre-fabs' were Europe's first post-war experiment in industrialised building. They were designed to be made in sections in factories no longer required for aircraft production. When erected on site they had a poor external appearance but inside there was a surprisingly spacious and carefully planned two-bedroomed home which was luxurious, compared with a pre-war council house. It had fitted cupboards, a heated towel rail, a refrigerator, ducted warm air to the bedrooms, an immersion heater, and a folding kitchen table for taking meals. The central core of the house contained a slow-burning solid fuel stove which backed on to the airing cupboard and bathroom from its position in the completely fitted-out kitchen. This meant that the water services, etc., were incorporated in one single portable unit. The cost of manufacture and erection on the site was borne by the Government. The bungalows were allocated to local authorities, who were responsible for their letting and management. Altogether 125,000 were erected before the project was brought to an end in 1948. They were intended to have a ten-year life but many were in occupation for more than double that time. Unfortunately, the 'pre-fabs' proved to be much more expensive than traditionally built houses. They cost around £2,000 to make and erect, whereas the cost of building a brick house in 1945 was about £1,100. The price today of these 'pre-fabs' would be about £20,000 or more. An eight-man team could erect one on a prepared site in one ordinary working day.

It was the policy of the Labour Government in 1945 to build council houses that were 'better and bigger' than those of the pre-war years. The new council estates were to be for a mixture of social classes and not exclusively for members of the working-classes. It was hoped, for example, that the family doctor and other professional people would be encouraged to live on the new estates and with this in view a few larger houses, with space for a garage, were built on some of the estates. The restriction on local authorities to build only for the working-classes was removed by the Housing Act 1949. The size of the ordinary three-bedroomed council house was increased from the pre-war 750 square feet to 900 square feet plus a 50 square foot outhouse, intended as a utility room and store.

Although the houses were no longer solely for the working-classes the Government decided that the rents should be subsidised so as to allow them to be let at about the same rent as the pre-war council houses but with a small increase to pay for the higher standards. On the assumption that the pre-war net rents of council houses averaged 7s.6d (37½p) a week, and that the higher standard of the post-war houses would merit an extra 2s.6d (12½p) per week, the rents of the new houses were fixed at 10s (50p) per week. Average weekly earnings for men had risen from 69s (£3.45) in October 1938 to 121s (£6.06) in July 1945.

To build a typical three-bedroomed council house in 1945 cost about £1,100, so for each house an annual subsidy of £22.00 was required to bring the cost rent of 93p down to 50p per week. The subsidy was made up of £16.10s.0d from the central Government and £5.10s.0d from the local rates. The power granted to local authorities in 1930 to vary the rents charged according to the income of the tenant was renewed, but the Government did not make this compulsory, with the result that in some areas of the country some of the tenants of the new houses were receiving financial assistance they did not need from public funds.

By the end of 1946 about 320,000 additional units of accommodation had been provided. These were: 80,000 'pre-fabs', 45,000 by conversion and adaptation, 107,000 war-damaged houses repaired, 12,000 in temporary huts and service camps, 25,000 in requisitioned houses, and 52,000 in new permanent houses.

It was the Labour Government's intention, in the longer term, to extend the housing functions of local authorities and to establish a comprehensive municipal housing service. One aim of this service was to improve the existing stock of houses to a standard comparable to pre-war municipal houses, but the municipalising of private rented housing was considered at the time not to be practicable. The Housing Act 1949 gave local authorities the power to make financial grants to private owners who wished to improve their houses. Very few owners made use of the scheme and by 1953 only 6,000 grants had been paid (Chapter 9).

From 1947 onwards Britain experienced a number of financial and economic crises and the number, size and quality of houses built in any year depended largely on the overall economic position of the country. In addition, building costs rose more than was expected. In consequence, the standards for new council housing were lowered. In 1951, for example, local authorities were encouraged to abandon the requirement for a minimum of 900 square feet of floor area for a three-bedroomed house. In 1952 local authorities were asked to economise in the design of houses and also in the services and equipment installed in them. The Government pointed out that a significant reduction in the cost of a house, and consequently in the rent at which it would be let, could be made if the essential was distinguished from the unessential (Chapter 6).

In spite of the periodic financial crises and other problems building resources gradually became more plentiful and the freeing of building materials from licencing control began. Building for private ownership, which in 1945 had been virtually prohibited and in 1948 had been restricted to one-fifth of the local authorities' total house building programme, was in 1951 raised to one half of their allocation. In 1952 building work not likely to exceed £500 in cost was permitted without a licence and there was a tendency for licences to build private houses under 1,000 square feet in area to be given without question. In 1954 the licencing of house building came to an end. The proportion of the houses built which were for private individuals rose from 15 per cent in 1952 to 63 per cent in 1961 and on average it has remained at about that figure since then.

The housing queues remained depressingly long and the housing shortage remained a very politically sensitive matter. Both major political parties published house building targets which they hoped to achieve when in office. One of the most publicised was that of the Conservative Government when returned to office in 1951, which was to build 300,000 houses per year. It was achieved and even surpassed but there was a fall in standards and a higher proportion of small houses was built. In 1954 357,000 houses were completed, the equivalent of seven per thousand people. The best year for house building, however, was 1968, when 426,000 dwellings were built. Between 1945 and 1979 nearly ten million new dwellings were built in Britain and in 1979 more than two families in every five lived in a post-war dwelling.

By 1980 nearly all houses being built had some form of central heating and the average floor space of houses built for families of four or five people was about 960 square feet. The average cost of building a three-bedroomed council house, exclusive of land, was £350 in 1930, £1,500 in 1949, £2,300 in 1964, £4,575 in 1972, £7,842 in 1975, and £9,505 in 1977.

In 1980 public housing authorities owned about 32 per cent of the total housing stock (about seven million houses and flats), about 54.6 per cent was owner-occupied and most of the remaining 13 per cent was privately rented.

The rents of most privately owned houses remained controlled at their 1939 levels until 1954, in spite of a considerable increase in the cost of repairs and management during the period (Chapter 4).

Housing associations existed in Britain in the 19th century. They were originally non-profit-making bodies established by philanthropists for the purpose of providing low-rent housing for people in serious social need, or large employers of labour who provided and managed housing accommodation for their employees. Towards the end of the 1950s it became clear to the Government, as the result of investigation, that council housing and owner-occupation could not between them provide new housing for all those in need of it, and in consequence in 1961 an attempt was made to promote housing associations of new kinds with the aid of Government lending. In 1964 a National Housing Corporation was established to provide technical advice and to administer the making of loans to new housing associations (Chapter 8).

With the outbreak of war in 1939 the clearance of slums was halted. It was not until 1954, nine years after the end of the fighting, that the Government felt that conditions warranted the recommencement of this work (Chapter 10).

The acute shortage of housing accommodation in the immediate post-war period forced some people, especially newly-married couples unable to find a house or flat which would give them privacy, to make their homes in caravans and boats, etc. The caravans included vehicles of many types and descriptions, from pre-war motor-buses to old caravans which were not insulated. Among the boats in use as dwellings were small wartime craft sold by the Government at low prices. No information about the numbers of people who were living in these types of accommodation was available until the census of 1951. At that time there were in England and Wales 31,335 caravans and house-boats in use as homes and these formed 0.25 per cent of all dwellings (Chapter 11).

During the Second World War the number of people over 65 years of age rose from 4,249,000 to 4,960,000. Up to 1948 the special provision for housing the elderly was relatively small. A few charitable organisations provided accommodation, mostly in the form of alms-houses, and a few local authorities had provided special bungalows; but in 1939 for the majority of the old people who were living on the State pension of ten shillings (50p) per week or on Public Assistance (the Poor Law) the choice of accommodation lay between the worst houses in the private sector – probably slums – or lodging houses, and the Poor Law Institution (Workhouse). In 1931, for example, 159,000 people in England and Wales were accommodated in Poor Law Institutions. It was not until the late 1950s that a greater emphasis was placed by the Government on the building of accommodation for the elderly (Chapter 13).

Between the end of the war in 1945 and 1970 little was done in the housing field to help the physically handicapped, probably because of other demands on very limited resources. In June 1968 there were just over three million people aged 16 or over, who had some physical, mental or sensory impairment, living in private households. In 1970 an Act of Parliament placed certain duties on local authorities with regard to the care of the chronically sick and disabled to ensure greater comfort, safety and convenience in the home (Chapter 13).

In May 1946 about 28,000 children were maintained in England and Wales under the Poor Law, either in homes provided by local authorities or in homes provided by voluntary bodies. In addition, on 31 March 1946 5,200 children were found to be homeless on the winding-up of the Government evacuation scheme. These children were in private accommodation, hostels or nurseries in wartime reception areas, and for various reasons were unable to return to their homes. Some were orphans, others had a parent or parents who could not provide a home for them. They would normally have been classified as paupers and dealt with under the Poor Law but the Government decided that their situation was largely attributable to the war and made temporary provision for their care by the payment of billeting allowances or an equivalent sum for an interim period. About 3,000 of these children were billeted in private households, about 1,200 in hostels and 1,000 in residential nurseries and special schools. The concept of pauper gave way in 1948 to that of children in need of care, and the law was changed accordingly (Chapter 14).

In the 1950s and '60s many thousands of coloured immigrants arrived in Britain, largely from the West Indies, Pakistan and Africa. In the three years 1960-1962 the total net immigration into Britain amounted to some 388,000 people, three-quarters of them from the Commonwealth. It has been estimated that in 1971 coloured Commonwealth immigrants and their families numbered about 1.5 million, about $2\frac{1}{2}$ per cent of the total population of the country. In some areas of the country their arrival aggravated the housing shortage which was already acute. From time to time allegations were made about racial discrimination and other unsocial practices, in respect of employment and housing, etc. In consequence, new legislation was passed making it unlawful to discriminate against a person on grounds of colour, race or ethnic or national origin (Chapter 12).

In the late 1950s homelessness, whether it involved an individual or a whole family, began to attract public attention. In the summer of 1961 homeless London families began to appear on the television screens and feature stories appeared in the newspapers about the people who were unable to find a place to live and who either slept in cars, vans, park shelters, or public toilets, or slept rough in the open air. A number of investigations were made by different bodies, and these revealed problems as to which authority or authorities had the statutory responsibility for providing accommodation for those who, for whatever cause, found themselves without a home (Chapter 15).

New towns did not figure conspicuously in any of the political parties' programmes during the first post-war General Election of 1945. The major emphasis was on promises of maximum speed in building houses, but all three parties accepted that there was a need of some decentralisation from overcrowded towns. Also, although during the war each party had continued its separate organisation and had formulated its own post-war reconstruction programme, all three programmes included some provision for new towns and this agreement between the parties was helpful when the New Towns Bill was introduced in Parliament in 1946. The New Towns Act 1946, with The Town and Country Planning Act 1947, created a system of land use control and machinery for the construction of New Towns that was revolutionary (Chapter 7).

This chapter has sketched in outline some of the problems which faced Britain both during the war and in the immediate post-war period in order that what has, or has not, been achieved in the housing field during the period 1945-1980 can be seen in perspective. At the end of the war in 1945 the British people indicated by the ballot box and other means that they wanted a new social structure in which there would be greater social justice than had existed in 1939. The expectations included full employment, a universally available comprehensive health service, the right to education according to capacity but without regard to class or wealth, a social security system which would abolish real poverty, and a decent individual home available for every household that wanted one. It was the hope that never again would there be mass unemployment with hundreds of people marching on London to demand the right to work in order to earn a reasonable standard of living, as had been the case in the 1930s. Nor would there be homelessness caused by a lack of accommodation available at reasonable prices.

Nearly forty years on there are two and a half million people unemployed and it is envisaged that the figure will reach three million in the very near future. Housing and social conditions in some parts of the larger urban areas are in some respects worse than they were in 1939. In 1979 riots occurred in some of these areas and in 1981 there were more serious and widespread riots which bordered on the complete breakdown of law and order, with the police as a symbol of the establishment as a prime target.

This book deals only with one aspect of Britain's very complex social problems of the post-1945 period. The fourteen chapters which follow show and explain the changes that have taken place in the various sections of the housing market between 1945 and 1980.

A small minority preferred primitive living to the bombing.

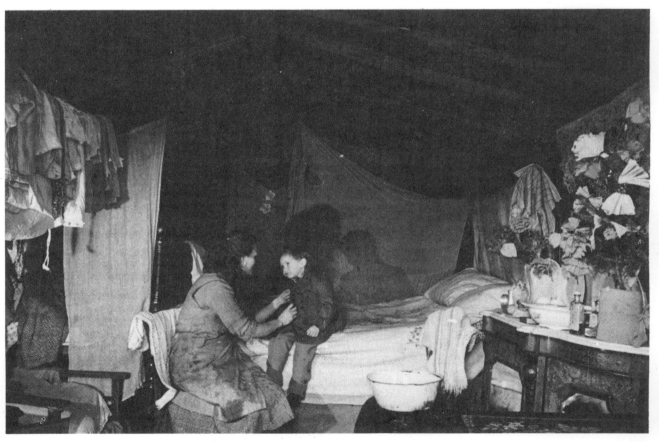

One family's refuge from the bombing.

Bomb damage in the 1940s

Small children playing among the remains of bombed houses.

9

In 1945 the amount of rebuilding required in the bomb-damaged towns was in a measure evident from the gaps where buildings had once stood.

Former war-time service hut in use as a house. (1954)

The inside of a corrugated iron Nisson hut converted into a house. (1954)

'Temporary' pre-fabricated bungalows.

Chapter 2

URBAN HOMES

In this chapter the terms 'city', 'town' and 'urban area' may be used interchangeably, although strictly speaking in Britain a city is a special town which usually has a cathedral or a university and has been raised to the dignity of a city by a charter or letters patent.

The United Kingdom is about 80 per cent urbanised, which means that four persons out of five live in a town. But what is a town? Many theories to describe and explain it have been put forward but there has been little unanimity about its precise nature.

Some countries have a legal definition of what constitutes a town, and in these countries a town is any place which the State is prepared to recognise as having sufficient urban characteristics. For example, the density at which people live, the amount of industry in the place, and whether or not employment is largely non-agricultural. Until the end of March 1974, the United Kingdom was divided for local government purposes into rural and urban areas, and the urban areas were recognisably towns. This distinction between rural and urban local authority districts was abolished by the reorganisation of local government which took place in April 1974. The new County Districts contain both rural and urban areas within their boundaries. Therefore local government boundaries are no longer helpful in our search for an explanation of what constitutes a town, and it is necessary to seek elsewhere for an answer.

Some people see towns as relatively dense conglomerations of streets and buildings. Others see them in terms of their functions rather than in terms of their physical form, i.e. as a centre for many kinds of services such as banks, shops, libraries, schools, hospitals, etc. To some people, however, a town is both a place and a way of life. Certainly a town is more than a mere conglomeration of streets and buildings, because a vital part of a town is the society which lives in it and which moulds its character and contributes to its physical form. But in Britain today town life and village life do not differ a great deal; certainly not as much as they did even as recently as the 1930s. So the way of life of the inhabitants of a place is not a reliable guide as to what constitutes a town. Although a familiar phenomenon of the British way of life, and one which is taken for granted, the town defies a definition which would be acceptable to everyone. Towns vary so much in size and in other characteristics that a common denominator may seem to be non-existent. There are, however, common elements in places in Britain which are regarded by most people as being towns. Four of these are: the number of people who live in the place, the size of the built-up area, the building density and the kinds of services which the place provides, e.g. shops, banks, schools, offices of solicitors and other professional people. All these elements are usually present in places which have a population of 5,000 or above. However, difficulties in definition arise at the point where a village is almost a town, or a town is nearly indistinguishable from a village. At that point it is suggested that a place is a town when it is recognised as such by the local people.

In some respects every town in Britain is unique, for example in its location, its size, population densities, and in the mixture of the services it provides; and, therefore, in a sense its housing can also be regarded as unique. But there are certain characteristics which are common to all British towns. There is usually a town centre which consists largely of shops and offices and a few of the older houses. All the main streets, apart from town bypasses, converge on it. Also, no matter what the size of the town, there is a great similarity in the design, layout and construction of most of the houses built in the same periods. In spite of the apparent differences, therefore, urban housing in Britain has followed uniform patterns and can be examined as a whole.

During the 18th and 19th centuries Britain changed from a predominantly agricultural society to an industrial one, and tripled its population. In the *laissez-faire* system of the time public responsibility for housing was confined to the laying down of very rudimentary standards. Manufacturing and mining attracted large numbers of semi-starving people from the over-populated countryside and from famine-stricken Ireland. The increased population of the towns could be housed only by the erection of numerous cheap houses packed tightly around the factories and other workplaces. The houses were built by private landlords for renting at rents which were low enough to be within the means of the tenants and high enough to give a reasonable profit to the investors. The rents had to be low, and therefore the houses cheaply built, because the weekly wage of a labourer was about £1, a great deal of employment was casual, and the compulsory holidays of Christmas and Good Friday, etc., were unpaid. There was no National

Health Service, so doctors' bills, etc., had to be paid out of wages, and education was not free. There were no subsidised council houses. In these circumstances the rents of houses for working-class families had to be about 10p to 12p a week.

Most of the houses erected for the working-classes in the early part of the period were built back-to-back and close to the factories, mines and shipyards, etc., as public transport was almost non-existent. By 1939 nearly all these back-to-back houses had been demolished, largely by slum clearance and redevelopment schemes, but a small number, mostly in the North of England, were still occupied in 1945. Some of the back-to-back houses still in use in 1945 had been built as late as the first decade of the 20th century and were of such sound construction that they were later improved and provided with bathrooms, etc.

By the latter half of the 19th century the real wages of the working-classes had increased and there was a demand for a better standard of housing. Stimulated by this demand the speculative builders began to provide houses which had both front and back doors. One type consisted of three small rooms, each less than 100 square feet in area, one on top of the other and connected by a narrow winding staircase. Although they had back doors these houses usually did not have any windows in the rear walls and were only a slight improvement on the back-to-back type. The back doors of these houses usually opened on to a common yard which contained a block of water-closets or privies which were used in common by the inhabitants of the houses in a long terrace. Sometimes there was a single water tap in the yard, which was the only supply for a block of about twelve or more houses. By the early 1930s most local authorities considered this type of house to be unfit for human habitation but in 1945 there were fairly large numbers of them, mainly in the industrial towns, still in use as dwellings.

A better type of house, consisting of four rooms, two on the ground floor and two on the floor above, was built in large numbers towards the end of the 19th century and during the first decade of the 20th century. Each such house was provided with a small yard at the rear, often about ten feet square, which contained a water-closet and ashpit. It was the common practice at the time to build both the three-roomed and the four-roomed houses in long terraces or rows, with as few breaks as the bye-laws would permit. The four-roomed houses, often called 'two up and two down' type, are to be found today in every town in Britain and in some towns they account for about 30 per cent of the total housing stock.

The industrialisation of the country resulted in a steep rise in the wealth of the factory owners, the iron masters, and the bankers, etc., and with it a movement away from the expanding towns with their smoke-polluted air to the open countryside. The houses they built were individually designed, mostly large and often ornate. They sometimes incorporated experiments in design and equipment such as bathrooms and hot-water systems which later trickled down to the houses built for the less rich. The rich people were, however, a very small minority of the urban population of Britain. Many of the houses they built have long since been pulled down and their sites used for other purposes. Some of them, however, remain and can be seen like islands surrounded by a large sea of small Victorian terrace houses. They have been put to a variety of uses such as small factories, offices, lodging-houses and hotels, etc.

At about the same time that the large detached houses were being built in the open countryside, terraces of large identical houses were being built on the fringes of many important towns. Sometimes the terraces were designed to form the sides of a square, the centre of which was laid out to form a garden consisting of flower beds and a lawn, in the middle of which was a shelter. The gardens were enclosed by railings so as to ensure the exclusive use of the garden for the inhabitants of the houses in the square. Examples of these beautiful squares are to be found today in many towns. In some cases the houses have been well preserved and may be in use as dwellings, consulting rooms and offices, but in other cases they have been allowed to fall into decay and have become lodging-houses or workshops, etc., and their former gardens are now waste lands used unlawfully for dumping waste materials and refuse. Some have been included in slum-clearance programmes.

Another type of layout for large houses used in some large towns during the latter half of the 19th century and the first decade of the 20th century was the private park or estate containing a number of large houses each standing in about an acre or more of land. These exclusive estates, or parks as they are usually called, are enclosed by railings or trees, etc., and are entered through a gateway or gateways, at which there may or may not be a lodge for the gatekeeper. The roads in these parks are usually not public highways and therefore have to be maintained by the householders collectively. Many of these parks still exist but some have been absorbed in the surrounding development. Of those that still exist some have long since lost their gates and gatekeepers, and in many cases the houses are no longer maintained to the standard one would expect in an exclusive park.

In the last quarter of the 19th century cheaper transport in the form of trams and workmen's tickets made it possible for many more people to live outside the towns, and so the areas which have become the middle zones of towns were developed. The houses in these areas were built in shorter terraces than those in the inner zones, and in different styles. Most of the houses had six rooms, two of which were provided by building a back addition projecting out from the main building into the yard space, which contained a water-closet. It was considered to be unhealthy to have a water-closet inside the house. The rooms and back yards of these houses were larger than those in the four-roomed type built in the inner zones. These larger terrace houses were built for renting by skilled artisans and white-collar workers. They are to be found today in large numbers in most towns and are often included in General Improvement Areas (Chapter 9).

During the same period numerous even larger terrace houses were built in select areas for renting by the business and professional, etc., classes. They were often three or four storeys high, and some had cellar kitchens. They varied in size from seven to ten or more rooms. Accommodation for a servant or servants was commonly in the attics, which had skylights instead of windows. This type of house usually had a bathroom and all the rooms in the earlier ones had gas lighting and those in the later ones electricity.

Until 1919 the Victorian suburbia which contained these later types of terrace houses partially encircled many of the industrial towns of Britain. Such terraces are to be found today in most, if not all, of Britain's towns. Many of them are very well built and in very good condition in spite of their age, and in recent years in some districts have regained their popularity as dwellings for the professional and business classes. They are often found situated on main or important roads. Today they have many uses: e.g. for single family occupation, as hotels, as flats, lodging-houses and offices.

Before World War I most urban housing was built in terraces or rows, irrespective of size. In 1919 there was a great demand for something better than the long dreary terraces with their small flagged or concreted back yards containing the W.C. at the far end away from the house. To meet this demand the estates of status-symbolising, semi-detached houses, the villas of the wealthier people, bungalows and council estates, all with gardens instead of back yards, sprawled over the agricultural land which at the time surrounded all the towns of Britain. Planning powers were almost non-existent, so the rape of rich agricultural land went on without hindrance. Imported food was much cheaper than home-grown food and in consequence British agriculture was so depressed that farmers were willing to sell land for building, often to avoid bankruptcy.

In the 1930s some urban local authorities began building blocks of flats on land which had been cleared of slums in the inner zones of cities. Although tenement blocks had been built during the late 18th and 19th centuries, largely by charitable organisations, this was a relatively new approach in Britain to the housing problem. A few of the larger local authorities sent delegations to European towns to study the design and layout of flats, which were very common in most European countries, and as their reports were generally favourable limited flat development went ahead in spite of the fact that it was known that most British people had a preference for houses.

By the outbreak of war in 1939 the proportion of terrace houses in towns had fallen from over 90 per cent in 1914 to something like 50 per cent. During the inter-war period the towns in the large conurbations, now called Metropolitan Counties, coalesced at a fast rate, with the result that some of them lost their separate identities and perceivable boundaries. It was only after 1945 that any real action was taken to halt the uncontrolled urban sprawl, and for some of the towns it was then too late to have much effect.

Most of the destruction of buildings which occurred during the 1939-45 war was in the industrial towns. The amount of land separating some of these towns in 1945 was very small, with the result that before long house-building began to go upwards in the form of blocks of flats of four, eight, eleven or twenty stories instead of the long terraces which the 19th century speculative builders had erected. Some towns became partially ringed with tower blocks of flats. By the 1960s some of the blocks of flats built in the larger towns began to give rise to serious problems, and on the whole the tall blocks were not popular with the people who lived in them. In consequence, in the late 1960s and 1970s most local authorities reverted to building some of the once-despised terrace houses. Chapter 6 deals with council housing.

Although the houses in all the towns in Britain follow certain broad patterns of design and construction according to the periods when they were built, decay and other bad features of urban housing exist to a greater degree and extent in the Metropolitan Counties. The six Metropolitan Counties in England and Wales were created when local government was reorganised in 1974. Each Metropolitan County consists of a continuously urbanised area containing a cluster of towns surrounding a very large city, such as Birmingham, Liverpool and Manchester, which is recognised as the nucleus. The Metropolitan Counties, together with the area of the Greater London Council, have a total population which amounts to about one-third of the total population of Britain. The housing problems of the Metropolitan Counties are considerable and complex. For example, most of the slums are in these areas. In addition they have a higher proportion of drab substandard housing than have the other urban areas. This is in part due to the rapid and unplanned industrial expansion during the 19th century and to air pollution which for nearly a century was coating the buildings with tar, soot and grime and was eroding brick and stonework.

In 1952 there was a sudden big increase in London in the number of deaths from respiratory diseases and this led the Government to set up a committee (Beaver Committee) to study the degree and the causes and effects of urban air pollution. As a result of the work of this committee the Clean Air Act 1956 became law. This Act allows local authorities to designate the whole or parts of their districts as 'Smoke Control Areas'. In general, but allowing for certain exemptions, it is an offence to burn bituminous coal (coal that yields tar or pitch and black smoke when burnt) within a Smoke Control area. The Beaver Committee expressed the hope that by the late 1970s the whole of the United Kingdom would be subject to Smoke Control Orders. This has not been achieved but there has been a considerable reduction in the amount of smoke pollution in urban areas, which has been brought about by the operation of the Clean Air Act, with its grants to householders, and by economic forces, e.g. the availability of natural gas at a lower price than that of solid fuel.

During the late 'fifites and 'sixties many of the large towns had ambitious programmes for the redevelopment of town centres and inner-city areas. These were usually very comprehensive and included the building of office blocks, shopping arcades, six-lane urban highways, ring-roads, subways and flyovers, etc. At this time the heavy industries and traditional manufacturing industries were being scaled down and were becoming less labour-intensive. Also some of the buildings occupied by these businesses were old and located on sites of high rateable value, so it seemed logical to prepare plans for comprehensive redevelopment of these areas. By use of the stick and carrot many industrial concerns located on inner-city sites were pursuaded to move to new factories built on cheaper, green field sites. Some of these businesses were small but profitable and capable of growing when carried on in old, low-rented properties, but doubtedly so in high-rented new factories. The gradual evolutionary change which had previously been the pattern of town development did not seem to the councils to be appropriate, and in any case comprehensive redevelopment was in fashion among the urban local authorities. Often the speed with which the plans were prepared and approved by the councils did not allow for discussions between the business owners, the land owners and the planners.

In these circumstances overspill housing became a necessity and to a large extent the building of new dwellings had to be concentrated on the fringes and outskirts where the new factories and workplaces were to be located. In some cases this required the building of what were virtually satellite towns (not new towns, which are dealt with in Chapter 7) or the expansion of smaller urban areas. Many of these places have matured into well-planned and pleasant places to live and work. Kirkby, near Liverpool, for example, in its mature state demonstrates the skill and ideals of its planners in spite of the bad publicity at times given to it.

Many of the city dwellers moved out of the inner-city areas to the new districts and the new towns, leaving behind the old, the permanently ill and the less skilled. Immigrants from overseas moved in at a time of full employment and their children, many of them born here, are now adults, some with children of their own. The corner shops, primary schools and churches, all in one way or another community centres, became empty. Some, perhaps many, of the houses in these inner-city areas were judged to be unfit for human habitation, and these with other houses not unfit, and shops, etc., were demolished by slum-clearance procedures in advance of the proposed redevelopment. Then the money ran out. Because of cuts in public expenditure the redevelopment had to be postponed, at first for what was believed to be a short time, for the duration of 'the freeze'. This, however, lasted for several winters and summers and in some cases for twenty years or so.

Large areas became waste lands yielding no rates or other income to the local authorities, who had to find the money to pay the loan charges on the buildings they had bought and demolished, and on the land earmarked for development at some future date. Meanwhile, the exporting of population meant that the burden of the debt fell on fewer people.

The devastation spread outwards, like a contagious disease. The houses in street after street on the periphery of the cleared areas became decayed, mutilated and vandalised, although had they been repaired and improved in time they would have provided comfortable homes. In some towns post-war council flats on the fringes of the devastated areas had to be protected from vandals by wire grills over windows, and any flats which became vacant had to be boarded up as the people were moving out.

Little or no maintenance or repair work was carried out to the houses in these now moribund areas because "everybody knew that they had a short life", and in any case the increasing vandalism would have made such a step an act of lunacy. Governments may try to control the money supply but they have no control over the weather. Rain, frost, storm and wind took their toll, so that disrepair increased at a progressive rate. There was no capital investment in these areas. Building societies were reluctant to advance money for the purchase of houses which had an uncertain future, and local authorities were hesitant about giving discretionary improvement grants. (The improvement of houses is dealt with in Chapter 9.) The infrastructures, e.g. sewers, water and gas mains, etc., were not adequately maintained because they were to be renewed when redevelopment took place.

With the further contraction of industry throughout the country the factories in these moribund areas became prime targets for closure, often with the result that more factories and commercial buildings became derelict and vandalised. Unemployment in these areas increased at a fast rate until it was easier to count those that had employment rather than those that had not.

By the 1960s many of Britain's inner-city areas were decayed and seriously crumbling at a fast rate, and in the eyes of the inhabitants nothing was being done about it. Many of the inhabitants, especially the young, lost all confidence in those in authority. The feeling of being trapped in poverty and squalor for the rest of their lives led to despair. They saw the promises of Government, both national and local, as being fraudulent. The despair of the young was intensified by the fact that their fathers were not only unemployed, but were humiliated by it, made to feel useless and had lost the will to fight. In some areas the young developed a strong sense of alienation from authority in general and from the police in particular, and began to believe that change would come about only as the result of violence. Consequently, riots occurred in different parts of the country during 1979-81. There have been suggestions that they were the result of the work of small groups who wished to overthrow the established order, or that they arose through racial disharmony. However, the study of the causes of social unrest is outside the scope of this book, except for the part bad housing conditions may play in it.

In 1973 it was acknowledged by the Government that the existing housing legislation had failed to meet the needs of the older and more decayed urban areas. Improvement grants were going to the better 19th century housing rather than to those areas in greatest need of rehabilitation. A new concept, 'Housing Action Areas', was aimed at giving priority to the improvement of areas in which the poor physical condition of the houses was combined with social stress and deprivation. These were areas in which the normal improvement grants would not have been available. The Housing Act 1974 provided means by which living conditions in these areas could be improved even though the houses were considered to have a relatively short life. (For more details of the Housing Act 1974 see Chapter 9.)

As the strict Government control of public borrowing continued it became obvious that a great deal of inner-city land, which was in the ownership of the local authorities, was unlikely to be developed by the local authorities themselves within the foreseeable future. The costs which the local authorities had incurred in acquiring the buildings on the land, demolishing them and clearing the sites, plus the price of the land itself, made it impracticable to put a realistic sale price on the land which would attract any private developer for the land earmarked for housing, or for the other land scheduled for other purposes should the council decide to change its mind about the use of the land, e.g. to permit the building of houses. By 1975 some local authorities had come to the conclusion that it was in the interest of their ratepayers to make at least some of this land available to private developers on terms which would permit the erection of low-cost housing for sale on a sponsorship basis. This meant the disposal of the land to the private developer on a very long lease for a minimal licence fee to build low-cost housing units for sale: predominantly to people on the council's waiting list or from slum-clearance areas, but also for sale in the open market. Theoretically, the benefits of such schemes are passed on to the purchasers of the houses

in the form of lower prices, but in addition no subsidies have to be found from public funds and there is no demand for capital from public funds at a time when public borrowing is strictly curtailed. There is also the prospect of middle-class people moving back into the inner-city areas and the local authority begins to get an income from the land in the form of rates from the houses, when built.

In 1980 it was estimated that the prices of these houses would range from as little as £12,000 for a single person's flat to about £25,000 for a three-bedroomed house. In Liverpool during 1981 three-bedroomed houses were on offer at £21,000, and because of the high cost of travel people were glad to move back into the inner-city areas.

From 1977 onwards this form of development has been encouraged by the Government but there has been resistance from some district councils who do not believe their role is to provide, or be involved in, private sector housing. However, the Local Government and Planning Act 1980 requires the keeping of registers of unused or under-used land and enables the Secretary of State for the Environment to force the sale of registered land.

The problems of Britain's inner-city areas are complex; however, apart from housing, they are outside the scope of this book. Since 1968 the Government has made available certain sums of money to alleviate some of the bad conditions in these areas, but money by itself has proved to be insufficient. There are signs that some of the very large urban areas may be unmanageable in their present form, but they have only been in existence since 1974. One solution to their problems might be the creation of community organisations consisting of local leaders, business people, members of the interested professions and politicians and endowed with powers similar to those possessed by the Development Corporations of the new towns.

People who are not bankers, civil servants, economists or politicians may have difficulty in understanding the rationality of the situation in which all the real resources necessary to revitalise our towns – e.g. unemployed skilled building labour and plant and building materials – are available but cannot be used because of money targets and statistical symbols. Perhaps money, a very useful tool, has become God!

In some ancient towns there is a rich diversity in the style and design of the houses.

Example of grim 19th century tenement blocks built in some large towns for renting to low paid workers. (1956)

Short terrace of late 19th century back-to back houses. (1959)

Before the days of cheap public transport workers' houses had to be close to the factories and therefore to the source of smoke, noise and vibration pollution. (1960)

Yard and W.C.s shared by a group of houses. A common feature in many towns of early 19th century houses built for factory workers. (1955)

Houses with both front and back doors but with no rear windows. (1955)

Small 19th century houses in a narrow court. (1957)

Rows of 'two-up-and-two-down' houses built on sloping site. (1957)

Rear of the same houses showing the very narrow passage separating the backs of two rows of similar houses. (1957)

In some areas although the yards are small the back streets are wide enough to permit the use of motorised vehicles for refuse collection. (1955)

Small terrace houses so crammed together that there is no back street or passage. (1955)

Land saving in industrial towns. Late 19th century tall terrace houses. (1965)

A 19th century long terrace. In 1980 in many towns about 30 per cent of the housing stock consisted of similar houses many of which were owner-occupied and had been modernised.

A shorter terrace of late 19th century houses. (1965)

*A larger type of terrace house built about the beginning of the 20th century
and now commonly found in the middle zones of towns. (1955)*

23

Tree-lined street of late-19th-early-20th century terrace houses built for renting to skilled and clerical workers but many of the houses are now owner-occupied.

Well preserved large Victorian terrace houses built for renting to higher income groups. Although they are likely to be now situated in the inner zones of towns some have maintained their value.

Large four-storey terrace houses with spacious cellar kitchens built in the 19th century for, and often still occupied by, the higher income groups. They have kept their high value because of their situation, e.g. away from industry etc.

Nineteenth century terrace houses built to form a square the centre of which is laid out as a garden. In select areas, like this one, the houses are well maintained and have retained their relatively high value in spite of their age. Some have been converted into high-class flats.

A crecent designed as a whole and not just as a group of similar individual houses.

Solid Victorian terrace houses situated within an inner zone of a large city after renovation in the late 1970s.

Semi-detached houses built about 1910 on a ring road around a large city.

Three-storey Victorian terrace houses with cellar kitchens built for professional and business men now in the middle zone of a town and allowed to fall into gross disrepair. (1959)

Early post-1945 flats which resemble those built in the 1930s.

Early post-1945 redevelopment with houses and flats.

28

The old road pattern has been retained but the worn out houses have been replaced with low-rise flats.

A valley in an industrial town packed with 19th century slums. (1956)

The recreation of the valley as a green open space flanked by tower blocks contrasts sharply with the previously slum area.

Aerial view of former slum area redeveloped with blocks of flats. (1966)

30

Industrial housing units instead of blocks of flats began to appear in the late 1960s. (1968)

Air pollution was a serious problem in many of Britain's towns until the late 1950s-1960s.

Narrow and tall 19th century terrace houses with cellar kitchens and windowless attic bedrooms intended for servants. In some towns in spite of its age this type of house is still in demand by high income group households.

A street in a decayed inner-city area. (1955)

A decayed inner-city area. (1955)

Large type terrace houses in a decaying inner-city area. (1958)

Terrace houses built in the 19th century for renting to professional and other white collar workers. As the towns spread these people moved out and the cellars were let as separate dwellings but were closed as unfit during the 1930s. The houses themselves fell rapidly into disrepair because it was impossible to let them for one family occupation. (1955)

Low-cost built for sale by a private developer on land in an inner-city area released by the local authority for the purpose. (1980)

Flats built for sale by private developer on land in an inner-city area released by the local authority for the purpose. (1980)

Chapter 3

RURAL HOMES

Although Britain is 80 per cent urbanised, which means that four out of five people live in towns, forty-seven million acres out of a total land surface of sixty million acres are in use for agriculture, and about a further four million acres are in use for afforestation. Between eleven and twelve million people out of a total population of about fifty-six million live in areas which until 1974 were called rural districts. In many parts of Britain there are not even villages but only hamlets, and in the hills and the mountainous areas there is often only a scattering of individual farmsteads.

It is as difficult to define a village as it is to define a town (see Chapter 2). A settlement which today might be called a hamlet in terms of its population, e.g. fewer than 200 people, would once have been regarded as a village. A better criterion for distinguishing a village from a hamlet is the services which each community can support. In the 19th century and before, a village was largely self-supporting. It had its church, school, pub, doctor and the various craftsmen to supply most if not all its needs. Today, for a settlement to support a single form primary school, a pub, a shop-cum-Post-Office and a doctor a population of at least 2,500 is needed.

The character of villages has changed irreparably since 1945 and the rural villages are no longer dependent on agriculture. There are villages which now largely rely on tourism, villages which provide homes for commuters and for weekenders, and there are villages with light industry. However, apart from the fishing communities and the industrial villages, it was agriculture which gave life and character to most of the villages in Britain.

Food, water, shelter and security were the reasons for the choice of the location of the primitive settlements, and the form of agriculture practised largely dictated the nature of the settlement. Geology, climate and the varying skills of the people who occupied different parts of Britain have all contributed to the considerable diversity.

Broadly speaking, but subject to numerous exceptions, for example that there is some arable farming in Scotland, Wales and the north of England, arable farming is more widespread in the east and the south-east of England, and pastoral farming is most common in the upland areas of the north and the west of Britain. Villages are the more characteristic form of settlement of the arable areas, and hamlets and scatterings of individual farmsteads predominate in the pastoral regions. The reason for this difference is that pastoral farming needs land more than people, and before mechanisation arable land required a relatively large pool of labour, especially at certain times of the year, such as harvest time.

During and after the Second World War the mechanisation and the efficiency of British agriculture increased considerably and this resulted in a big drop in the number of agricultural workers required. Also many of the rural craftsmen, such as carpenters, masons, blacksmiths, boot and shoe makers and tailors, were forced out of business by competition from urban industries and had to seek employment in the towns. One result of this movement of people from the rural areas was that in the 1950s and early 1960s some farmhouses and cottages were abandoned and allowed to decay and become derelict because there was no demand for them. However, in the late 1960s and 1970s the position changed, as it had become more difficult to find plots of land with planning consent for housing, whereas no planning consent was required to repair existing houses, and it was almost certain to be forthcoming for extensions. There developed a big demand not only for farmhouses and cottages, no matter what their condition, but also for barns, disused railway stations and other buildings which were capable of being converted into dwellings, from people who wished to commute, and from retired people.

The prices asked for the broken-down buildings increased with the demand for them. The prices of the farmhouses and cottages rose steeply, and in 1975 other buildings with planning consent for conversion into dwellings were bringing something like £5,000 to £20,000 in the open market in their unconverted state. The costs of conversion were often very high, perhaps between £20,000 and £60,000, depending on how they were converted. It became the fashion amongst those who could afford to do so to find a derelict building in a rural area and convert it into a dwelling, often of a very high standard. All these factors helped to speed up the changes which had been going on for some time in the social structure of the rural population. In the 19th century village people lived and worked as though they were one big family, with a strict hierarchy: the squire, doctor, parson, teacher, craftsmen and so on down to the farm labourer living in a tied cottage with a garden and pigsty attached. The old social hierarchy was gradually eroded and the idea of a self-sufficient community in the villages faded away. Today in many villages the agricultural worker is in the minority. Some of the inhabitants work in towns, and some agricultural workers live in towns and come to work in cars. The inhabitants of many villages are approaching a cross-section of the total population of the country. Since 1945 some villages have been so extended with new houses that they resemble housing estates, with the old village forming a core. Today nearly all villages in Britain have electricity and a piped supply of water and have been sewered, but in 1945 25 per cent of rural parishes were without a piped supply of water and had to rely on wells and springs, some of which were polluted.

Many of the villages on the present-day map of England existed at the time of the Domesday survey which was carried out by the Normans and completed in 1086. The coastal villages are often more recent than the inland ones because it was only in the 15th century that improved building techniques enabled large-scale construction of quays and jetties. However, there are some inland villages which did not evolve from small groups of primitive farmhouses and cottages but were planned. These are the estates and the industrial villages which came into existence largely in the 19th century. However, the English village as we like to picture it with its farmhouses, cottages, a church and a school was to a great extent shaped between the latter half of the 16th century and the 18th century.

In Scotland, rural development was somewhat different from that in England. Until the 19th century agriculture and rural settlement were based on large farmsteads or small hamlets, and later on the 'clearances' in the Highlands.

The estate villages were the creation of the land-owning classes and were originally under the sole ownership of one man – the landowner, who lived in the big house or mansion set in a parkland. These estate villages commonly originated from the demolition of shacks and hovels which were clustered close to the big house before it was enclosed by parkland. When the owner decided to isolate his domain from the farms and other lands he let at rents, he first had to sweep away the ugliness of poverty and deprivation so that the land around his house could be beautifully landscaped and made to produce food, nearly always more than adequate for his household, besides flowers and often exotic fruits grown in glass-houses or on south-facing walls heated by the sun in summer and fires in the spring and autumn. He also had to ensure that there was a sufficient depth of land all round the house to isolate it from roads and other houses and so ensure privacy.

The shacks were replaced by a row of identical cottages, usually built fairly close to the gates of the estates so that the labour necessary for the estate would be readily available. Sometimes the new cottages were constructed of similar materials to the large house, e.g. stone or red brick, and there was a

relationship in their designs. Later, with unplanned random development, which usually included an inn and a shop, the settlement developed into a village, but its economic and social life depended to a great extent on the whims of the landowner or squire.

Some landowners engaged architects to plan and design settlements for small rural communities on a grandiose scale, and some of these picturesque villages remain almost unaltered today, while others can be seen as beautiful cores in much enlarged villages. Many of the prosperous Victorians who built mansions away from the towns also built villages near their estates. These villages, amongst other things, provided housing for the fairly large staffs needed to run the estates, e.g. gamekeepers, gardeners, carpenters, farm labourers, domestic staff, etc. The building of a village also often satisfied an urge for philanthropy, which at times was fashionable amongst the rich. It was believed that good housing reinforced the moral fibre of the labouring classes and gave them a pride in their surroundings.

During the period of the industrial revolution some rural landowners found that their estates contained mineral deposits, such as coal and iron, and they became mine-owners or otherwise financially interested in the extraction of the minerals. Other rural areas contained the water power for the new manufacturing businesses that were rapidly growing up. Housing had to be provided for the labour required in the new industries and so the new industrial villages grew in the countryside. The differing industries gave rise to varying patterns of workers' houses, but on the whole the standard in the industrial villages was much lower than that in the estate villages and tended to follow that of the towns, but there were exceptions. In most of the industrial villages the houses were arranged in dreary terraces, some back-to-back, close to the mine or factory they had been built to serve. Although they were often set in beautiful countryside the view from their windows was frequently that of the factory building. Rarely was any provision made for community activities, except perhaps for the erection of a mission hall. A great many of these industrial villages were engulfed by town expansions but some are still in existence and are to be seen straggling main roads between towns or in valleys once the source of water power for the factories, which are probably now defunct.

Improved transport and alternative housing has made the industrial village no longer essential but during the inter-war period a very small number of firms with factories outside a town built villages close to them so as to be sure of a reliable work force. No industrial villages have been built in Britain since the end of the Second World War but the Forestry Commission has built a few hamlets in isolated and remote places in England and Scotland.

Villages in Britain today can be placed in one of three categories. These are: the carefully preserved village, often picturesque and with special architectural features; the scattered village, that is an original village with a certain amount of infilling and surrounded by a conglomeration of inter-war and post-1945 estates; and the industrial village built around a factory or a mine which is likely to be defunct.

In 1919 there were about one and three-quarter million dwelling-houses of all descriptions in the rural areas of Britain. These houses accommodated a population of about seven and a half million people, representing somewhere between 10 and 20 per cent of the total population of the country. Many were small, dark because of inadequate window areas, damp because they had no damp-proof courses, and without a piped supply of water and proper drainage. In many cases the sanitary accommodation consisted of pail or earth closets, or privies which had to be emptied by hand every few weeks. Artificial lighting was provided by candles or paraffin lamps. Some of the houses were in isolated positions away from the villages.

Besides agricultural workers, considerable numbers of other people were living in the villages, such as teachers for the village schools, small shopkeepers, craftsmen of many kinds, Post Office workers, railwaymen, retired people and the families of all these. The people not directly employed in agriculture amounted to something between one-third and one half of the population.

Between 1919 and 1939 about 871,000 new houses were built in rural areas, and out of these 707,000 were built by speculative builders for sale largely to workers in neighbouring urban areas and to retired people; 159,000 were built by rural district councils. Some of the houses built by the rural district councils between 1919 and 1933 were sold for owner-occupation, but the bulk of them were let at rents which for the most part were higher than the agricultural worker could afford to pay on the rates of wages then common. The average rent for a council house in a rural district was about 30p a week exclusive of rates, or 40p including rates. After 1920 the minimum agricultural wage dropped to a range of between £1.50 and £1.75 per week. This meant that many agricultural workers were unable to accept the tenancies of the new houses, ostensibly built for them, because to have done so would have meant their families going without some necessities. Even in 1936 the minimum agricultural wage averaged only £1.60 a week. In the circumstances, rather than leave the houses vacant many rural district councils were forced to let the new houses to non-agricultural workers, who often included people from adjacent urban areas. Because of the problem of balancing the rents of new houses with the wages of agricultural workers some rural local authorities did not build any houses during the inter-war period.

Between 1933 and 1939 private builders continued building houses in rural areas for sale to any willing buyers, and rural district councils switched their house building programmes to deal with the clearance of slums and with overcrowding, which had been revealed by a national survey carried out during 1935-36.

In 1938 the Housing (Financial Provisions) Act made bigger subsidies available to local authorities for building new houses for agricultural workers. The intention was that the new houses would be let at a rent of about 25p a week, including rates, and this was thought to be within the rent-paying capacity of most agricultural workers. The outbreak of war prevented any of these houses being built but the rural district councils had in total prepared plans to build 1,000.

On the opening of hostilities in September 1939 there were at least 68,000 unfit houses in the rural areas of England alone. Most of them lacked a piped supply of water and were dependent upon wells or springs which were often polluted. They very often lacked satisfactory drainage and were a great distance from an electricity supply. One quarter of the rural parishes in the country were without an adequate supply of water. Some of the unfit cottages were occupied by old people who had lived in them for many years and were opposed to leaving them. They had survived in reasonably good health for a long time without a water tap and a flush toilet and did not want these new-fangled ideas if it meant moving to get them. On the whole the rural authorities were sympathetic and reluctant to force the old to move. The councillors were countrymen themselves.

After the death of the tenants most of these houses became derelict and remained so until the late 1960s and 1970s when there was a demand for them from urbanites who were willing to spend large sums of money on reconditioning them either for permanent homes or for holiday retreats.

During the war, building was virtually suspended and slum clearance brought to a halt, as was the case in urban areas, but limited new building, amounting in all to 1,500 houses, was carried out in a few rural districts in which war industries had been established. Also, to meet the special difficulties which arose in certain districts as a result of a substantial development in wartime agriculture, the Government built 3,000 cottages, spread over 377 rural districts. However, the general shortage of housing for agricultural workers remained and much of the stock of houses in the rural areas deteriorated from lack of maintenance.

Agricultural wages rose during the war and in consequence the rent-paying capacity of agricultural workers improved and put them in a position whereby they were able to compete on closer terms with most other inhabitants of rural districts for such accommodation as was available. Also, so far as rent-paying capacity was concerned, there was little or no difference between the people living in rural villages and similar people living elsewhere in Britain.

In 1942 a quasi-Government committee (Hobhouse Committee) was asked to review the subject of rural housing and especially to examine any changes brought about by the war and to make recommendations for the policy to be pursued after the war. The committee published its report in 1944. It made recommendations in relation to the building of new houses in rural areas, about the reconditioning of existing houses, and the financing of these projects. In addition it recommended that all rural district councils should as soon as possible make a comprehensive survey to ascertain the housing needs of their areas. These surveys proved to be of great help to the rural councils in the immediate post-war period.

By 1942 the minimum agricultural wage had risen from £1.70 in 1939 to £3.25, and on this basis the Hobhouse Committee recommended that the rents of the new council houses to be built in rural areas should not exceed 40p a week, exclusive of rates. In 1939 the cost of building a council house for an agricultural worker was about £500 for the non-parlour type and £550 for a house with a parlour. In 1944 the estimated cost of building similar houses was £966 for the non-parlour type and £1,047 for the parlour type. The Government accepted the recommendations in the Hobhouse report, and most rural councils made surveys to ascertain the housing needs of their areas.

In spite of the fact that the rural areas had escaped most of the bombing, agricultural housing started the post-war period with much more leeway to make up than had urban housing because of the lag in the general improvement in agricultural housing during the inter-war period. Rural councils, however, had the advantage of having up-to-date information from the surveys they had made in 1945. In the immediate post-war period many of them made a quick start and good progress in building houses, often in proportion to their size, i.e. the number of houses built per thousand of population, building more houses than urban areas.

During the inter-war period substantial parts of some rural areas, with large numbers of modern houses, were transferred to adjacent urban districts. This reduced the rateable value of these areas and therefore their revenue, and increased the proportion of their housing stock which was substandard and needed replacing or reconditioning. However, even up to 1974, when the rural districts were abolished by local government reoganisation, some rural districts contained the suburban fringes of the adjacent towns so that their populations were not predominantly agricultural.

The statistics and other information given in this chapter relate to the local government units which until 31 March 1974 were known as rural districts. Although in Britain there are many areas which are undoubtedly rural in character, since 1 April 1974 they have been incorporated for local government purposes into larger districts which are predominantly urban in character. There is therefore no demarcation now, for administrative purposes, between rural and urban areas. However, the illustrations included in this chapter are of the types of houses which before 1974 were commonly to be found in areas described as rural districts but which are now incorporated in predominantly urban local government districts.

Remoteness. No piped water supply, no gas, no electricity; heat for cooking and warmth obtained from peat and paraffin. (1955)

Remoteness. Cooking and even the baking of bread is done on an open fire. (1957)

39

Small farmhouse close to a wind-swept coast. (1955)

The living-room in a crofter's cottage. (1957)

A new crofter's cottage built in 1956. It has a piped water supply, electricity and a telephone.

A 200-year-old farmhouse.

A small farmhouse with barn and dairy amongst the Lakeland fells.

House, barn and byre built integrally.

The home of a dairy farmer.

A larger type of farmhouse.

43

A renovated farmhouse offered for sale with 3 acres of land. (1980)

*In the late 1960s and 1970s there was a demand for barns and other farm buildings
capable of being converted into dwellings.*

A barn before conversion into a house.

The same barn after conversion into a house.

45

Former railway station converted into two dwellings.

Cottage at gateway to abbey. Design follows closely that of abbey.

A village that has kept its character. (1964)

A village that has remained unaltered in spite of modern traffic which passes through it.

47

An ancient and beautiful village. (1964)

A picturesque Cotswold village.

Former industrial village now straggling a main road. (1978)

Houses in a post-1945 Forestry Commission village. (1980)

Attractive, but the new limewash conceals the defects.

A dream cottage: the picture which many townspeople have in their minds of rural living. (1979)

Weather-boarded cottages.

Old cottages built with local stone and slate in the vernacular style.

More rural cottages built in the vernacular style of more than a century ago.

Old whitewashed cottages with thatched roofs.

Flint-stone cottages.

Old timber-framed rural cottages.

53

House near fells and lakes built in traditional dry walling.

Modern house with thatched roof showing the skill of present-day craftsmen.

54

Post-1945 privately owned bungalow built in a rural area.

Post-1945 privately owned timber-built rural houses.

55

Chapter 4

PRIVATELY RENTED HOMES

For a period of about 150 years, which finished at the beginning of the First World War, the great majority of houses in Britain were owned by private landlords for renting at a profit, and until the end of the first decade of the 20th century housing was considered to be such a sound investment that some other investments were described as being "as safe as houses". During the earlier part of this period there was little or no Government intervention in housing. Dwellings were built at a cost which would allow for rents that tenants could pay and also yield a profit on the investment. Many of the houses built for the working-classes were of poor quality, often back-to-back and packed tightly together in narrow streets or courts. They were frequently kept in bad repair and were overcrowded.

By about half way through the period the housing conditions of the working-classes in many towns gave rise to public concern and Government intervention followed, requiring the speculative builders and landlords to meet gradually rising standards. However, house building for renting remained a profitable and sound investment until about the beginning of the present century. By that time it had become increasingly difficult to meet the rising standards and yet provide housing at rents which the lower paid worker could afford. The supply of houses in many parts of the country exceeded the effective demand, but not need. Housing became much less attractive as a speculative venture and there was a rapid decline in house building, resulting in considerable unemployment amongst building workers by 1911. Very little house building for private renting took place in the inter-war period and since 1945 there has been virtually none.

Since 1919 there has been a decline in the proportion of the housing stock rented from private landlords. At the beginning of the First World War about 90 per cent of houses in Britain were privately rented. By 1951 the proportion had fallen to 45 per cent, by 1973 to 17 per cent, and by 1980 it was down to 13 per cent. There are many reasons for this rapid decline. They include government intervention through the enforcement of gradually rising minimum standards, rent control, slum clearance and redevelopment, the provision of municipal housing, changing economic circumstances, and the greater availability of other forms of tenure. For example, it was estimated that a house which would have cost £250 to build in 1914 would have cost £1,000 in 1919-20 and could not have been let at a rent within the means of the working-classes.

The freedom of the private landlord was significantly affected in 1915 by the Rents and Mortgage Interest Restriction Act of that year, which fixed rents, gave tenants security of tenure against eviction, and prevented an increase in the interest rates on mortgages and the calling-in of mortgages. Although this law was intended to be only a temporary measure, there has been rent control in some form ever since. Efforts were made between the wars to decontrol the rents of some houses when it was felt that the shortage had been overcome, but decontrol was limited to higher rented dwellings and on the landlord obtaining vacant possession. Limited increases were also permitted in the rents of houses which remained controlled, to take account of changes in the costs of maintenance and inflation.

At the outbreak of the Second World War in 1939 the rents of all but the very expensive houses were frozen at their 1939 levels. They remained controlled at this level until 1954 in spite of a considerable increase in the costs of repairs and management during the period. In 1953 a Government committee (Girwood Committee) estimated that housing repairs which cost £100 to do in 1939 would on average, in April 1953, have cost £316. It was argued that since the costs of repairs were just over three times what they were in 1939 the repair element in rents should be increased to allow landlords to repair and maintain their houses to the standard they had adopted in 1939. In consequence, the Housing Repairs and Rents Act 1954 allowed for increases in the controlled rents of houses to meet the higher cost of repairs but did not allow a general increase in rents or the decontrol of houses. The rent increases could be claimed only if the house was in a good state of repair and not unfit. Tenants who were not satisfied with the condition of their dwellings could, if they wished, apply to the local authority for a certificate that the house was not in good repair, and if it was granted the landlord could not claim the increase while the certificate remained in force, but he could apply for its cancellation when the necessary repairs had been completed.

During the first six months after the Act came into force about 18,000 disrepair certificates were issued in England and Wales, but after that the number of applications for them rapidly declined. It is likely that a proportion of the tenants of the several million controlled houses considered their rents to be unreasonably low and paid the rent increases without the repairs having been done by the landlord, or else did the repairs themselves. Also, many of the landlords did not claim the increases either because they considered the small permitted increase did not warrant the high cost of the necessary repairs or because they did not have the capital to pay for them. The repairs had to be completed before the rent increase could be claimed from the tenant.

The Government expressed high hopes that the provisions of the 1954 Act would encourage landlords to put, and to keep, millions of rented houses in a state of good repair and therefore preserve an important national asset; but the Act did not have the hoped-for effect. The permitted rent increases came too late, and were insufficient to remedy the ravages of years of forced neglect. In addition, the British taxation system does not encourage private investment in housing for renting, because no provision is made in it for amortisation and depreciation in respect of housing.

In general the landlords of private houses have had a bad public image. They are often seen as a symbol of the exploitation of man by man, an image which probably originated in the period before 1914 when real poverty was fairly widespread in Britain and the Government intervention in housing was small compared to what it is today. Before the age of subsidised municiple housing, rent control and social security, rent arrears in times of trade recession were fairly common and the sight of bailiffs seizing the meagre possessions of those who had not done a moonlight flit with their goods on a hired handcart when they realised their position was hopeless was not rare. Fairly recent studies of present-day landlords, however, have shown them not to be a homogeneous group of shrewd investors. Most landlords of this type withdrew their investments from the housing field a long time ago.

Studies of London landlords carried out for the Committee on Housing in Greater London (Milner Holland Committee) in 1964 revealed that a great proportion of landlords were not in 'business' as landlords, but merely let property to relatives, friends or employees. About 60 per cent owned only one dwelling and 85 per cent owned between one and nine dwellings. Another study was made by Professor John Greve, with the help of the British Market Research Bureau, of a sample of 269 landlords drawn from all parts of England. It suggests that three-quarters of this country's private landlords are responsible for less than six tenancies, and that the majority of them are individuals who have not established a limited company.

Perhaps the best evidence about the social and economic status of landlords came from J.B. Cullingworth's study of landlords in Lancaster in 1962-63. There were 853 private landlords there who between them owned 2,631 houses. Well over half owned only one house. A third of them were 70 or more years of age, and a further quarter were aged between 60 and 70. Their average weekly income, including net income from rents, was less than £10. Nearly three-quarters of them obtained their dwelling by inheritance. Very few had sufficient capital to improve their houses even if they had been inclined to do so, and most considered their houses a responsibility to be shed at the first opportunity. Also, most were from the same social class as their tenants and lived on the same economic level and often in very close touch with them. Landlord and tenant relationships were sometimes on a social and friend to friend basis.

At the other end of the housing market a study of landlords in St. Marylebone in the centre of London revealed a large number of big business-like landlords who were efficient in the management of their property. Also in other parts of London and in some other big towns there are property companies which own blocks of high value rented accommodation, largely in blocks of luxury flats. However, large-scale private investment in housing ended before 1914, and since then there has been a movement of private investment away from housing into more profitable fields. Private investment that has remained in housing is mostly in blocks of luxury flats and in furnished lettings, which until 1965 were not subject to rent restrictions, and the tenants did not have security of tenure.

Predominantly, then, the landlords of the present day are not able and efficient business people, but individuals who entered the business of renting houses more or less by accident rather than by a clear-cut business decision. They include, for example, those who became landlords by inheritance or because they bought the house next door, or a house for a relative to live in, or with insufficient knowledge bought a house in the hope of providing an additional income when they retired. Amongst them are the few who gambled on the chance of obtaining vacant possession at an early date and then selling at a good margin of profit.

Another attempt to deal with the problems of disrepair in privately rented housing was made by the Conservative Government in 1957. The Rent Act 1957 was intended to create a rational and equitable rent structure. It freed houses with a rateable value of over £30 in England and Wales, excluding London, and over £40 in London and Scotland, from any rent control, but landlords were encouraged to offer their tenants a three-year lease. All other privately rented houses remained subject to rent control, but rents were permitted to rise to a new ceiling related to gross rateable value and to the extent of the landlord's responsibility for repairs. It was assumed that the worst houses which remained controlled would gradually be acquired by local authorities for slum clearance or because they were incapable of repair at reasonable cost. All new tenancies, created after a landlord had obtained vacant possession, were released from rent control.

The Government hoped that the Act would

improve the standard of maintenance of rented houses, maintain the supply of privately owned dwellings available for renting by encouraging new building for the purpose and discouraging the sales of rented houses for owner-occupation, allow greater mobility of labour and reduce under-occupation and overcrowding by allowing people to move into dwellings more suitable to their needs rather than clinging to the security of tenure, etc., guaranteed by the Rent Acts.

As an alternative to the measures contained in the Rent Act 1957 a section of the Labour Party advocated that all privately rented houses should be acquired by local authorities. But others in the party expressed grave doubts about the wisdom of saddling local authorities with such a heavy financial burden.

Although the effects of the Rent Act 1957 varied in some degree from place to place, on the whole it did not achieve its objectives. For example, since 1957 the private rented sector has continued to contract. In some areas there was evidence that the Act had made the housing situation worse, and in a minority of cases it led to the exploitation of tenants by unscrupulous landlords. In some of these cases dogs were used, and in others the electricity and water supplies were turned off in order to harass the tenants into moving and thus giving the landlord vacant possession, or into paying illegally high rents. The activities of these landlords were personified in the person called Rachman, who operated this kind of racket in north-west London, and referred to as Rachmanism. By the Protection of Eviction Act 1964 harassment was made an offence.

The Labour Government's Rent Act 1965 introduced the concept of 'fair' rents, and by its provisions, under certain conditions, 'regulation' took the place of 'control'. Unfurnished tenancies newly brought within its provisions of rent control were known as 'regulated' tenancies. The security of tenure granted by earlier Acts was extended to every tenancy of an unfurnished dwelling-house of up to £400 rateable value in Greater London and £200 in the rest of Great Britain, and to new dwelling-houses of these rateable values. The first step to establish the fair rent of a dwelling was for the landlord and tenant to try to reach agreement on what was the fair rent, and if this was not possible either of them could ask the rent officer to determine it. The provisions of this Act were consolidated with others in the Rent Act 1968.

The Rent Act 1977 both consolidated and amended the law with respect to privately rented dwellings and further amendments were made by the Housing Act 1980. Under the latter Act all controlled tenancies became regulated tenancies for which the rent officers can determine the 'fair' rents and, furthermore, controlled rents can be increased only by an application to the rent officer for the registration of the fair rent. The present position is that most lettings of non-resident private landlords will create a 'regulated' tenancy. It does not matter whether the letting is furnished or unfurnished provided its rateable value is not higher than £1,500 in Greater Lon-

don or £750 elsewhere in Britain. Dwellings with higher rateable values may still fall within the provisions of the Rent Act if their rateable value on the valuation list which expired on 31 March 1973 was £600 or less in Greater London, or £300 or less elsewhere in the country.

In fixing a fair rent the rent officer must take account of all the circumstances, except the personal circumstances of the landlord and the tenant. In particular he must take account of the state of repair of the dwelling, its character, locality and age. In the case of furnished lettings he will also take account of the quantity and quality of the furniture provided. He must ignore any disrepair for which the tenant is responsible and also any improvements that the tenant has made without being obliged to do so by his lease. He must assume that the demand for similar houses or flats available for letting in that particular area does not substantially exceed supply.

Over the years, because of the security of tenure granted to tenants of private rented properties, dwellings which otherwise might have been available for renting for short periods remained empty in spite of any housing shortage in the area. To deal with this situation two amendments to the law have been made. The first, under the Rent Act 1977, is the "mandatory ground for possession", which means that if at the start of a tenancy a written notice is given to the tenant that the possession might be recovered, an application can be made to the court for a possession order. The person making the application must have lived in the dwelling before he let it and must satisfy the court either that he wants to live in the dwelling himself or alternatively that a member of his family who was living in the dwelling at the time he occupied it wants to live in it. The second was made by sections 51 to 55 of the Housing Act 1980. It introduced a new type of protected tenancy – "the protected short hold tenancy". The main feature of this is that the tenancy lasts for a fixed period agreed at the start of the letting, at the end of which the landlord has a clear right to repossession provided he has complied with certain conditions.

The rents charged for privately owned dwellings vary throughout the country. The following are examples of the median annual net rents charged in the early 1960s. In Lancaster it was £36; in Beeston and Stapleford, on the fringe of Nottingham, it was £51; and in the Metropolitan Borough of St. Marylebone it was £55, but here there was a wider variation than in the other two towns, for example about 25 per cent of the tenants paid £70 or more per year.

Most privately rented housing in Britain is old, obsolete, of poor quality and suffers from years of neglect. The Government's 1971 House Condition Survey of England and Wales revealed that about 70 per cent of privately rented houses had been built before 1919 and that 23 per cent of them were statutorily unfit, as compared with 7 per cent of all houses. 40 per cent lacked one or more of the basic amenities, and 30 per cent were in need of substantial repair. The 1976 House Condition Survey showed that 15 per cent of privately rented houses were unfit as compared with 5 per cent of all houses, and 26 per cent lacked one or more of the basic amenities, as compared with 9 per cent for all houses.

Where the lease of a house is for less than seven years, e.g. a monthly tenancy, the landlord has a duty under the Housing Act 1961 to keep in repair its structure and exterior, and also to keep in repair and proper working order all installations in the house for the supply of water, gas, electricity, sanitary fittings and space and water heating.

In addition to the foregoing, under the Housing Act 1957 if a local authority is satisfied that any house is unfit and is capable of being made fit at a reasonable cost it can serve a notice on the owner of the house requiring him to carry out specified works to make the house fit. If the owner fails to do the works specified, the local authority can do the work and recover the cost from him, which might mean collecting the rent until the cost is recovered. It all seems to be straightforward, but when does a house become unfit? This is discussed in Chapter 10. And what in practice is meant by 'reasonable' expense?

A case (Phillips v London Borough of Newham) which was heard before Lord Denning in July 1981 cleared away some of the confusion which had existed for many years about what constituted 'reasonable' expense.

There has to be a realistic approach to the value of dwelling houses as saleable assets in the hands of the landlord when considering the reasonableness of the expense required to make a house fit and, therefore, regard must be had to the presence of tenants and their rights to continued occupation and the effect that they have on the market value. So what would appear to be the right way of solving the problem of 'reasonable' expense is to consider the value of the house as it is – unrepaired and dilapidated – with the tenant there, probably protected by the Rent Acts, and having regard to the age etc. of the tenant. Then compare this value with the value of the house as it would be if the works were completed and the tenant in occupation, protected by the Rent Acts. Taking these two figures compare the difference between them with the amount of money required to make the house fit. For example, if the estimated cost of repairs was £5,000 plus VAT, and the value of the unrepaired tenanted house was £3,000, which after the repairs had been done and with the tenant in possession is likely to be increased to £7,000, then to insist on the execution of the repairs would mean that the owner was being asked to spend over £5,000 in order to increase the value of his saleable asset, the house, by only £4,000. However, an offer by the local authority of a repair grant, say one half of the proposed expenditure, may alter the position. In that event the landlord would only have to find less than £3,000 to increase the valuation of his property by £4,000.

At least since 1945 local authorities have been faced with problems about what to do about many of the older privately rented dwellings which are in need of repair. An owner of an unfit house faced with a repair notice served by the local authority can appeal to the courts, and if successful the local authority would be faced with making a decision about buying the house and carrying out the repairs it tried to make the owner do.

Until 1974 local authorities had to wait until houses fell into a state of unfitness before they could take formal action to have them repaired, but in that year the law was amended by the Housing Act 1974. Now, if a house is not unfit but is in need of substantial repair, the local authority can serve a notice on the owner requiring him to carry out works which are necessary to bring the house up to a reasonable standard, having regard for the age of the house, but in such a case the local authority is not required to enquire into the cost of the repairs or the value of the house, but this would seem to be a wise thing to do.

A further amendment to the law was made by the Housing Act 1980. This new power enables local authorities to deal with houses which are neither unfit nor in need of substantial repair, but in which there are items of disrepair which interfere materially with the personal comfort of the tenant. Formerly these items of disrepair were regarded as giving rise to a nuisance and were dealt with by powers contained in the Public Health Act 1936, but the courts have held this was a wrong use of these powers.

Privately rented housing contains a wide variety of dwelling types and sizes, and the bulk of it is let at comparatively low rents to tenants, many of whom will never be able to buy a house or obtain the tenancy of a council house. Something like 40 per cent of the tenants are over 65 years of age and over 50 per cent are in the lower income groups.

In 1968, Birmingham City Council pioneered a scheme contained in a Private Act of Parliament, which gave it the power to pay rent allowances to tenants in furnished and unfurnished privately rented dwellings. In 1971, the Conservative Government published proposals for changes in the system of housing finance, which included provisions for rent rebates and allowances on a national scale. The following year, the Housing Finance Act 1972 made it compulsory for housing authorities to have schemes for rent rebates for council housing and the payment of rent allowances to certain tenants of unfurnished privately owned lettings. In 1973 the duty was extended to tenants of furnished lettings. Also, since 1974 tenants of furnished accommodation have the same protection as tenants of unfurnished dwellings, and may apply to the rent officer for a fair rent determination. However, the security of tenure does not apply in those cases where the landlord lives on the premises.

In Britain the sharing of houses by two or more households, whether in furnished or in unfurnished accommodation, has existed at least since people poured into the towns at the commencement of what is called the 'industrial revolution'. Even by the end of the first decade of the 20th century, although in many towns there were empty houses, a large proportion of lower paid workers were living in lodging-houses or in rooms because they were unable to pay the rent, and for heating and lighting, of a whole house. During the inter-war period the proportion of households which were living in shared accommodation fell, but in 1951 about one million households, out of a total of thirteen million, were living in shared accommodation. During the next two decades the number of sharing households fell, but the 1971 census showed that 270,000 dwellings in England were in multiple-occupation, 152,000 of which were in Greater London. The types and the condition of the houses which are in multi-occupation vary widely. For example, some are very large houses, which in former times were the residences of the very wealthy, but are now in such a bad condition that they await demolition in slum clearance areas. Others are well maintained, fairly modern houses situated in good-class areas.

For many years local authorities had the power to make bye-laws with respect to conditions in what were then called 'houses-let-lodgings', but they were not very effective. In the late 1950s conditions in some of these houses gave rise to concern by various organisations and following a number of deaths as a result of outbreaks of fire led to publicity in the newspapers, etc. At that time conditions in some of these houses, especially many of those in the large towns, were appalling. The cooking facilities for several families often consisted of a single gas cooker placed on a staircase landing, and one sink had to serve for the preparation of food and for the general ablutions of a number of tenants. The landlords of many of the houses exercised little or no control or management over the houses, except for the collection of rents, which were often very high. The result was that staircases and passages used in common by the inhabitants were cleaned only very infrequently. Gross overcrowding was common but there were no means of escape in the event of fire. Local authorities were hesitant to take action about the provision of additional facilities in the houses because of the danger of aggravating the housing shortage.

The Housing Act 1961 now gives local authorities powers to insist on a reasonable degree of management of houses in multi-occupation, and to require the person having control of the house to provide sufficient of certain facilities, such as sinks, baths, wash-hand basins and cooking facilities; and also to ensure that there are adequate means of escape in case of fire. In cases where the person in control of the house fails to carry out the work required the local authority can do the work and recover the cost from him. Also, in extreme cases of neglect in respect to management, the local authority may take over the management of the house for a specified period. The Housing Act 1969 contains further powers for local authorities to deal with conditions in houses in multi-occupation. For example, there is power to make registration of a house with the local authority a pre-requisite of new multiple-occupation. Also, improvement grants are now available for the provision of basic amenities in houses which are in multiple-occupation.

Since the middle of the 1960s conditions in houses in multi-occupation have improved considerably, on the whole. For example, it is now common for each dwelling unit to have its own cooking facilities and either a sink or a wash-hand basin; and there has been a big improvement in the means of escape in the event of fire. However, in some areas of the country the shortage of housing accommodation still hampers the enforcement of reasonable standards in these houses.

Houses in multi-occupation cater for various groups of people who often need accommodation at short notice. They include mobile workers and their families, students, trainees and other young people who for a variety of reasons have left the parental home, the newly-married, immigrants, and those suffering from family break-up. The accommodation provided meets housing needs which would be difficult to satisfy in any other way. If the standards enforced by local authorities are unreasonably high in the prevailing circumstances, there will be a reduction in the amount of the accommodaton available and consequently an increase in homelessness.

Private investment in rented housing commenced to decline about the beginning of the 20th century. At that time in many parts of the country numbers of working-class houses were empty or had become difficult to let because would-be tenants could not afford the rents. The building of new houses slumped and by 1911 there was considerable unemployment among building workers. Also, there were alternative channels of secure investment, primarily overseas, which provided a higher rate of return than in the circumstances could be obtained from housing.

In 1914 about 90 per cent of the housing stock in Britain was rented from private landlords, as compared to about 13 per cent in 1980. The main reasons for the decline have been the operation of rent and other legal restrictions, a big increase in both the facilities and in the demand for owner-occupation, the availability of subsidised publicly owned dwellings and slum clearance. Out of these reasons, the way in which rents have been controlled during the last sixty years has been the most important.

Privately rented housing, both furnished and unfurnished, still plays an important, but diminishing, role in the life of Britain. However, it consists of a high proportion of the older and substandard property which is becoming unfit at a fast rate because of prolonged neglect. Larger and earlier permitted rent increases during the last sixty years would have reduced some of the present-day housing problems, especially in the inner-city areas. Since 1954 successive Governments have made changes in the law with respect to housing. A great deal of emphasis has rightly been placed on the interests of tenants but more regard should have been paid to the need to preserve more of the existing stock of houses which were capable of providing reasonable homes. If private rented housing is to continue providing accommodation for a variety of types of households not adequately catered for by other means, and often at short notice, then there must be a new and positive approach to the needs of the private housing sector.

Example of the larger houses which remained privately rented during the 1960s-1970s. (1979)

Large Victorian houses converted into flats for private renting.

62

In 1914 about 90 per cent of all houses were privately rented. During the inter-war period some of the larger houses in the better areas remained in single family occupation but after 1945 the demand for them fell off. Some were converted into flats, others fell into multi-occupation without the necessary adaptations.

Post-1945 eight-storey, high-value, privately rented blocks of flats. (1960s)

Post-1945 infilling of prestige site with high-class privately rented flats.

Solid Victorian houses built for renting by skilled artisans and white-collar workers but by the 1950s regarded as substandard because they lacked modern amenities.

Four-roomed terrace houses; a type built in every town in Britain during the late 19th and early part of the 20th century for renting to the working-classes. To-day they account for about 30 per cent of the housing stock of many towns.

Double bay-window terrace houses built late 19th century on what was then the outskirts of towns but now to be found on the inner rings of many towns. Originally intended for renting to semi-professional and other white-collar workers but by the 1950s occupied by a mixture of classes depending upon the degree of the housing shortage in the area.

Privately rented working-class houses packed tight in a narrow court. (1955)

Three-storey terrace houses, with cellar kitchens, built in the 19th century for renting to businesses and professional families. By the 1930s many had become obsolete for single family occupation and were in multiple occupation. (1955)

Dwellings, built in the middle of the 19th century for renting to the working-classes, over stables and adjacent to factories etc. (1958)

19th century terrace houses built for renting to the working-classes. Some have cellars (bricked up), which up to the early part of the 20th century were let as separate dwellings. (1957)

Once a proud crescent; now the drabness and decay which goes with over-occupation. (1965)

Change and decay caused by age and lack of maintenance. Once fine houses now in multiple occupation. (1965)

Sinks provided on flat roofs for the use of several families. (1959)

Cooking facilities for several families on staircase landing. (1958)

One of several single-room homes in a large house once the splendid residence of a wealthy family, (1956)

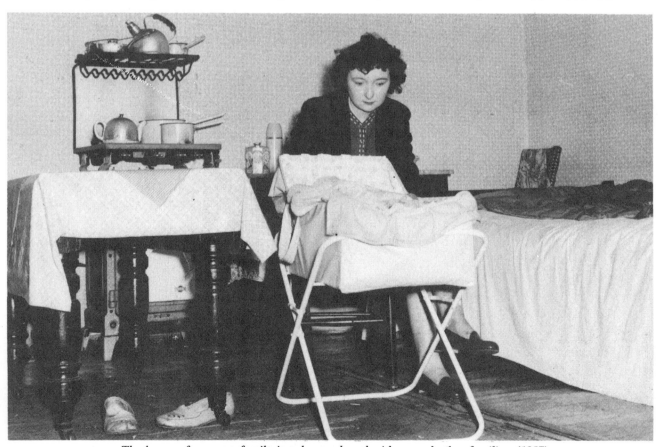

The home of a young family in a house shared with several other families. (1957)

The rear of a terrace of large 19th century houses occupied by several families. (1956)

The rear of the same terrace after improvement and conversion into flats. (1964)

One house occupied by 7 families (11 adults and 3 children). The other house occupied by 6 families (12 adults and 1 child) (1959)

The two houses after conversion into seven one-bedroomed flats. (1964)

Chapter 5

OWNER-OCCUPIED HOMES

For many people in Britain home ownership is the most rewarding form of house tenure. It satisfies a primeval desire of the individual to have independent control of the place which gives shelter and ensures privacy for himself and his family. Also the name 'owner' implies a higher status than that of tenant, and although tenants have a very large measure of security of tenure, that of the owner-occupier is even greater in spite of the probability that he has replaced his landlord with a mortgagee. If the householder is buying his house on mortgage, by steady saving he is building up a capital asset for himself and his dependents, and if the building is free of mortgage, in all probability its value will have risen continuously over the years.

In spite of these and other advantages not every householder in Britain wishes to become an owner-occupier. To some of these people owner-occupation is a risky business and involves responsibilities they prefer not to have, for example for the structure of the dwelling. Others choose to keep current housing expenditure at a modest level through rent payment, leaving a larger proportion of the family income for other things, rather than to make larger payments in the short term in the expectation of a capital gain and reduced housing payments in the future.

There are also traditional tenants, householders whose cultural and family backgrounds are in opposition to ownership. A survey made for the economic development committee for the building industry during 1970-71 showed that three out of five council and private tenants did not wish to own but preferred to rent their houses. This group probably included those who thought that they would never be in the financial position to buy their houses.

Between 1919 and 1939 there was an enormous swing towards owner-occupation. The prime factors in this swing were the ability to pay the prices, which indicates a substantial rise in real wages since 1914, and the existence of institutions which were able to provide the finance and allow the phasing of repayments over a sufficiently long period of time to bring costs and incomes into a feasible relationship. During the period about two and a half million houses were built for owner-occupation – predominantly by speculative builders who were able to buy land relatively cheaply and were not controlled by strict planning requirements as is the case today. Some of the houses were poorly built, and inferior materials were often used. To keep costs down workmen were frequently paid piece rates, e.g. bricklayers so much per thousand bricks laid, and the plumber, if he was to keep his job, had to fix all the pipes in a house in a single day. The result was poor workmanship. However, most of the houses were sufficiently well built to survive to the present day, that is about half a century's wear and tear, without considerable deterioration.

During the 1930s both building costs and interest rates fell. At one period in some parts of the country a three-bedroomed speculatively built house could be bought for as little as £300, and building society interest rates were 3 per cent. Owner-occupation was brought well within the reach of the average skilled workman who could count on a reasonable degree of continuous employment. In 1919 less than one-tenth of households were owner-occupiers, but by 1939 the proportion had risen to just over a quarter. In the thirty-five years since the end of World War II, the number of people owning or buying their homes has more than doubled. Owner-occupied dwellings in Britain in 1980 accounted for nearly 55 per cent of the total housing stock of the country.

The housing stock which is in owner-occupation is immensely variable – ranging from houses officially classified as slums and small four-roomed terrace houses, to houses in London commanding prices around M£1. Owner-occupiers are similarly a heterogeneous group in terms of age, occupation, income and social class.

Dwellings become available for owner-occupation predominantly in two ways, i.e. by new building and by the sale of existing rented accommodation, which may be privately or publicly owned. Existing accommodation may be sold either to sitting tenants or with vacant possession. The sale of existing council houses to sitting tenants is discussed in Chapter 6.

Most new dwellings built for owner-occupation are provided by private speculative builders and developers, but a few local authorities and new town corporations also build houses for sale to owner-occupiers. In addition, each year there are a relatively small number of houses built to order, but these are usually the larger and more costly types. Private building for owner-occupation accounted for 14 per cent of all completions in 1952, 41 per cent in 1956, 54 per cent in 1960, and 63 per cent in 1973, and has remained somewhere around that figure since then.

No reliable information is available on how the majority of speculative builders determine the number, types, and prices of the houses they will build in any one year. From observations on some of the sites it would seem that there is a great deal of guess-work and conformity with certain norms, such as design and local selling prices, etc., but of consider-able importance is the availability of cash. With the small builder money is borrowed on the security of the land to buy materials and to pay for the labour for the first one or two houses and as these are sold money is available for further building. The speed at which the houses are sold depends a great deal on the availability of mortgages, which is in turn linked to the lending rate. The larger developers, however, probably do some market research and costing.

There is no precise information available about the number of houses which change each year from being rented to being owner-occupied, but the speed at which the private rented sector has shrunk, even after allowing for demolitions, indicates that it must be quite large.

Owner-occupiers, and especially first-time buyers, frequently have insufficient capital to pay for their houses in cash and in consequence have to negotiate a loan. The loan is made for a fixed period during which repayment of principal, and the payment of interest on the outstanding debt, are made until the debt is discharged. Lending agencies are constrained by the amount of money they have available for loan pur-poses. Interest rates influence both the availability of funds and the cost of the loan to the borrower. The lender must be concerned with the security of the loan and in consequence must ensure that the borrower can meet capital and other repayment requirements, which involves consideration of the borrower's age, income and financial commitments. Also the lender must be satisfied that the mortgaged property will maintain its value during the period of the loan, which involves consideration of the age, structural condi-tion, value and location of the house.

House purchase loans are obtained mainly from four sources. These are: building societies, local authorities, insurance companies and banks. In addi-tion there are other sources such as some housing associations and individuals who include the back-street mortgagees who demand very high rates of interest from borrowers who cannot satisfy the requirements of banks, building societies and local authorities, either because of unstable income or because of the condition of the houses. This type of mortgage business is more likely to thrive in inner-city areas and in particular in the parts predominantly occupied by immigrants. In some of these cases the mortgagee is also the vendor.

The building society movement has a long history. The first society on record was founded in Birming-ham about 1775. The early societies were actually concerned with building, as the name suggests. They were mutual aid groups, in which members used their accumulated savings to buy a plot of land and build houses on it. Each member agreed to pay the building society a fixed sum of money each month until all the members were housed – at which point the society went out of existence.

Funds were augmented by borrowing money from investors not seeking a house, but receiving interest on their investment. To cover these interest payments the society charged interest to borrowing members. From these beginnings the modern building society has evolved to its present important position in the housing system of the country. In the process of evolution changes have occurred. The modern build-ing society is 'permanent' in the sense that it does not terminate when a certain objective is completed, and the word 'permanent' has been incorporated in the name of some societies. Societies are not now con-cerned with house building – in fact they are prohi-bited by law from erecting dwellings for sale.

The principal function of building societies today is to supply long-term loans on the security of private dwelling-houses purchased for owner-occupation. Their funds are derived mainly from the general public who invest in shares or deposits. The Building Society Act 1962, which consolidated a number of earlier Acts, prescribes the general way in which societies must conduct their business. The Chief Registrar of Friendly Societies has discretionary power to stop a society either advertising or accepting money from investors if he considers that the way in which the society's business is conducted is jeopardis-ing investors' money. The amount of share capital of a society is not fixed, and the shares, which have a fixed value, are not dealt in on the stock exchange but may be withdrawn in cash if notice is given.

In the 19th century building societies were small but numerous: there were about 2,250 societies in 1900 with total assets of about M£70. By 1939 there were fewer societies but their assets had grown to M£773. At the end of 1980 there were 273 building societies in Britain and their total assets amounted to M£53,793. However, the five largest societies held M£29,799, or 55.4 per cent of these total assets. Building societies' net advances for house purchase amounted to M£5,418 in 1980, or 78.6 per cent of all advances for house purchase, and they had outstand-ing balances of M£42,404, or 82 per cent of the total balances outstanding for house purchase.

In 1980 199 societies were members of the Build-ing Societies Association, which was founded in 1869. The Association is concerned particularly with the financial security and practices of the member societies and recommends interest rates, but the recommendations are not binding. The larger societies operate throughout Britain but most of the small ones operate only within a very restricted area, for example a single county.

Local authorities have the power to make loans to any person for the purpose of acquiring, constructing, converting, altering, enlarging or improving houses, and this power may be used in respect of houses or buildings inside or outside the local authority's area. They also have power, with the approval of the Sec-retary of State for the Environment, to make certain guarantees with respect to house mortgages to building societies. However, from the late 1960s there have been Government restrictions on the amounts which local authorities can lend for house purchase in any one year, in the interest of the national economy. Also local authorities have been advised by the Government to use their limited resources mainly for the purpose of helping those borrowers who are least likely to be able to obtain an adequate loan elsewhere. Local authorities have thus become large lenders of last resort, providing mortgages of up to 100 per cent of the local authority's valuation, to borrowers regarded as having priority of need, for example the homeless, people high on the council's waiting list, people displaced by redevelopment schemes and those wishing to buy the older property which is not likely to attract a building society mortgage, and first-time buyers of new dwellings. Besides increasing opportunities for access to owner-occupation, local authorities' lending has also implications for the rehabilitation of older housing which otherwise might be unsaleable or available only to cash buyers, or at the higher rates of interest charged by money lenders or back-street mortgagees or other non-orthodox mortgage institutions. On average local authorities lend about 5 per cent of the total amount advanced in a year for house purchases, but in 1974 because building societies experienced difficulties in attracting new investments it was 14 per cent of the total. In 1979 local authorities advanced 4.6 per cent of the total amount advanced and in 1980 it was 6.5 per cent, or M£448. Local authorities' outstanding balances amounted to M£3,646, or 7.1 per cent of the total balances outstanding.

Insurance companies' mortgages are usually linked to endowment or similar polices. They provide only about 4 per cent of the funds for house purchases. In 1980 it was 3.7 per cent, or M£255 and they had outstanding balances for house purchases of M£2,082, or 4 per cent of the total.

During 1980 the banks were freed from some of the restrictions under which they had previously operated and this enabled them to compete more aggressively for savings. As a consequence they announced a number of new mortgage schemes. That same year 9 per cent of all advances for house purchase were made by the banks and this amounted to M£620. They had outstanding balances of M£2,910, 5.6 per cent of all outstanding balances for house purchases.

In 1972 about a quarter of the houses mortgaged by building societies were newly built, that is since 1945, and only 19 per cent were built before 1919. In 1980 28 per cent were built before 1919, inter-war built houses accounted for 18 per cent, 39 per cent were built between 1945 and 1979, and 15 per cent were new houses.

In 1972 over one-third of the houses were semi-detached and less than one-quarter were terraced. 6 per cent of mortgages were given on flats or property other than houses and bungalows. Bungalows accounted for 9 per cent of the mortgages granted by building societies during 1980, detached houses accounted for 20 per cent, semi-detached houses for 32 per cent, terraced houses for 30 per cent, purpose-built flats 7 per cent, and converted flats 2 per cent.

Between the end of the war in 1945 and 1969 the price of houses rose steadily, i.e. in line with the general increase in wages. For example, in 1968 the prices of new houses rose by 8½ per cent, the prices of existing houses by 6½ per cent and earnings rose by just under 8 per cent. In 1971 house prices began to rise more steeply and in 1972 they rose very steeply. A survey conducted in 1959-60 by the Co-operative Permanent Building Society (now the Nationwide Building Society) showed that during that same year a quarter of its mortgagors bought houses costing less than £1,000 and nearly three-quarters of them bought houses costing less than £2,500, which was about the cost of most new houses. Slightly more than half the mortgagors earned less than £750 per annum, as did most industrial workers, but average earnings were £813 per year in the last quarter of 1959 and the average price of all houses in the same period was £2,330, which gives a house price/earnings ratio of 2.87.

In the last quarter of 1971 average earnings rose by 9.8 per cent and house prices on average by 26.7 per cent and the house price/earnings ratio was 3.46. In the last quarter of 1972 average earnings rose by 15.2 per cent and the average price of houses rose by 42.4 per cent, giving a house price/earnings ratio of 4.07. In the last quarter of 1980 the average price of new houses was £26,790 and of second-hand properties £21,390, which gives an average price for all properties of £23,470. Average annual earnings for the period was £7,095, which gives a house price/earnings ratio of 3.31.

The price of houses, like that of any goods or service, is affected by many factors, for example the normal supply and demand equation and the prices of land, labour and materials, but very important is the amount of money available for mortgages. Building societies provide about 70 to 80 per cent of all mortgage advances and their interest rates are a key factor in determining the supply of mortgage funds. The building societies' net inflow of funds depends largely upon the differences between their borrowing interest rates and other short-term borrowing rates. Between 1967 and mid-1972 building society borrowing rates remained fairly stable, i.e. between 7.23 and 8.50 per cent, while short-term money rates varied between 4.8 and 9.8 per cent; consequently the flow of funds into building societies was erratic. During 1970 and 1971 the societies maintained their borrowing rates around about 8 per cent but short-term money rates dropped from 8.5 per cent to 4 per cent at the end of 1971, which resulted in a substantial increase in the flow of funds into building societies. The rate at which mortgage funds flow into the housing market has an effect on house prices. When mortgage money is more freely available this increases peoples' ability to buy houses, and because in the short term the supply of houses is fixed, this is bound to lead to increases in house prices which cannot be attributed to any other cause. The relationship between the amount of money available for the purchase of a commodity, which has a fixed supply, and its price is close. The more money available the higher the price, and this is one explanation for the steep rise in house prices during 1972.

Some people and organisations have put forward other explanations for it. One of these is rising land prices. Between 1952 and 1974 land prices in the south-eastern region of the country rose by 350 per cent and in the rest of the country by between 200 and 250 per cent, but these increases took place over a long period and therefore would not account for the big jump in house prices in 1972, because the price of land represents what a developer is prepared to pay for a site after deducting from the anticipated selling price of the house his financing costs and target profit. Another explanation which has been put forward is that the rise in house prices is directly linked to rises in incomes, but in 1972 house prices rose by between 40 and 70 per cent but incomes rose only by between 15 and 20 per cent. There are therefore grounds for saying that the volume of money available for mortgages must have a significant effect on house prices.

In 1973 a mortgage crisis occurred, when withdrawals of savings with building societies rose to a record height. The Building Societies Association revealed that during March 1973, for instance, withdrawals amounted to M£412 and the net receipts for the month were M£30, compared with nearly M£100 in the first two months of that year. To stem this outflow of funds, in April 1973 the rate of interest charged on home loans was increased from $8\frac{1}{2}$ to $9\frac{1}{2}$ per cent and in September 1973 it was further increased to 11 per cent. In the last quarter of 1980 it was 14 per cent, having fallen from a peak of 15 per cent in the previous quarter.

Since the last quarter of 1972, although the rate of increase in house prices has fluctuated, the general trend has been downwards and has never in any quarter approached the level of 42 per cent it was then. In the last quarter of 1980 the average percentage increase in the price of all properties was 6.9 per cent, which was much lower than the rate of inflation and in real terms means a fall in house prices. Since 1945 there has been a continuing increase in the proportion of householders embarking upon home ownership and there seems to have been a general assumption that in real terms house prices will continue to rise. However, the boom in house prices may be over, or at least drawing to an end, and the price of some of the older houses may shortly begin to fall in real terms, perhaps steeply. Current prices and high interest rates have made home ownership increasingly costly, especially in the case of the older houses when the costs of maintenance and improvement are taken into account (see Chapter 9). During the last few years, when assessing ability to make mortgage repayments building societies have been prepared to take into consideration the earnings of both husband and wife, which in times of virtual full employment was not unreasonable, but in 1980 there are about three million unemployed people in Britain and little prospect of this number being appreciably reduced. In these circumstances the number of mortgagors who find that they are unable to keep up their mortgage repayments is likely to increase, perhaps considerably, and the length of time a mortgage can be extended must have a limit. A wide-scale inability to keep up mortgage repayments would raise serious problems for local authorities because they hold in mortgage a high proportion of the older and less saleable houses. In the 1980s areas of older owner-occupied houses may become as big a problem to local authorities as was much of the private rented housing during the 1950s and 60s. Should the houses fall into such a state that they have to be included in clearance programmes, local authorities will have to pay full market value to the owner-occupiers in spite of the fact that they are unfit for human habitation. Some, perhaps many, of the owner-occupiers will be glad to be relieved of a heavy burden on this basis.

During the 1930s speculative builders provided houses for as little as £300-350. The houses were sometimes built in blocks of ten or more with a tunnel access to the rear between each pair.

Low-cost housing built at a cost of £150 in the 1930s for renting, but later sold for owner-occupation.

Middle price-range semi-detached houses of the late 1930s.

An example of landscaping by a private developer of the late 1920s. Middle price-range houses built for sale. (1967)

A closer view of a middle price-range semi-detached house of the late 1930s.

The 55 per cent of the housing stock which is owner-occupied contains many types of dwellings. (1980)

A inter-war, architect-designed, detached house built by a private developer for higher income groups.

In 1954 when house building licencing ended speculative builders with land rushed into building for sale, often to pre-1939 plans.

Infilling: two detached houses built on a plot of land left vacant in 1939. As building land became more difficult to find the demand for small undeveloped plots increased.

In the 1950s the craze for television was reflected in house design. This three bedroomed semi-detached house had a selling price of £2,600.

The T.V. house, looking from kitchen into dining-room.

After 1952 land prices rose steeply and speculative builders increased densities. The small individual front garden, universal during the inter-war period, gave way to open landscaping.

Chalet-type semi-detached houses built middle 1950s to sell at about £1,775. Tile hung dormers and large glass areas built when fuel was cheap.

The Clean Air Act 1956. Builders responded to the demand for smoke control by providing oil fired central heating which required only small bore flue pipes instead of chimneys.

The demand for detached houses rose as incomes increased. This one was built in 1955 to sell at £3,500.

Changes in design in the early post-1945 period. Speculative building often resulted in large glass areas and the consequent greater heat loss.

The 'Town' house built for sale in the 1960s.

A larger detached house built in the 1950s to sell at £4,575.

The living room of the 'Town' house.

Semi-detached houses built in the 1970s for selling at about £20,000.

Speculatively built detached houses in N.W. England, built 1978-80 for selling at about £32,000.

Speculatively built Georgian style houses for sale in N.W. England in the late 1970s for over £70,000.

A detached house built on a sloping site to owner's requirements in the 1970s.

A bungalow in the higher price range built to owner's requirements in the 1970s.

During the 1950s private developers began to build flats for sale, sometimes on prime sites which they had acquired by buying large houses standing in their own grounds. In the middle 1950s prices ranged from about £4,000 - £16,000 but by the 1970s they had risen to £16,000 – £50,000.

Flats built for selling in the late 1950s for about £4,000.

A superior type of house likely to be converted into luxury flats in the post-1945 period.

Chapter 6

COUNCIL HOUSING

In 1980 about seven million dwellings in Britain (31.9 per cent of the total housing stock) were owned by public housing authorities. These include local authorities, new town development corporations and housing associations. The last two are dealt with in Chapters 7 and 8 respectively.

Since 1919 council housing has become increasingly important in Britain. More than a century has passed since local authorities were first given permissive powers to build houses, but by the outbreak of war in 1914 the number of dwellings in public ownership was small – about 5 per cent of the total housing stock and confined to a very few towns.

World War I resulted in great social changes. People of all classes had come forward to fight for "their King and Country", many of them from squalid tenements, rat-infested cellar dwellings, crowded lodging-houses, and even the workhouses. The mobilisation revealed serious deficiences and neglect in the educational and other provisions for the well-being of a large section of the population. For example, the medical examination of men for the Armed Forces between 1 November 1917 and 1 October 1918 showed that only 36 per cent of the men examined were up to the full normal standard of health and physical fitness, and that 10 per cent were totally and permanently unfit for any form of military service. The unsatisfactory physical condition of such a large proportion of the male population was clearly related to poverty and the unhealthy conditions in which many were forced to live. There developed a general resolve to raise the living standards of the poorest section of the population when the war was finished.

In 1918 when the fighting ended it was estimated that there was a net shortage of one million dwellings and that houses which had cost £250 to build in 1914 would in 1919 cost £1,000. At that price the cost rents of the new houses, i.e. a rent sufficient to cover all outgoings, would have been £1.50 per week exclusive of rates, or three times higher than the controlled rents of most of the houses then occupied by the working-classes. Available information indicated that most working-class families would have been unable to pay a rent higher than 62p per week.

A failure on the part of the Government to take effective measures to deal with the acute housing shortage would have resulted in a large, and no longer docile, section of the nation becoming discontented and angry to a degree which would have undermined the stability of the State, and perhaps led to a revolution.

The Government had two choices. One was to remove rent controls and let rents soar to a point where speculative building would have become highly profitable and therefore attractive to investors. However, because of the mood of the nation, such a step was politically dangerous. The alternative, which the Government was forced to adopt, was to reduce the rents of the new houses to be built, by means of a subsidy. This was a revolutionary step, but it was made easier by the belief that it was only a temporary measure which would have a limited life during a short period of high building costs. There was at the time considerable support throughout the country for subsidising the rents of new houses intended for the lower paid workers, but at the same time there was also a strong feeling in certain quarters against the permanent subsidising of house rents on the grounds that it was the responsibility of a husband to provide for his wife and children. It was said that it would be a disaster if the housing crusade led to the permanent dependence on the State of any class for so vital a commodity as housing, because it would lead to a fresh form of pauperism. Some people argued that unless wages were high enough to allow people to pay for their own houses the social system would collapse. After more than sixty years of rent subsidies, during which time public assistance towards the cost of housing has been considerably expanded, the social system has not collapsed.

Another revolutionary step taken by the Government in 1919 was to impose on local authorities a legal obligation to provide for those housing needs of the working-classes in their districts which were not otherwise likely to be met. The houses built by the local authorities in discharge of this duty set a new and much higher standard of working-class housing than had ever been know in this country before. At the time, however, this duty was seen as a temporary one to cope with an emergency which for the time being was beyond the capacity of the private speculative builder.

From 1919 until the outbreak of the Second World War in 1939 Government subsidies, in one form or another, were paid to reduce the rents of houses built by local authorities for the working-classes. Sometimes they were for houses built to meet general needs, at other times they were directed towards houses built only for special purposes, e.g. for the replacement of slums or for families who were overcrowded. An overcrowding survey carried out in 1935-36 showed 341,554 houses in England and Wales, i.e. 3.8 per cent of the houses surveyed, to be overcrowded on a standard based on two adults living and sleeping in a room of not less than 110 square feet in area.

Between 1919 and 1939 one and a half million houses were built by local authorities for letting at subsidised rents. When subsidies were first introduced there was a widespread belief in Government circles that house building costs would fall and remove the need for subsidies. Costs did fall, but not as expected. In 1921 they fell considerably as a result of severe internal deflation, but they rose again within a short time. In 1927 a standard three-bedroomed house was costing on average £440 to build, against £350 in 1923. It was not until the early 1930s that prices fell again to about the 1923 level, as the result of a worldwide economic depression. During this period the income of the majority of working-class families was between £2.75 and £3.00 per week, and housing standards had to be reduced to enable the subsidised rents to be within the rent-paying capacity of the tenants. At the same time there was a large body of unemployed building labour and a growing mass of unused capital in the hands of the banks which resulted in very low interest rates. These factors contributed to the creation of the position where it was possible to build a three-bedroomed council house for about £350.

During the 1930s the Government recognised that some of the families to be housed by local authorities, especially many of those forced to move because of slum clearance or overcrowding, would be financially worse off than others. In consequence, local authorities were permitted to pool their housing subsidies and to use the total in a way which would give the poorest families bigger subsidies than the better off.

Changes in Government policy from time to time influenced the numbers and types of houses built. However, the majority of the council dwellings built during the inter-war period were two-storey three-bedroomed houses of about 760 square feet in floor area, erected in pairs or in short terraces. The houses had either one or two living rooms. The latter were called the parlour-type. In some of the large towns, municipal building included, in addition to houses, four- and five-storey blocks of flats, with balcony access, built in the inner-city areas following slum clearance. Many of these blocks of flats were designed with large open areas and some had incorporated in them ground-floor shops fronting on to the local main road. These flats were regarded by some architects and councillors as being 'model homes for the working-classes'. The first tenants were usually families rehoused from slum clearance areas in the immediate vicinity and that helped to maintain a community spirit among the tenants. Over the years,

however, the tenants changed, and especially since the 1950s some of these flats have deteriorated to a degree that has made them difficult to let. Some have been so vandalised that they have been considered by the local authorities as being beyond repair.

In 1919 the provision of a bath in new municipal housing was made a condition for claimimg the Government subsidy but in some of the earlier homes it was sited in the kitchen and did not have a piped supply of hot water, which had to be ladled out from a clothes boiler. After 1924 the provision of a bathroom and a piped supply of hot water became general. On a few council estates experiments were made in providing hot water from a central point and with water-borne refuse disposal, and communal laundries were provided in a few blocks of flats.

In spite of the relatively large number of houses built by local authorities between the wars, in 1939 there was still an unsatisfied need for low-rented dwellings that could only be met with the aid of public funds.

In March 1945, as the war was drawing to an end, the coalition Government proposed in a White Paper (Cmnd 6609) that the first two years after the end of hostilities in Europe should be treated as a period of national emergency, when exceptional measures would be taken to meet the grave housing shortage. These measures have been discussed in Chapter 1. The Labour Government elected in the summer of 1945 decided to concentrate all house building resources in the hands of local authorities, but that designs, layouts, methods and materials would be controlled by the central Government. The new houses were to be allocated to families strictly according to housing need, and without regard to capacity to pay the rent and to social class. Doctors, it was hoped, would live on the same estates as their patients, and teachers alongside their pupils. The restriction on local authorities to build dwellings intended exclusively for the working-classes was removed by provisions in the Housing Act 1949. Thus during the immediate post-war period local authorities became responsible for meeting the general housing shortage in their areas. The national target was set at 240,000 houses a year.

In 1947 127,541 were completed, and by the following year output had reached 206,559, but the building industry had become stretched to its limit and the target was reduced to 200,000 a year. During the next three years the yearly average production was 170,000.

At the end of the war knowledge about the size and composition of family incomes was inadequate. On the assumption that the pre-war rents of municipal houses averaged 37½p a week and that the higher standard of the post-war houses would merit an extra 12½p a week, the net rents of the new post-war houses were fixed at 50p, a sum it was thought most families could afford to pay. Building costs were much higher in 1945 than they had been in 1939 and it was estimated that an annual subsidy of £22 a house was required to bring the cost rents of the houses down to

50p a week. In consequence, in 1946 the Government fixed the Exchequer subsidy at £16.50 a year for sixty years and required the local authorities to pay a further subsidy of £5.50 throughout the period out of the local rates.

Early in 1947 an enquiry conducted by the Government Social Survey provided some information on the wage rates of heads of families. The 6,000 families included in the enquiry were divided into five economic groups. The lowest income group, comprising about 11 per cent of the total, consisted mainly of what were called 'social pensioners', with weekly 'wages' of less than £3; 8 per cent of the total had wages of between £3 and £4 per week; 44 per cent had wages of between £4 and £5.50 per week; and 29 per cent of the sample had weekly wages of between £5.50 and £10. The remaining 8 per cent had an income of more than £10 per week.

In 1944 a sub-committee of the then Central Housing Advisory Committee (the Dudley Committee, named after its chairman, Lord Dudley), examined the question of what should be the standards and designs of post-war council houses. In its report the committee recommended an increase in area from the pre-war standard of 760 square feet (70.6 m²) for a three-bedroomed, five-person house, to a minimum of 900 square feet (83.6 m²). The committee also made recommendations for room sizes and equipment. Many of the recommendations of the Dudley sub-committee were incorporated in the Housing Manual, 1944, which was issued as a guide to local authorities by the then Ministry of Health, which at the time was responsible for housing. The Manual also contained type plans and technical appendices, so that municipal housing followed a uniform pattern throughout the country.

In 1949, taking advantage of four years' experience in post-war house building and the progress of research in techniques and methods, the Ministry of Health issued another Housing Manual. In the period immediately after the war the most urgent task was to provide homes suitable for the younger families who, because of war conditions, had been unable to obtain a separate home of their own. In the 1944 Manual, therefore, emphasis was laid on the provision of three-bedroomed two-storey houses. The longer-term housing problem, however, called for a variety of types of houses, some larger and some smaller than the three-bedroom type, so the 1949 Manual covered a wider field than had the 1944 Manual. The types of accommodation illustrated in the 1949 Manual were for small and large families, single persons and aged couples, in a variety of plan arrangements. The Manual did not seek to lay down rules as to the percentages of the different sizes of dwellings to be built in any locality, but left this for the local authority to decide. However, the standards of accomodation for the various types of houses were based on the standard of 900 to 950 super feet in area of the three-bedroomed houses, the sizes of the other types of houses varying in proportion. The Manual paid special attention to the importance of layout in both town and country, the siting and design of the dwellings, and the grouping of the buildings in relation to each other, the neighbouring area and the landscape. It contained plans of model layouts and of the individual dwellings. The manual was used universally by local authorities.

By 1952 the Ministry of Housing and Local Government was in existence and in that year it issued another Housing Manual. At the time there was an economy drive on, but also an effort by the Government to achieve an increased output of new dwellings. In consequence, space standards were reduced but emphasis was laid on the need to use the reduced space so that there was no or little loss of convenience in the houses.

Seven years elapsed before housing standards and design were again reviewed by the Government. In 1959 another sub-committee of the Central Housing Advisory Committee, under the chairmanship of Sir Parker Morris, was set up to consider the standards of design and equipment applicable to family dwellings and other forms of residential accommodation, whether they were to be provided by public authorities or by private enterprise. The report of this committee, "Homes for Today and Tomorrow", was published in 1961.

It suggested that the starting point for thinking about housing must be the activities which people wished to undertake in their homes. Amongst the many recommendations were: more space for activities demanding privacy and quiet, and for satisfactory circulation; provision for more and better storage space; and that kitchens be arranged for easy work and large enough to take some meals in. Recommendations were also made about heating, lighting and safety in the home. The minima net floor areas recommended ranged from 320 square feet for a one-person single-storey house to 1050 square feet for a six-person three-storey house. Publication of the report coincided with one of the frequent periods of economic restraints and the standards were not made compulsory for local authorities until 1969.

The cost and availability of land are important factors for determining the types of dwellings to be built and their costs and rents. Also the layout of a housing estate is influenced by the topography and other conditions of the site. Between the wars most of the council housing was built at a density of twelve houses to the acre and on sites fairly easy to develop.

In the 1950s pressures to increase the density of housing development were growing as shortages of readily available sites in the larger towns became apparent. It was argued by some architects, planners and others that industrialised building techniques, high-rise building and increased population dispersal were needed to deal with the competing claims on land in the bigger towns. One idea put forward was for tower blocks built in steel and concrete in a park-like setting, with all the social facilities for the families provided in the block. Another suggestion on the same theme was for a two-mile deep band of point blocks, up to twenty storeys high, to be built on the fringes of the inner cities. It was argued that such a scheme would reduce transport problems, minimise the need for overspill development and attract middle-class people back into the towns if a number of prestige blocks were constructed specifically for them. There was a growing belief among many architects and planners that in towns vertical housing in the form of blocks of flats would supersede the horizontal development of houses with gardens so much favoured by the public. Architecturally, these were exciting proposals but they seemed to have over-looked the fact that they were concerned with homes.

Throughout the 'fifties and early 'sixties, in circulars sent to local authorities the Government supported the idea of high densities in pressure areas, and backed up this support by increased subsidies for high-density development. For example, after the Housing Subsidies Act of 1956 the annual subsidy for a twenty-two-storey block of eighty flats was approximately £6,000, while that for eighty houses was £800. The result was that the proportion of flats and maisonnettes in local authority schemes rose from 23 per cent in 1953 to 55 per cent in 1964. The proportion of local authority dwellings constructed in blocks of five storeys or over rose from an average of 6.9 per cent between 1953 and 1959 to a peak of 25.7 per cent in 1966, whilst dwellings in buildings of over fifteen storeys rose from an average of 0.5 per cent in 1953-1959 to 10.6 per cent in 1965.

It is doubtful whether the ideas of the planners and architects who favoured high-rise development would have been put into practice had they not had the support of the large building and civil engineering contractors, some of whom had acquired the rights to use foreign industrial systems. For the large companies a change to high-rise and systems building had definite attractions. Industrialised building methods meant all-weather production, greater control over the workforce, and less dependence on local labour because much of the work was carried out in factories away from the site and there was a reduction in the amount of skilled labour required. The research, setting up a system, marketing it and getting the production flowing required a large capital investment and only a very few large companies had the necessary resources. This placed these companies in a near-monopolistic position which could yield high profits. On the other hand, local authorities stood to gain from the advantages of large package deals. The contractors usually undertook to do the preliminary site investigations and surveys and to provide the professional services of architectural design and engineering consultancy, normally provided and paid for separately by the authorities. In addition, the local authorities were assured of a faster and continuous production of housing units. For example, in one north-west town in 1956 the concrete shells of six eleven-storey blocks of maisonnettes were completed in nineteen days. At the time speed was to some degree as important as economy. Industrialised building of housing units spread to towns large and small throughout the country. Large contracts were profit-

able to the big contractors and had advantages for the local authorities who, as it were, could buy their dwellings 'off the shelf'.

It was not long, however, before serious problems arose in some of the blocks of flats and maisonnettes. These included condensation, excessive heat loss, poor sound insulation, and in some cases penetrating dampness. There were cases where structural defects arose within a short period after completion of the buildings. Also, structural weaknesses were brought to light following an internal gas explosion in 1968 in a high-rise block in London (Ronan Point). It became clear that some of the industrialised systems had not been adequately tested, especially for the British climate.

By 1966 high-rise flats had become unpopular with some of the people who were living in them. In some cases the cost of maintenance was found to be excessive, and matters were not helped if the local authority was dilatory and inefficient in carrying out the repairs, which was commonly so, not only in relation to flats but also to council dwellings in general. One effect of delaying the execution of repairs is a steep rise in the cost when they are eventually done. For example, in 1975 repairs and maintenance to local authority dwellings in England and Wales cost over M£200, as compared with M£126 in 1971-72.

Vandalism has increased during the last decade or more and seems to have become a normal pattern of behaviour for large numbers of children between the ages of 12 and 16, but it is more common in large blocks of flats, which in some cases have been damaged beyond repair and have become unusable. Although studies have been made the causes of vandalism have not been clearly identified. In 1979 two blocks of maisonnettes built for families about twenty-two years earlier in Birkenhead were in such a bad state that the local authority decided that they could not be made suitable for occupation and ordered their demolition, in spite of the fact that the loan charges for them would still have to be paid for about another forty years and in addition the council stood to lose the Government subsidy for them. In other parts of the country local authorities had blocks of flats that were either difficult or impossible to let.

The expectations of major gains in terms of land use and falling costs after a period of initial development were not fulfilled, and high-rise building became subjected to detailed criticism. The Housing Subsidies Act 1967 abolished the previous arrangement whereby each storey above six attracted a progressively rising subsidy. The general effect was that the percentage of dwellings in tenders involving blocks of five storeys or over fell from 25.7 per cent in 1966 to 19.9 per cent in 1968, 9.8 per cent in 1970, and by 1975 it was down to 1.2 per cent. The Ronan Point incident in 1968 was also a contributory factor in this decline, because many local authorities found themselves faced with considerable expenditure in making some of the high-rise blocks safe to live in.

The 1965-70 period, therefore, saw a rapid decline in high-rise construction, especially of blocks of over fifteen storeys, but the construction of low-rise flats using industrialised methods continued.

Experience has given rise to the opinion that high-density living in blocks of high-rise flats is generally unsuitable for families with young children, is unpopular, and exacerbates many social problems. This view, however, has been challenged by a few who believe that apart from the difficulties associated with children's play there are major advantages, such as quietness and a good view, and that the main problem revealed by many social investigations was that of the unreliability of the lifts. However, during the 1970s many local authorities built terrace houses instead of high-rise flats and there has been a general tendency for local authorities to reduce the densities of new dwellings in the inner-city areas.

The average cost of building a three-bedroomed council house, excluding land, rose from about £350 in 1930 to about £2,300 in 1964, £4,575 in 1972 and £9,502 in 1977. Some of these increases are due to inflation.

Local authorities in Britain meet the capital costs of new house construction by raising loans on the open market or by borrowing from the Public Works Loan Board. The loan term is usually for sixty years, the notional life of the house. The amount of capital invested in housing by local authorities in any one year exceeds the capital expenditure in any of the other services. Housing loans account on average for 64 per cent of all the capital liablities of a local authority.

Besides the loan charges (capital repayments and interest) on its houses, a local authority has to meet the costs of management and repairs, but rents, excluding rebates, very rarely meet all the outgoings. For example, in 1975 rents contributed on average only about 53 per cent of the total housing expenditure. About ten years earlier the proportion was around 67 to 70 per cent of the total housing expenditure. Where large new housing or improvement programmes are undertaken the rent contribution is likely to be even lower than 53 per cent.

Local government housing finance is a subject far too complex for discussion in any detail in a book of this character, but it is clear that if the cost of providing, managing and maintaining houses is not paid for by the tenants it has to be paid for by somebody, in this case the taxpayer or ratepayer, or both.

Most developed countries make provision for financial assistance in some form towards the cost of housing to the individual. In Britain housing subsidies from the Government have been available since 1919. By 1954 the housing subsidies fixed by the Labour Government in 1946 at £16.50 per house for sixty years from the Exchequer and £5.50 from the local authority were costing the country about M£60 per year. Because, since 1945, the criteria for obtaining a council house had been solely housing need, by 1956 some of the new council houses were occupied by people not in need of the subsidy, while at the same time there were families who were living in bad housing who could not afford to pay the council rents because both building costs and interest rates had risen since 1945. The Government therefore passed the Housing Subsidies Act 1956, which reduced the subsidy for housing built to meet any general shortage to £10 per house a year and gave the Minister power to abolish it, which he did in November 1956, except for dwellings intended for old or single people. At the same time subsidies were made available for dwellings built for rehousing families from unfit houses in slum clearance areas, and for houses built in new and expanding towns, for overspill populations and for schemes connected with industrial expansion. Higher subsidies were made available for building flats and for building on expensive sites. Local authorities were encouraged by the Government to pool all their housing subsidies and to rationalise their rents by charging higher than cost rents for houses that were built when costs and interest rates were low, and reducing the rents of houses built at a higher cost and when interest rates had increased. The Housing Subsidies Act 1956 also relieved local authorities of the duty to make contributions from the local rates towards the cost of their houses.

With the abolition of the subsidy to meet the general housing shortage there was an immediate decrease in the number of houses built by local authorities. In 1956 completions in England and Wales dropped to 149,139 as compared with nearly 221,000 in 1954, and the fall continued until 1961 when only 98,466 dwellings were completed. On the other hand, building for owner-occupation increased and reached 170,366 in 1961 against 124,087 in 1958.

The main purpose of the Housing Act 1961 was to introduce a new principle into the subsidy system. The Government was optimistic that by the end of 1965 the majority of local authorities would have completed their slum clearance programmes. On the other hand, it considered that there was still a need for houses for overspill populations from certain congested areas, and a further need for one-bedroomed dwellings. The 1961 Act provided for subsidies at two basic rates: £24 per house and £8 per house. The rate payable in the case of any particular local authority was determined by a resources test. The housing expenditure of the authority, as shown in the housing revenue account, was compared with the income available to it from rents and Exchequer subsidies on the assumption that the income from rent equalled twice the gross value of the dwellings for rating purposes. Any authority whose income measured in this way was less than its actual expenditure qualified for the £24 subsidy; other local authorities received the £8 subsidy.

This method of paying subsidies encouraged local authorities to rationalise their rents and to have a rebate scheme so as to make those tenants able to do so pay cost rents, and thus provide larger subsidies for those in need. There were supplementary subsidies for housing provided for certain special needs, e.g. for comprehensive redevelopment.

Changes in the rates and the purposes of housing

subsidies over the years had brought the housing finance system for local authority housing into a chaotic state and during 1970-71 there was general agreement amongst all interested parties that it needed reform. House building subsidies (not including rent rebates, etc.) which had cost the country about M£60 in 1954 were growing inexorably. For example, by 1973-74 they had reached M£363 in England and Wales and M£66 in Scotland. The Government accepted the view that there was a need for a comprehensive review and set up a study group, the Finance Review Advisory Group, to examine the matter. However, the project was quietly shelved.

In the meanwhile, the Housing Finance Act 1972 introduced eight new subsidies. Some of these were intended as temporary measures to cover the transition to a new system which it was hoped would be developed from the work of the Review Advisory Group. Others gave financial assistance to local authorities with the rising costs of slum clearance, and with the costs of rent rebates and rent allowances (see Chapter 4). In addition the system of 'fair' rents was applied to public housing with the expectation that the subsidies paid to council tenants might ultimately be abolished.

Prior to 1969 local authorities were enabled to fix the rents of their houses at levels they considered to be reasonable. However, this led to inequalities between local authorities, with tenants paying very different rents for similar houses. For example, in 1971-72 the average weekly unrebated rent of a three-bedroomed house built after 1964 was £1.79 in Wakefield, £4.65 in Birmingham and £5.26 in Portsmouth. This independence of local authorities to fix rents was challenged, and the Government referred the matter to the then Prices and Incomes Board. The Board found it to be incompatible with the Government's prices and incomes policy and made recommendations. These led to legislation, the Prices and Incomes Act 1968; Rent (Control of Increases) Act 1969, which limited any rent increases local authorities could make.

The Housing Finance Act 1972 (and the equivalent Scottish Act) removed local authorities' discretion for setting rent levels, and applied the principle of 'fair rents', which had applied to private rented housing since 1965. This meant that the rent of each dwelling had to be assessed by reference to its character, location, amenities and state of repair, but disregarding any market value which was due to the shortage of similar accommodation.

A number of local authorities initially refused to implement the terms of the 1972 Act relating to the charging of 'fair rents'. There were provisions, in this event, for the appointment of Commissioners to take over the housing functions of local authorities. However, by the end of 1972 most local authorities had agreed to fulfil their duties under the Act, but the council of Clay Cross, in Derbyshire, decided not to do so. A Commissioner was appointed and eleven members of the council were surcharged with the deficit due to their non-operation of the Act.

In 1975 the Labour Government repealed the provisions relating to fair rents for council housing by the Housing Rents and Subsidies Act 1975, and restored to local authorities the power to fix rents. However, it was later forced to impose a rents standstill on local authorities to help its pay policy and its attack on inflation. The Labour Government also passed the Housing Finance (special provisions) Act 1975, which prevented surcharges being made arising from the provisions of the Housing Finance Act 1972. Local authorities are now required to charge their tenants reasonable rents (e.g. which keep a balance between the interests of tenants and the interests of ratepayers).

Local authority rent arrears during the last few years have risen, especially in the larger urban areas, where they seem to be a symptom of other social problems. A report by the National Consumer Council gives the figure of M£27.5 in owed rent for half the local authorities in England and Wales for 1974-75, and for London alone a figure of about M£12. A definite remedy for the problem is difficult to find. The use of the threat of eviction is no longer effective in a high proportion of cases, because local authorities have a legal duty to house the homeless.

The tenant is legally responsible for seeing that the rent reaches the landlord, or his agent, who is under no obligation to collect it. In practice it is in the landlord's interest to provide facilities, e.g. by collection, for tenants to pay their rents, and rent collection is a major part of the work of housing departments of local authorities. But door-to-door collection, once the only method, has in many areas been abandoned for security and other reasons. Present-day systems include payment by banker's order or Giro, and payment in cash by the tenant at a branch office of the local authority.

Since the 1930s local authorities have been urged by the Government to use their housing subsidies through rent rebate schemes to help tenants who could not otherwise afford the rents of council houses. A model scheme was included in a circular sent to local authorities in 1967 (MOHLG 46/67); under this a rent was fixed for each dwelling and the tenant could apply for a rebate related to his income and family responsibilities. However, in 1968 more than 50 per cent of local authorities had no rent rebate scheme. In 1972 the requirement that local authorities should charge fair rents for their dwellings would have resulted in hardship for some council tenants had it not been for a provision in the Housing Finance Act 1972 requiring every local authority to introduce a rent rebate scheme. Details of the computation of rebates and allowances were contained in a schedule to the Act. In view of the considerable social changes which have taken place since housing subsidies were introduced in 1919 and the compulsory provision of rent rebate schemes, the application of the principle of fair rents to council housing was not unreasonable.

The methods for allocating council housing are complex and in some degree vary with local circumstances, but there are common factors. For example, local authorities have a legal duty to make provision for the rehousing of people from slum clearance areas, those that are overcrowded, and the homeless. This limits their freedom to reject people who are known to have been evicted because of rent arrears or are otherwise potentially unsatisfactory tenants. Guidance on the selection of tenants is from time to time given to local authorities in Government circulars, etc. For example, attention has been drawn to the special needs of the elderly and the disabled. Most authorities operate a 'points' system of some kind, so that it is the officers who actually select the tenants, but this is done within a framework laid down by the council.

There is a considerable variety in the types of households accommodated in local authority housing, but the majority of heads of households are manual workers. About half of the households contain children. In 1971 a tenth of heads of households were aged under 30, and 15 per cent were aged 70 or over. This means that the majority of the tenants were in the middle age groups. About one-tenth of the tenants had an income of less than £500 a year, and 9 per cent had an income of £3,000 or more a year.

Many households are likely at some time to need temporary or permanent help from the social services. These include the elderly, the disabled, the poor, problem families and immigrants, so local authority housing management must include an element of welfare, even if it is only for maintaining the value of the houses. Since 1945, however, there has been a move away from the paternalism and condescension which existed in municipal housing management of the 1930s. Up to 1939, the tenants of local authorities were largely the lower income groups who had moved from the slums or from houses let-in-lodgings; and it was said in some quarters that these tenants would keep coal in the bath and use the toilet seats for picture frames, but as a general proposition this turned out to be wrong. On the other hand, there were more problems connected with rehousing than there are today.

Sometimes during the 1930s tenants rehoused from one slum-clearance area were evicted because of rent arrears, then drifted into another slum area from which they were again rehoused, perhaps for a second or third time. Also, many of the families rehoused by local authorities in this period had come from dwellings which were in such a bad structural state that any attempt to keep them clean was fruitless. Many of the housewives had never cooked on anything but an open fire or a paraffin stove, nor had they and their families ever been able to take a bath in a bathroom at home. Electricity and gas cookers were unknown quantities. It was not surprising, therefore, that some families needed a great deal of help and instruction in how to use the equipment in the new houses.

Many of the houses in slum clearance schemes, and others, were infested with bed bugs and other vermin. The furniture and other household effects of the tenants were also infested. To try to prevent the spread of the infestation to the new houses some local authorities insisted that all tenants' furniture, clothing and other articles likely to harbour the vermin be disinfested by the council. Other local authorities limited the requirement to the goods of families living in houses shown by inspection to be infested.

Some of the tenants when offered local authority housing were living in dire poverty. Often the only furniture they had was a rickety bedstead, a makeshift table and a few broken chairs, but no floor coverings. Few, if any, of these tenants had the money for extra furnishings and were afraid to purchase by deferred payments because they only had casual employment. Tenants such as these could not make full use of the available accommodation and desperately needed help.

Local authorities had the power to provide furniture for tenants in suitable cases, but only a few used it. Those who did generally took the view that having provided good housing they would be failing in their duty to assist tenants to achieve a higher standard of living if they did not do something more. Some of these authorities purchased a limited range of furniture at wholesale prices, and sold it to their needy tenants at less than the retail prices, allowing the tenants to pay by weekly instalments collected with the rent. In the 1930s the total cost of furnishing a dwelling consisting of living-room, kitchen and two bedrooms, with this limited range, was about £50. In addition, some local authorities accepted gifts of furniture from many sources and distributed it free to the most needy tenants.

British people do not take kindly to interference in matters affecting their private lives or to paternalism on the part of landlords. During the 1930s there was a great deal of unemployment and poverty in Britain, and in the absence of many of today's sources of help municipal housing was essentially a social service and housing departments devoted a great deal of attention to social matters. Since 1945 new social services have been established and the great majority of people have a standard of living much higher than that experienced by the working-class in 1939.

Also, the housing responsibilities of local authorities are no longer confined to members of the working-classes, so council tenants are much more representative of the population as a whole than they were in 1939 and consequently do not require the guidance and instruction which was often necessary in the past. Although the basic functions of housing management remain the same, local authorities on the whole have slowly recognised the social changes which have taken place since 1945 and have accordingly adjusted some of their management methods. However, there are still special groups, for example the elderly, the disabled and problem families, that require support.

Prior to 1945 most local authority dwellings were subject to strict tenancy agreements which included prohibitions on keeping animals, taking in lodgers and subletting, and requirements about keeping gardens, etc., tidy. During the post-war period a proportion of council tenants considered that these requirements were too restrictive and that they were being treated as second-class citizens. Also, there was a growing, but not a big, demand from tenants to buy the houses they occupied. Pressure for change was exerted by tenants' associations in many parts of the country and in consequence they were given certain rights.

The Housing Act 1980 established a charter for public-sector tenants, giving them statutory rights such as security of tenure, provision, on their death, for succession to the tenancy by a resident relative, rights of subletting, and for taking in lodgers, and reimbursement for improvements made by the tenant. With certain exceptions public-sector tenants of at least three years' standing can buy the freehold of their houses, or a long lease of their flats, at a discount on the market price of from 33 per cent to 50 per cent, depending on the length of their occupation. The discount must be repaid in part or in full if the property is resold within five years. Tenants also have the right to be given a mortgage by the local authority to effect the purchase. Similar provisions for Scotland are contained in the Tenant's Rights, etc. (Scotland) Act 1980.

The provision of subsidised council housing began in 1919 as a short-term operation. Since then, and especially since 1945, there have been considerable social changes in Britain. Local authorities have become important providers of housing accommodation not exclusively occupied by the working-class. Some of the conditions that gave rise in 1919 for a need to subsidise the rents of council housing have disappeared, new social services have been created, and local authorities now have a duty to make provision for rent rebates and the payment of rent allowances. There is, therefore, a need for a review of the place of municipal housing in the present social structure of Britain.

Tenements erected in 1869 which were probably the first municipal dwellings built in England for the 'labouring' classes. They were improved during the 1950s.

Late 19th century municipal tenements substantially built and structurally capable of a long life. (1955)

Municipal tenements built in 1914.

Semi-detached council houses built in 1921.

100

Council houses of the 1920s built in concrete blocks made to resemble the local red sandstone. (1965)

Council houses built in the early 1930s for £350 each.

High standard, council housing of the middle 1930s.

A council estate completed in 1938.

Council flats built in 1938 to replace slums.

Blocks of flats built in the late 1930s to replace slum houses, in a state of gross disrepair. (1980)

103

Factory-produced aluminium bungalow designed and erected by the Bristol Aircraft Company in the early 1950s.

The living-room of an aluminium bungalow made by the Bristol Aircraft Company.

104

Permanent houses constructed largely of steel, designed by the British Iron and Steel Federation. (1950s).

Timber council housing of the early post-1945 period.

A matured, early post-1945 council estate. (1957)

An early post-1945 council estate with large open space reserved as a play area.

Relatively low densities with land left for leisure purposes were common features of many early post-1945 council estates.

The condition fifteen years later of blocks of flats built in the early post-1945 years.

Three-storey block of flats built in the 1950s as part of a new housing estate.

Early post-1945 flats in a redevelopment scheme built in the style of 1939.

Four-storey blocks of flats built in the 1950s with no-fines concrete.

Barrack-like blocks of flats built in the early 1950s.

109

*A closer view of a superior type
of middle 1930s council house. (1970)*

The grim rear to the barrack-like block.

The lounge in one of the barrack-like flats. (1957)

Industrialised building: two-storey houses and three-storey block of flats in a redevelopment area. (1966)

A return to the once despised terrace house.

New development: a small scheme of two-storey houses.

Terrace houses in a redevelopment scheme.

A small council estate which has retained some of the natural features.

Front of terrace houses on sloping site. Living rooms on upper floors. Entrance through patio garden. (1960s)

Rear of terrace houses on sloping site.

114

A new development of the 1960s.

New development, 1960s. Four-storey, two-bedroomed maisonnettes with garages/stores in basement.

Small terrace houses with two bedrooms, designed for south facing sloping site. The living rooms are on the first floors.

New development: eight-storey blocks of flats. With few exceptions the early post-1945 municipal flats did not exceed four storeys and had no lifts. During the 1950s a trend towards greater densities and high-rise development began.

Eleven-storey tower block.

Block of industrialised system-built flats derelict after about twenty years' use. Local authority will be liable for loan charges on them for about another forty years. (1978)

This development consists of five eleven-storey maisonnette slab blocks and two separate groups – fifteen in all – of twelve-storey point blocks, providing a total of 1,035 dwellings.

Twenty-two-storey tower blocks.

Early post-1945 council houses. The one on the left is tenanted, the one on the right is in owner-occupation.

118

Chapter 7

HOMES IN NEW TOWNS

The increase of wealth and population in the large towns and cities of Britain during the 19th century paradoxically resulted in a big section of the inhabitants having to live in extreme poverty, in crowded, insanitary and squalid dwellings. No small part of the money raised by rates in the towns had to be spent on measures to alleviate those conditions which were a positive danger to the health of the public. Both rents and rates were high and consumed a large part of the low wages of the working and labouring classes.

It was Ebenezer Howard, the son of a small shopkeeper in the City of London, who in 1898 first suggested a cure. Howard had no special advantages of class or education but for most of his working life he was a parliamentary reporter and this gave him a good background knowledge of many subjects. He advocated a policy of building on virgin land what were then thought of as 'satellite' towns. He put forward the idea that when a town had reached its optimum size (which was not defined) it should not be allowed to expand further, but new towns should be built which would be separated from the parent town by a green belt, and the new towns themselves would also be surrounded by green belts so they in turn could not become too large. Each of the satellite towns was to be for a moderate-sized industrial and trading community, living in close contact with a surrounding agricultural countryside from which it would obtain fresh food at reasonable prices because there would be little or no transport costs. These towns were to be planned in such a manner that there would be areas for homes, other areas for workplaces, and areas for shopping and for cultural activities. Each area would be easily accessible from the others so that there would not be long and expensive journeys to and from work and from home to the schools and shops. There was to be single ownership of the land, coupled with leaseholds, thus reconciling the public interests with freedom of choice and enterprise. The towns were to be administered for the common good and not predominantly with a profit motive. In consequence profits from land and buildings were to be limited and used to pay for the town's services and for improvements. The new towns were to be stepping stones to a higher and better form of life in the industrial towns of the country.

Largely because of Howard's efforts a company was formed in 1903 which purchased 3,818 acres of land in rural Hertfordshire, thirty-five miles from central London, and thus Letchworth, the 'First Garden City' was conceived. The architects appointed to plan the new town were very conscious of the social pressures and popular aspirations which later transformed housing design so that the semi-detached-house-and-garden standard became universal in Britain during the inter-war years. This standard had been anticipated at Bournville and Port Sunlight (see Chapter 8). The foundation of Garden City Associations in many other countries gave Letchworth world-wide fame and the town became the Mecca of housing and planning reform.

In 1919 Howard's 'Second Garden City', Welwyn, was founded, but it had not been completed by the outbreak of the Second World War in 1939.

The establishment of Letchworth did not lead to a growth of 'garden cities' as Howard had hoped. Instead, during the inter-war period there were vast expansions of Britain's towns with suburbs. This resulted in the transference of large numbers of people from the congested inner cores of towns to new estates developed by municipalities and speculative builders, and to long and costly daily journeys to and from work, which in some cases led to a fall in the living standards of lower paid people who had moved to the suburbs. This unhampered spread of towns, and especially the spread of London, gave rise to increasing concern. Advocates of new towns and garden cities, headed by the Town and Country Planning Association, were persistent and persuasive in their arguments. These pressures and the vulnerability of the concentrated centres of population to aerial attack in the event of war, which was becoming increasingly likely, led to the appointment in 1937 of the Royal Commission on the Distribution of Industrial Population, under the chairmanship of Sir Montague Barlow. The Barlow Report published in 1940, contained a great many facts and figures and other information about British towns and was an impressive study of the disadvantages of exceedingly large ones. Prominently featured in the report were the social and economic drawbacks of large towns, and the overcrowding, ill-health, noise, smoke and traffic congestion which existed in them. In the early years of the war, because the first priority was the nation's survival, the report lay on the shelf almost forgotten, but eventually it proved to be the turning point in post-war urban planning which had to take account of the acres of rubble and vacant sites result-

119

ing from the bombing of many of Britain's towns and cities.

The Coalition Government of the 1939-45 war was made up from members of all three democratic parties. However, the parties continued their separate organisations, and each set up a post-war reconstruction committee to study the problems of post-war housing and planning and to formulate policy for them. Although differing in some respects, all three parties included in their reconstruction programmes planned redevelopment of the centre of towns, dispersal of population, the maintenance of green belts around towns and new towns. This degree of agreement proved to be important when legislation for the creation of the new towns was introduced in Parliament in 1945. However, although all three political parties mentioned the building of new towns in their manifestoes for the 1945 General Election, the matter did not figure conspicuously as an election issue. As in 1919, the main emphasis was on the speed in building houses.

The Ministry of Town and Country Planning was established in 1943. Following the General Election of 1945 the Minister of Town and Country Planning appointed a committee, the New Towns Committee, with Lord Reith as chairman, to examine methods of promoting new towns. In its three reports this committee covered a wide variety of topics. The recommendations made by the committee were followed fairly closely in the New Towns Act 1946, now consolidated in the New Towns Acts of 1965 and 1968 for England and Wales, and in the New Towns (Scotland) Act 1968 for Scotland. The New Towns (Northern Ireland) Act 1965 makes similar provisions for Northern Ireland.

The New Towns legislation gives the Secretaries of State for the Environment, Scotland, Wales and Northern Ireland power to designate as the site of a new town any area of land (which may include an existing centre of population). The appropriate Minister must consult the local authorities concerned and make provision for public comment on the proposed designation. The Reith committee recommended that a designated area should include all the land needed for the built-up area, together with a peripheral belt about three-quarters of a mile across, and that assuming a general density in the built-up area, including recreational parks, of roughly twelve persons to the acre, the approximate area of land should vary from 5,500 acres for a population of 20,000 up to 11,000 acres for a population of 60,000. However, the Government has tended as a general rule to keep a designated area as small as possible because the mere inclusion of land in a designated area tends to be discouraging to farmers, who cannot be sure whether or not their land will be taken for the development in the course of a few years.

After an area for a new town has been designated the appropriate Minister appoints a development corporation to plan and create the growth of the new town. The corporation is responsible for the preparation of the master plan, which is drawn up in consulta-

tion with the appropriate Minister, Government departments and the local authorities in the area. In addition, existing residents are given an opportunity to state their views and if there are objections to the plan a public inquiry might be necessary. When the plan has been agreed, the development corporation draws up detailed proposals for particular sections of the designated area and submits these to the responsible Minister for approval which (given after consultation with the local planning authorities) constitutes planning consent. A development corporation has extensive powers. For example, it can acquire by agreement or compulsory purchase any land or property within the designated area necessary for its purposes, and it is empowered to provide houses, factories, offices and other essential buildings, estate roads and in certain circumstances the main services essential to the development of the town.

The capital required for creating the new town is advanced from public funds and is repayable over sixty years. Under the New Towns Act 1946 Parliament approved a fund of M£50 to provide for advances to the development corporations but this has been increased by subsequent Acts and in 1980 stood at M£3,250 (net of repayments). After something like a decade most new towns are able to meet all their loan charges and thereafter there is usually a revenue surplus. It would be difficult to estimate accurately what would have been the cost of any conceivable alternatives to the new towns but it is very doubtful if they would have been less costly.

In the allocation of houses the corporations of the new towns work on guidelines laid down by the Government. For example, those of the new towns around London were expected to give priority to households living in London who established a housing need. Generally the applicant must have obtained work in the new town or close to it, or because of his skill be likely to do so. Also, new towns make provision for housing a proportion of retired people so that the parents of the younger householders can be accommodated and thus give mutual support. However, in all new towns there is a great deal of emphasis on matching employment with housing but this is not entirely exclusive of meeting housing needs not connected to the availability of employment in the new towns because the availability of labour is a factor in encouraging industries to move into a new town.

One of the biggest problems for the management of the new towns, when it has built the houses and factories, is to attract industry and to equate the numbers of the right type of workers with the jobs available or likely to be available. This problem increases if, for any reason, factories close or new factories remain unoccupied. In these circumstances houses can also remain empty and may become vandalised.

New town development corporations are not allowed to use any of the profits they make from commerce or industry to reduce the rents of their houses, and unlike local authorities they have no cheap pre-war houses to aid their rent pools. However, they do receive Government subsidies, which take account of the fact that development corporations have no income from rates. Rents of houses in the new towns tend to be higher than those of local authority houses in the area, but rent rebate schemes cushion the effect for the lower-income households.

A feature of the new towns has been the small proportion of owner-occupied dwellings but in 1970 the Government requested the development corporations to sell existing houses to sitting tenants. The price was fixed at market value with vacant possession, less a standard 20 per cent reduction. During 1970-73 24,000 houses were sold, but in 1974 the Labour Government stopped further sales on account of the shortage of rented accommodation in relation to the demand for it. Since then the law has been changed. The Housing Act 1980 establishes a charter for public-sector tenants (which includes new town tenants), giving them certain statutory rights such as security of tenure, etc., and the right in certain circumstances to purchase the houses they occupy at a discount on the market price of from 33 per cent to 50 per cent, depending on the length of their occupation.

A new town means a new community, but this is less easy to create than the new town itself. Where a nucleus exists, for example a small town or village, integration between the old and the new communities is essential but sometimes difficult to achieve. Also, if the new community is to be a healthy one, it needs to be balanced, e.g. with a mixed social strata and a mixture of age groups. The facilities for social activities and leisure need to be provided at an early stage so as to help develop the sense of community. In the first post-1945 new towns the provision of facilities for social and leisure activities lagged far behind the provision of housing and this led to social problems which were featured in newspapers as 'new town blues' and 'neurosis in new towns'. Some young housewives suffered from loneliness and depression. They missed the old and familiar surroundings, the support of their parents and the social contacts with relatives, friends and neighbours in shops and pubs, and taking a bus ride to see friends. Facilities for dealing with complaints and for listening to grievances were either non-existent or inadequate, so small irritations were exaggerated into questions of life and death.

The Government's original plan was to build up to twenty new towns and during 1947-50 fourteen were started, twelve in England and Wales and two in Scotland. In 1956 a third new town was authorised for Scotland, but no further new towns were authorised until 1961. Eight out of the first fifteen new towns were intended primarily to disperse people and workplaces from the London conurbation. These were Basildon, Bracknell, Crawley, Harlow, Hatfield, Hemel Hempstead, Stevenage and Welwyn Garden City. Two, East Kilbride and Cumbernauld, were to serve the same purpose for Glasgow. Two others, Peterlee and Glenrothes, were designed to collect populations from scattered villages and place them into more satisfactory urban centres and also provide supplementary industries. The other three were to bring more and better housing and community services to industrial settlements that were for various reasons socially and economically inadequate. These were Corby, Cwmbran and Newton Aycliffe. Between 1956 and 1960 Government policy seems to have been to encourage the voluntary expansion of small towns instead of planning more new towns.

The second generation of new towns was commenced in 1961, and by 1968 eight were in progress. Six are in England: Skelmersdale, Telford, Redditch, Runcorn, Washington and Milton Keynes. Two, Livingston and Irvine, are in Scotland. Four of those in England were based on existing towns with populations ranging from 20,000 to 30,000 and their planned future populations ranged from 80,000 to 100,000 people. Two new towns, Telford and Milton Keynes, were planned to integrate a number of towns and villages into regional complexes with populations of 200,000 to 250,000. By 1980 Milton Keynes was nearly half-way to achieving its maximum population target of 200,000 by the year 1990, it had become a pleasant place in which to live and work and in its development had managed to avoid the 'new town blues'. Telford was not so successful.

During 1967-68 the Government adopted a new policy of using development corporations to co-operate with local councils in planned major expansions of existing towns to form regional or sub-regional centres which would also absorb small towns and villages in the vicinity not suitable for individual expansion. The towns planned for expansion were Peterborough, seventy-seven miles north of London, and an adjoining area consisting in total of 15,940 acres and a population of 80,500 but planned to accommodate 150,000 by 1981; Northampton and surrounding area consisting in total of 21,280 acres, and a population of 120,000 planned to double by 1981; Warrington with a surrounding area containing in total 21,000 acres and a population of 127,000 which is to be increased to 200,000; and Ipswich, 22,000 acres and a population of 120,000 which is to be increased to 190,000.

The designation of the central Lancashire new town in March 1970 was another step away from the original concept of new towns as moderately sized communities. The area designated for this town covered fifty-five square miles and included the major towns of Preston, Chorley and Leyland, and many smaller communities. The population of the area when designated was about a quarter of a million people and it was planned to double this figure in about twenty years. The primary purposes of the central Lancashire new town were urban regeneration, which included the clearance of blighted areas, and the stimulation of economic growth in the region. It was hoped that as the project proceeded it might contribute to a reversal of the flow of population from the north to the south-east of the country, and arrest the decay and industrial stagnation of the sub-region.

Because the main purpose of this new town was not that of catering for overspill the development corporation was not under pressure to build large numbers of houses in a great hurry but was able to carefully plan the grafting of new units on to the established major communities so that they would not lose their identity, and at the same time to plan the area as a sub-regional complex. The functions of the central Lancashire new town development corporation are not those of a mere developer, but are pre-eminently those of a sub-regional planning authority, planning not only for the most efficient use of land, but also for the economic and social welfare of the sub-region.

The decision of the Government to plan and develop regional cities or complexes instead of continuing to create new towns of moderate size was probably taken because of an official forecast of a big increase in the population of Britain by the year 2000. This forecast has been revised in the light of a fall in the birth-rate but the designation of such large areas was a new and bold use of the new town machinery. A Government review of the new towns policy, after substantial reductions in population forecasts, and because of the clear need to revitalise the inner-city areas of many towns, has led to a reduction in the long-term target populations of some of the towns and will probably result in a reduction in the momentum of new town development.

The question of the ultimate ownership of the new towns was first raised in Parliament during the debates on what became the New Towns Act 1946. Since then the matter has been debated many times inside and outside Parliament. In England four of the new towns have been substantially completed and the development corporations dissolved. Target dates have been announced for the dissolution of a further eight new towns' development corporations by the early 1980s. In Wales responsibility for one of the two new towns has been taken over by the Development Board for Rural Wales. In Northern Ireland development of the new towns has been incorporated in a new District Towns Strategy, which is the responsibility of the Department of the Environment for Northern Ireland. The present Government (1980) plans substantial disposals of the completed assets of the new towns in order to release resources for investment and to reduce the involvement of the public sector.

The new towns are one of Britain's greatest successes of the post-1945 period. Mistakes were made because of the lack of experience, economic stringencies have left their mark, and with ideas rapidly changing some of the developments of thirty years ago are out of date, but the achievements of the development corporations in housing and planning have not been equalled by local authorities, or by private developers. Lessons have been learned since the early years. Social facilities are now provided at an early stage in the development of a new town. Also there are usually adequate facilities now for dealing with complaints and for giving help and support to newcomers and others who may need it. The early new towns have become established communities in which people have deepening roots. The later ones planned as regional or sub-regional centres were bold attempts to deal with certain economic and social problems of the time. Two million of Britain's fifty-seven million people live in the new towns.

In 1980 the situation in relation to the need for new towns is different from what it was in 1945. The population of Britain is not increasing at the same rate that it was in the immediate post-war period and there are some indications that it might become static or even fall. The new towns have drawn population and industry from the inner zones of many of the larger towns and cities and these have decayed and become almost derelict. In the last few years this has called for a switch of economic resources to rebuild them, but both Government and local authorities should have seen what was happening before it reached crisis proportions. Virgin land in Britain is very limited and what there is left should be kept for food production, because in the longer term food is likely to become more valuable than the manufactured goods we now export. It seems unlikely that any more new towns will be created in the foreseeable future but valuable lessons have been learned and experience gained which can be useful in the task of rebuilding many of Britain's inner-city areas. The Reith Committee stressed that for the building of new towns an organisation was needed that could concentrate wholly on the task. This can be said of the job of rebuilding the old and worn-out inner-city areas, which with proper planning could become the next generation of new towns.

First generation new town – Crawley – typical short terrace.

First generation new town – Stevenage – grass courts instead of pavements.

First generation new town – Stevenage – pedestrian way through terrace housing.

First generation new town – Cwmbran – terrace houses around close.

Second generation new town – Skelmersdale – houses with front doors which open on to a pedestrian way.

Second generation new town – Skelmersdale – landscaping at rear of dwellings.

125

Second generation new town – Runcorn – rented housing.

First generation new town – Cwmbran – flats with view of open country.

Second generation new town – Runcorn.

Second generation new town – Runcorn – Castle Fields.

Second generation new town – Runcorn – flats Windmill Hill.

Second generation new town – Runcorn – private housing at Marina village on the Bridgewater canal.

Second generation new town – Milton Keynes – rented housing with pedestrian access.

128

Second generation new town – Milton Keynes – rented housing with play area.

Second generation new town – Milton Keynes – front entrances of rented houses.

129

Second generation new town – Milton Keynes – front view of terraced housing.

Second generation new town – Milton Keynes – housing for the elderly.

Second generation new town – Milton Keynes – solar house, rear aspect showing solar panels.

Regional complex – Central Lancashire new town – purpose-built single persons' accommodation at Clayton Green, Chorley.

131

Regional complex – Central Lancashire new town – rented housing at Leyland.

Regional complex – Central Lancashire new town – more rented housing.

*Regional complex – Central Lancashire new town –
a close up of a house in the development at
Penwortham, Preston*

Regional complex – Lancashire new town – kitchen of rented house.

Chapter 8

HOMES PROVIDED BY HOUSING ASSOCIATIONS

Housing associations, as they are now called, emerged about the middle of the last century to alleviate the awful squalor and poverty in which many sections of the working-classes lived in most of the large towns of Britain. At the time they were not called housing associations.

The first housing society or association on record was established in 1830 as The Labourer's Friend Society, but it only began its housing work in 1844 when it built blocks of flats, or what were then called tenement blocks, to let at low rents. However, although the rents were low, they were high enough to cover all the costs and allow a small return on the capital invested. The Labourer's Friend Society survived for over a century until the 1960s, when it was taken over by the Peabody Trust, which had been endowed in 1862 by George Peabody. Some of the dwellings built by the Labourer's Friend Society are still in use.

George Peabody was an American, born of poor parents, who started life as a grocer's apprentice. He prospered first in America and later in London, where he settled down in banking after giving up his American business. He made gifts totalling half a million pounds to ameliorate the conditions of the London poor, and suggested to the trustees of the fund that the money should be used for the construction of improved dwellings for the poor but, in accordance with the philosophy of the time, should show a 5 per cent return. Although the 5 per cent was never achieved, by the end of the first twenty years of its existence the Peabody Trust owned 3,500 dwellings which housed 14,600 people.

The Peabody Trust and the Metropolitan Association for Improving the Dwellings of the Industrious Classes, both of which started about the same time, had as an objective the building of model dwellings for lower paid workers which it was hoped would be copied by private landlords and others. However, sufficient investment capital was not forthcoming and in the latter part of the century a number of housing trusts were endowed by certain philanthropists. Some of these are still in existence and a few continue to bear the name of their founders. Examples are: the Guinness Trust, founded in 1889 with an endowment of £200,000 given by Sir E.C. Guinness; the Samuel Lewis Trust (1906) operating then in London; and the Sutton Housing Trust, endowed with M£2 under the will of Richard Sutton in 1900 and which owned

and managed, in 1975, over 12,000 houses and flats in industrial towns throughout England. Other housing associations founded by philanthropists include Port Sunlight in Wirral, commenced by Price Brothers, candlemakers, in 1853 by building seventy-six cottages for their work people and which were let at weekly rents of between 15p and 30p. The firm later became the soap manufacturing company of Lever Brothers which developed the estate into a model village containing a library, art gallery, sports ground, church and school. The houses were well planned and laid out in wide tree-lined roads. Port Sunlight, as it was called, grew and in 1975 covered 130 acres, had nearly 1,300 dwellings, besides shops, a swimming pool and assembly halls, etc. The firm is now part of the giant Unilever group and some of the houses have been sold to the tenants.

In 1879 Cadbury Brothers Ltd. built a new factory four-and-a-half miles to the south-west of Bimingham on a site in a rural area which they called Bournville. The business grew rapidly and in the first few years a small number of houses were built near the factory gates for key employees. One of the brothers, George Cadbury, kept in mind the terrible squalor and human misery he had seen in the slums of Birmingham and the people he had met there whilst teaching in the adult school. He was convinced that little progress was possible while the squalor and misery remained. In the 1890s George Cadbury found the time and the money to try out his ideas for promoting social betterment through improved housing. In 1893 he bought 120 acres of land close to the factory and the following year began building. Within six years 313 houses had been built and the estate had grown to 330 acres. The layout of the roads and the design of the houses followed the pattern of a 'garden city'. The estate was, and is, independent of Cadbury Brothers Ltd., now Cadbury Schweppes Ltd.

The first inhabitants of Bournville had various backgrounds. In 1902 only 40 per cent of the 405 households were connected with the factory and the proportion has remained fairly constant.

To ensure that his purposes and ideas would have some permanency George Cadbury founded the Bournville Village Trust. By the Foundation Deed he gave the twelve trustees a wide discretion to initiate further experiments aimed at improving living conditions of the working-class and labouring population. The trust was registered as a charity and the trustees of the time became responsible for property worth £172,724. George Cadbury wanted the houses to be self-supporting, and any surplus money from their management to be re-invested in estate development and housing reform. This resulted in the rents being higher than most working-class families were paying in Birmingham at the time.

In 1906 the Bournville Village trustees formed a co-partnership society and named it Bournville Tenants Ltd. They wished to demonstrate a method by which ownership of land and planning control could be vested in the municipality while at the same time the responsibility for development, design, selection of tenants and general housing management was in the hands of a co-partnership housing society to which all the tenants would belong.

The trustees have continued to follow the purposes and ideas laid down in the original Foundation Deed. For example, through different societies houses have been built for renting and for sale. One society built forty-nine self-contained flats for business and professional women. Since 1946 there have been self-build housing associations, and associations providing accommodation for special groups of people, for example the elderly, and retired professional people.

The Rowntree Trust is another body which has been concerned with the housing of the working-classes.

Before 1919 housing associations were alone in attempting to do something about the bad conditions in which most of the labouring classes lived, but in that year the position changed because a legal duty was placed on local authorities to provide housing for the working-classes (see Chapter 6). However, during the inter-war period housing associations continued in a limited way to be active in the field. At the end of the 1939-45 war the spate of welfare legislation made it look as though housing associations had served their purpose and would not expand further. In the event they did expand in certain ways to meet fresh needs.

In the early years after the 1939-45 war some industries were expanding rapidly in places which had been developed for war production, with workers living in temporary accommodation or billets, and in other places where previously there had not been a great deal of industry. In some cases the local authorities were incapable of providing the homes at the speed required and in consequence some firms sponsored industrial housing associations by putting up much of the required capital, often at preferential interest rates. These housing associations were eligible for Government subsidies.

Self-build societies, groups of young people with a core of skilled building craftsmen, were formed in many parts of the country to build houses for their members. This was another way housing associations expanded in the post-war period. Also, before local authorities were able or willing to provide accommodation for the increasing number of elderly people, some existing charitable trusts, some housing associations, and some newly-created local associations

stepped into the breach and provided accommodation by converting large houses and by building bungalows and flats.

Over the years the various bodies which have grown up to meet various kinds of housing needs on a charitable basis have adopted different titles, but since 1957 they have all been included in the generic term of housing association, which is defined in the Housing Act 1957. Briefly and loosely this definition says that a housing association is a body of trustees or a company established for the purpose of providing, constructing, improving or managing houses or hostels, and which does not trade for profit. In spite of this generic term in the Housing Act 1957, in law housing trusts are sometimes classified seperately from other housing associations. For example, the Rent Act 1968 has a long definition which broadly says that a housing trust is a body which devotes its funds to working-class housing. There are other legal definitions for specific purposes. For example, 'housing society' in the Housing Act 1964, and 'registered housing association' used in the Housing Act 1974. These terms have to be interpreted in relation to the context in which they are used but broadly speaking they all fall within the generic term 'housing association' which in this chapter is used inclusively. Broadly, then, a housing association is a group of people who have combined together with the object of constructing dwellings, or of improving existing ones, or of managing dwellings, or a combination of any of these functions on a non-profit-making basis. The association may, or may not, be recognised as a charity. It may operate on a national or local level, and may restrict its operations to the housing needs of a single group, for example old people. In addition to its housing functions, it may provide certain other services such as a warden service, the provision of meals, and facilities for hobbies, etc.

There are many kinds of housing association. Some are small and have very limited assets, but some are large and are run by professionals. Some were formed a long time ago for philanthropic purposes, whilst others have been formed within the last decade with the sole object of providing homes for their members on a self-build basis, and others on a co-ownership basis.

A housing association is usually formed: (a) by people concerned about the living conditions of others less fortunate than themselves; (b) by industrialists who want to provide good housing conditions for their workers; or (c) by those who wish to secure accommodation for themselves on a co-operative or co-partnership basis with people who are similarly minded.

Housing associations can be classified according to their objectives and the way they are financed. Many enjoy the status of a charity, which means they can obtain exemption from the payment of taxes. Others are incorporated under the Companies Acts and are not registered charities. The main types are listed below.

General family associations

This group includes associations whose main work is both new building and the improvement and conversion of existing buildings. Some of these associations were founded as charitable trusts in the 19th century to provide dwellings for the poor. The work they pioneered has to a large extent been taken over by local authorities since 1919, but since the 1960s they have been very active in the acquisition and improvement of older housing, especially in Housing Action Areas (see Chapter 9).

Special need associations

A special need association usually aims to help one particular group in the community. The groups concerned are broadly the old, the disabled, students, ex-patients of mental hospitals, ex-prisoners, refugees, ethnic minorities, and the homeless. For some of these groups hostels are more appropriate than houses or flats and the associations provide accordingly. Many special need associations were sponsored by religious and philanthropic organisations. Some provide more than housing, e.g. food and special care, and in recent years some have taken over for management short-life property awaiting demolition, and have carried out the necessary repairs.

Industrial housing associations

These associations were set up in connection with industrial firms, commercial organisations and public corporations, primarily for housing their own workpeople. They were among the earliest type of association but since the 1950s they have declined considerably both in numbers and in importance. Their origins were closely linked with tied housing, i.e. where the house went with the job and meant eviction in the event of dismissal or resignation. Examples are associations such as the Coal Board Housing Association, which took over a number of colliery housing associations after nationalisation of the coal mining industry, and those formed by the railway companies for their workers more than half a century ago. The day of the industrial housing associations seems to be over and some, perhaps most of them, have disposed of their houses and gone out of business.

Self-build housing associations

A self-build housing association is one in which the members have agreed to build houses for themsleves. They do all or most of the work themselves and thus reduce the capital required and the cost of the houses. A self-build association usually lasts only until the houses for all its members have been built and then it is dissolved. In 1975 it was estimated by the National Federation of Housing Associations that over 10,000 houses had been built by more than 1,000 associations since 1949. Self-build associations are able to borrow from local authorities or the Housing Corporation to enable them to purchase land and materials. When the houses are completed members arrange their own mortgages in the usual way and purchase the houses from the association, enabling it to repay its loan and wind up.

Cost-rent associations

As the name implies, cost-rent associations let dwellings at rents which cover the costs of capital repayments and interest, management, repairs and insurance, etc., but without a landlord's profit. During the 1950s there seemed to be a demand for rented accommodation from people who did not want to live in a council house and did not wish, or could not afford, to buy a house. In 1961 the Government made money available for making loans to approved housing associations, and in 1964 the job of making loans to housing associations was taken over by the newly-created Housing Corporation. However, by 1975 circumstances had changed, owner-occupation was more attractive than cost-renting and no new cost-rent associations were being formed.

Co-ownership housing associations

Co-ownership is a mixture of renting and ownership. The members of a co-ownership association are in one sense tenants because they make regular payments to the association under a tenancy agreement, but these payments are also the means by which they become one of the corporate owners of the property. Although they do not own the particular house or flat in which they live they are one of the corporate owners of all the property owned by the association, and are therefore in this capacity owner-occupiers. Co-ownership was in existence in Britain before 1964 but it was the Housing Act of that year which made provision for its expansion by making Government funds available for the purpose.

The Housing Corporation is a Government agency. Its Board members are appointed by the Secretaries of State for the Environment, for Scotland and for Wales acting jointly. The Corporation presents to the Secretaries an annual report and audited accounts which are laid before Parliament. It is responsible for financing, supervising and promoting non-profit-making housing associations throughout the United Kingdom, and in certain circumstances has powers of compulsory purchase. It has extensive inquiry powers into the affairs of a registered association, and power to remove committee members or officers of a registered association and appoint others where necessary. During 1979-80 the Board approved loans for new building and rehabilitation of dwellings estimated to cost in total about M£600.

Scotland and Northern Ireland

In Scotland and Northern Ireland there are Government sponsored bodies and housing associations. The Scottish Special Housing Association and the North Eastern Housing Association were formed between the wars to operate in what were called 'special areas'. These were areas severely affected by the economic depression of the time. These associations built houses for workers with funds advanced by the Commission for Special Areas and thus relieved the burden on the local rates. At the end of 1975 the Scottish Special Housing Association owned and managed about 86,000 dwellings. The North Eastern

Housing Association ceased building with the reorganisation of local government in 1975, but by that time it owned and managed about 18,500 dwellings.

In Northern Ireland action has been taken to stimulate the voluntary housing movement, and with the encouragement of the Department for the Environment in conjunction with the Northern Ireland Federation of Housing Associations registered housing associations are undertaking a large programme of schemes for groups, such as the elderly and disabled, and are also playing a significant part in the rehabilitation of older dwellings, especially in Belfast. Also the concept of shared ownership is being developed in the public sector by the Northern Ireland Housing Executive and in the private sector by the Northern Ireland Co-Ownership Housing Association.

By the early 1960s people in Britain wanting to rent housing accommodation could virtually only do so from local authorities and this lack of choice was in many circles considered to be unsatisfactory. In consequence, a pilot project for building houses to let at cost rents was launched by provisions contained in the Housing Act 1961. Loan capital amounting to M£25 for England and Wales and M£3 for Scotland was made available from public funds to housing associations that were prepared to build cost-rent housing. No subsidies were made available for these houses and local authorities were not expected to take any part in the scheme except for their normal functions of planning and building controls. By the end of 1963 the whole of the loan capital had been used up and about 7,000 dwellings had been built under the scheme. This encouraged the Government to launch a more ambitious scheme. Under the Housing Act 1964 the Housing Corporation was created and given the primary duty of encouraging the formation of housing associations to provide dwellings either to be let at cost rents or for group ownership by the occupiers. The Housing Corporation was initially provided with a sum of M£100 by the Government for the purpose. The housing associations in the scheme usually borrowed two-thirds of the capital needed from the building societies and one-third from the Housing Corporation.

It was not long, however, before the cost-rent associations found that the rents they needed to charge to cover all their outgoings were too high, especially when compared with the rents of local authorities for similar houses. In consequence there was a move away from the formation of new cost-rent associations and towards co-ownership associations. But by 1974 the Housing Corporation reported that the co-ownership societies were also finding that the payments required from their tenants were also too high in relation to other tenures. By 1975 no new societies were being formed but by the end of that year loans for 43,000 co-ownership dwellings had been approved by the Housing Corporation.

During the inter-war period some housing associations had concentrated their resources on the improvement and conversion for their particular purposes of older houses, and during the 1960s and 1970s other associations moved into this field. The special role of housing associations in this work was recognised when the discretionary grant was fixed at a higher limit for them when acquiring property for conversion or improvement. In some towns housing associations are now playing a major role in the restoration of areas of housing which otherwise in a few years' time would have to be cleared, e.g. in Housing Action Areas. They are also buying blocks of houses from private landlords and improving them, and in some cases then selling them to sitting tenants.

The Housing Act 1974 introduced new forms of financial assistance for housing associations, e.g. grants towards covering losses incurred on housing projects, and grants to help meet certain revenue deficits.

Because housing associations are eligible for financial assistance from public funds and have certain other privileges it is recognised that they should be subject to a degree of control. Provisions in the Housing Act 1974 require the Housing Corporation to maintain a register of housing associations, and any association which satisfies certain criteria of the corporation is entitled to be registered. At the end of 1980 there were about 3,000 associations on the register. Only those on the register are eligible to receive financial help from public funds and certain tax privileges. In exchange for these privileges a registered housing association must submit to certain controls. For example, it may not sell, lease or mortgage, or dispose of land except with the consent of the Housing Corporation, unless it is a registered charity, in which case it needs the consent of the Charity Commissioners.

The Housing Corporation has the legal power to investigate suspected misdemeanours and mismanagement of a registered housing association and, on either of these being substantiated, has the power to replace committee members or officers, transfer property and petition for the winding-up of the association. It may also specify maximum fees payable to association members and conditions of any contract involving them. Audited accounts and details of committee membership of registered associations are available on the public register maintained at the Corporation's headquarters.

Housing association rents are within the 'fair' rent system (explained in chapter 4). Under the Housing Act 1980 tenants of housing associations, like council tenants, have certain rights, e.g. security of tenure, the right to sublet and to take in lodgers. Also, in certain circumstances they have the right to purchase the house they rent at a discount on the market price.

The tenants of housing associations are usually selected in accordance with the objectives of the individual association and the application of the generally accepted criteria of housing need. For example, associations which provide accommodation for special categories of people select their tenants from these categories, but since 1972 it has been a condition of sanction for local authority loans to an association that the local authority should be entitled to nominate up to 50 per cent of the tenants of a scheme. However, in 1974 the Government suggested to local authorities (DOE circular 170/74) that housing associations be allowed to preserve the flexibility they had previously enjoyed in tenant selection. Most associations take great efforts to select as their tenants those who are in the greatest need for the accommodation they have available.

The management of housing associations is usually in the hands of a group of people who give their services free, but the management committees of the larger ones are helped and guided by paid professionals. In 1980 housing associations together controlled about 340,000 dwellings, or about 1.3 per cent of the country's housing stock. Today their main role is to complement and supplement the housing work of local authorities, in particular by providing accom-

modation for special groups such as the elderly and the disabled, etc., and in areas of housing stress supplementing the work of local authorities in relation to the repair and improvement of blocks of substandard housing, especially in Housing Action Areas, in which during the last few years they have become considerably involved.

Over the years housing associations have shown versatility and flexibility in meeting needs and circumstances as they have arisen and often long before central and local government were aware of their existence. It would be a great loss to the country if the voluntary effort in the housing field were killed or allowed to die. There is a good argument for allowing housing associations to take over certain aspects of the management of some council estates and for their greater involvement in the improvement of areas of older housing in towns.

conclusion

Port Sunlight, Bromborough Pool, cottages built by the Price Brothers in 1853. (1960)

Port Sunlight, Bromborough Pool, garden for growing food at rear of cottages built in 1853.

140

Port Sunlight, some of the early houses built for the factory workers.

Port Sunlight, terrace houses overlooking sunken garden.

141

Port Sunlight, Primrose Hill.

Port Sunlight, timber-frame construction.

Port Sunlight, mixed development, Lower Road.

Port Sunlight, semi-detached houses.

143

Bournville. (1955)

Bournville – early type of house built near the factory gates.

144

Most houses built at Bournville before 1939 had fair-sized gardens; the earlier ones averaged 600 square yards. A survey in the early 20th century showed that the produce from the average garden was valued at 12½p a week throughout the year. House rents averaged 37½p a week and wages were about £1.00 per week.

Bournville – until 1914 some houses were built without separate bathrooms but various devices were used to provide baths, e.g. the tip-up bath which lifted up into a cupboard in the kitchen.

Houses built in 1907 by a Bournville co-partnership society.

A group of alms-houses built by Richard Cadbury primarily, but not solely, for old Bournville employees, endowed by the rents of 33 houses on the estate.

A group of bungalows built in 1909 for elderly people.

146

Weoley Hill Ltd., a society formed under the village trust in 1914, built nearly 500 houses which were sold on 99-year leases. The houses were built at prices ranging between £300 and £2,000.

Bournville – between 1923 and 1925 smaller houses were built for sale and in conformity with the government subsidy regulations.

147

Small, low-cost, two-bedroomed houses built in 1923 to meet the needs of the newly married and the elderly.

Between 1924 and 1925 Cadbury Bros Ltd. leased land from the trust and built 96 bungalows for single women employees.

Bournville – blocks of furnished flats and bed-sitting-rooms with catering and other services built for professional and business women. In 1955 flats were let at £9.70 and the bed-sitting-rooms at between £5.40 and £7.00 per month. The rents included rates, essential furniture and some services.

The Bournville Trust began to build again in 1946. To obtain the Government rent subsidy the houses had to conform to Government standards, hence the similarity with council houses of the period.

Bournville – in the immediate post-1945 years the economic use of available materials was essential. In these houses it was achieved and the best use of limited space made to reduce the need for tenants' furniture.

Bournville – bungalows built in 1949 for retired professional people. Edward Cadbury believed that there were people with a relatively good income who needed smaller houses in which they could have a comfortable life with reduced housework.

An example of blocks of tenements built in the middle of the 19th century by charitable associations for the working-classes. (1958)

One- and two-bedroomed flats built by a housing association.

Bournville – post-1945 houses built for sale.

Housing built by the Scottish Housing Association. (Civic Trust award 1971)

Family houses built by the Scottish Special Housing Association. (1972)

Another example of housing built by the Scottish Special Housing Association. (1972)

Chapter 9

NEW HOMES FROM OLD
Conservation, Conversion and Improvement

Houses are not permanent things. They age and decay, and even if they are kept in good repair are likely to become obsolete unless they are re-equipped. Until the early part of this century the useful life of buildings was largely determined by the growth of towns and industrial expansion and by their capacity to remain standing. Effort to preserve the existing housing stock was small.

After the end of the First World War it became Government policy to encourage the improvement of some of the worst of the working-class houses. Local authorities were given powers to deal with areas, or 'aggregations', of houses which were not sufficiently unfit as to warrant demolition but were in a bad state of disrepair, badly arranged and overcrowded, in what were called 'improvement areas'. The general pattern was that in these areas some houses were demolished in order to provide additional daylight and ventilation to those remaining, sinks and individual piped water supplies replaced common stand-pipes, pail-closets were replaced by water-closets, and ash-pits, often rat infested, were replaced by dustbins.

Local authorities, however, were not the only bodies interested in improving working-class houses; some housing associations used a part of their resources to that end. A pioneer in this work was the Liverpool Improved Houses Association, which was formed in 1928 by well-known local people. In October of that year the association published its first report, describing the 'ten months' experiment on the possibility of improving housing conditions in Liverpool, which at the time was experiencing an economic depression which had contributed to widespread social problems. The report was not only an appeal for funds to further the work, but also a statement about the direction of that work.

The association had bought fifteen houses in Swan Street, Edgehill, and had "mended the roofs, put in gas lighting, improved the sanitary arrangements, increased the number of windows and cleaned and decorated inside and out". Paying less than 25p per week, "the tenants in Swan Street greatly appreciated the alterations". The association had also bought a large Victorian house in Queens Road, Liverpool 6, and divided it into three flats, with additional accommodation for a caretaker. In its first report the association stated: "This house has been filled with tenants from very inferior accommodation. One woman, who

has just come from a cellar dwelling, tells us that her little boy eats twice as much as he did in the old place."

By 1930 unemployment in Liverpool had reached catastrophic proportions, about 25 per cent of the workforce. For the new landlord – the infant housing association – the tenants' welfare was of major importance and it struggled to improve houses without Government assistance, relying only upon voluntary subscriptions and its own direct income from rents.

A 'New Homes for Old' exhibition, organised by twenty associations and held in the Central Hall, Westminster, in December 1931 was designed to show the conditions in which many people in Britain were living and what needed to be done. The exhibition was a success, and amongst other things showed by the display of maps, photographs and models of houses how existing houses could be improved by voluntary effort.

Since 1945 housing associations have again taken on the task of improving older housing. For example, Merseyside Improved Houses, formerly the Liverpool Improved Housing Association, has widely expanded its field of operations which have included the conservation of houses of outstanding architectural merit which otherwise would have been demolished.

During the inter-war period general housing standards in the rural areas were well below those in urban areas, partly because of the low rent-paying capacity of agricultural workers. In 1942 a sub-committee of the then Central Housing Advisory Committee was asked to review housing conditions in rural areas. The report of the committee, published in 1944, dealt in considerable detail with the matter and made many recommendations, amongst which were some relating to the repair and improvement of existing cottages and for the payment of Government grants towards the costs of such work (see Chapter 3). In 1945 both the wartime coalition and the new Labour Governments had in their housing objectives the improvement and the re-equipping of the older housing stock. The 1951 National Census, the first after the end of the 1939-45 war, showed that in England and Wales 12 per cent of households did not have the exclusive use of a piped water supply, 2 per cent were entirely without a cooking stove, 6 per cent had no kitchen sink and 37 per cent were without a fixed bath.

For the first few years after the end of the war in 1945 the housing shortage was so great that building resources had to be concentrated on the provision of additional units of accommodation. However, by 1949 the Government was satisfied that sufficient progress had been made in the provision of new houses for a start to be made on improving the older housing stock. It was accepted that although landlords had a legal duty to keep their houses in a reasonable state of repair, it would be wrong to expect them to install additional equipment such as baths and hot water systems, etc., at their own expense. Therefore the Housing Act 1949 offered financial inducements in the form of grants to landlords willing to improve their houses. The grants were known as discretionary grants and amounted to half the cost of the work which the local authority had approved in advance of its execution. The local authority was entitled to recover three-quarters of its outlay from the National Exchequer, which meant that one-quarter had to be a charge on the local rates. For this reason many local authorities were reluctant to make improvement grants. In the areas where the grants were available, however, house improvement was sporadic, e.g. one house in a street of thirty or forty houses, and these were mostly owner-occupied. Although between 1949 and 1958 160,000 discretionary grants were approved, the 1949 Act did not achieve its objective, which was wide-scale reconditioning of the older housing stock.

The House Purchase and Housing Act 1959 introduced a new type of grant, the standard grant, which could be claimed by an owner as of right for installing certain equipment (called amenities), provided that certain conditions were met. In respect of this grant, therefore, the local authorities had no discretion. However, the discretionary grants under the Act of 1949 remained available in those areas where the local authorities were willing to pay them.

Standard grants were fixed in amount in relation to each of the pieces of equipment installed. Originally these were: a fixed bath or shower, a washhand basin, a water-closet, a hot- and cold-water supply and a ventilated food store, and the house had to have a further life of at least fifteen years as against thirty years for the discretionary grant. Later the ventilated food store was omitted because it was not considered necessary since domestic refrigerators were increasingly being installed. Instead, a sink with a supply of hot and cold water was added to the list. For an owner to claim the grant the house had to have all the standard amenities but grant was paid only for those which had formerly been lacking.

At first the 1959 Act resulted in an increase in the rate at which houses were being improved, but the increase was not maintained. One reason for this was that whilst the grants remained static building costs were rising fast and there was no grant for repairs except for those made necessary by the improvement.

The improvement of houses, whether with discretionary or standard grants, continued to be a piecemeal and spasmodic affair with a tendency for the better houses to be improved whilst those in urgent need of reconditioning were left untouched and allowed to decay further.

The Labour Party's strategy for the municipalisation of private rented housing to obtain an increase in the rate of rehabilitation was abandoned because of the cost of compensation.

The 1964 Housing Act empowered local authorities to deal with the improvement of houses on an area basis. Where within any area there were 50 per cent or more dwellings which lacked at least one of the five standard amenities, the local authority could designate it an improvement area. It was hoped that this would lead to the improvement of areas of housing instead of odd houses here and there. For such a scheme to succeed, however, it was not sufficient to improve only the interior of the houses, the environment around the houses needed to be improved also, but the Act made no provision for works of this nature. A few local authorities implemented the new powers but the procedures under the Act were cumbersome and took a long time to complete.

The provisions of the 1964 Act were given a great deal of publicity, which included exhibitions and the use of demonstration houses in different towns in each region of the country. Many of the industries concerned, e.g. manufacturers of the equipment such as baths and fire-grates, and the nationalised industries concerned with the supply of energy, such as the National Coal Board and local gas boards, took part in these exhibitions and sometimes independently staged their own exhibitions and publicity. In spite of this considerable publicity progress in improving the older housing stock was poor.

In 1966 two important publications of the Ministry of Housing and Local Government focussed attention on the need to improve the whole environment of residential areas. The first of these, a report of a sub-committee of the Central Housing Advisory Committee (the Dennington Committee) called "Our Older Homes; A Call for Action", examined minimum standards of fitness for housing and expressed the view that the environment in which houses stood was as important to living conditions as the houses themselves. The second, The Deeplish Study, "Improvement Possibilities in a District of Rochdale", described a survey of an area of older houses and argued that the existing population would be better served by improvement of the area instead of by clearance and redevelopment. A pilot project to improve the streets by traffic management, planting trees, the provision of better paving and street lighting, etc., was carried out in the area.

In 1967 the then Ministry of Housing and Local Government made the first national sample house condition survey which revealed that there were 1.8 million dwellings in England and Wales which were beyond repair and that a further 4.7 million were in need of major repairs and improvement. For the first time the Government had a reasonably accurate picture of the amount of unsatisfactory housing in England and Wales and this pointed to an urgent need for a national comprehensive housing policy. In 1968 the Government published a White Paper, "Old Houses into New Homes" (Cmnd. 3602) which set out a policy for improvement and promised new legislation. Area-based improvement was posed as a cheaper alternative to wide-scale clearance and public-sector redevelopment, and it was reasoned that this would stimulate private investment in housing rehabilitation.

The Housing Act 1969 made needed changes in the law relating to housing improvement. The amounts of the discretionary improvement and standard grants were increased. Previously no grants were available for improving houses in multiple occupation because each letting was not a separately constructed dwelling. The Act made available a special grant for installing the standard amenities in these houses. Grants were also made available for certain approved repairs, and higher grants for the improvement of houses with three or more storeys. Local authorities, the New Towns Commission, new towns development corporations and housing associations became eligible for financial help for the acquisition of houses for improvement or conversion as well as the improvement work itself, the grant for which was increased. Housing associations were also able to use a special subsidy of three-quarters of the annual loan charges on the approved cost of improvement and conversion, which put them in a more favourable position than the private owner. The provisions of the 1969 Act for the payment of an Exchequer subsidy towards the cost of environmental improvements were of considerable importance.

Local authorities were asked to designate as 'general improvement areas' areas which were capable of upgrading as a whole. These areas were to be free from disadvantages of position as residential areas and not to have a significant proportion of dwellings which were in such a bad state that demolition was the only satisfactory solution. In a Government circular (MOHLG 65/69) guidance was given to local authorities on the assessment of the relative advantages of redevelopment or rehabilitation as applied to different cases. In addition, local authorities were advised to seek general improvement areas where the local population were favourably inclined to them, otherwise the success of the project would be in doubt. The result was that many local authorities reviewed their redevelopment plans and this led to a long-term fall in the number of dwellings cleared after 1973.

After the 1969 Act came into operation the number of houses improved with the aid of grants increased considerably. For example, in 1970 in Britain as a whole 116,379 grants were approved and in 1971 the number jumped to 137,364 and in 1973 to 260,364. There was also a marked increase in the modernisation schemes for the older council estates. The Housing Act 1971 made provision for increased financial assistance for housing improvements in areas of high unemployment, i.e. in development and intermediate areas. Unfortunately, the increase in the number of houses being improved with grants was not maintained and by 1979 the number had fallen to 64,709 for that year.

In the early 1970s some researchers began to question the criteria used by local authorities in selecting areas for improvement. They proffered the view that the choice of area largely depended only on the first two of the three factors that ought to be taken into account, i.e. physical, economic and social, that only rarely were the social problems of an area considered. The result was that the better types of houses and areas, easier to deal with, were being chosen, and this, together with long-term slum clearance proposals, was resulting in the worst areas of housing where there was often considerable social deprivation being left untouched in the belief that in ten years or so the houses would have further deteriorated and be in a state to warrant their being included in slum-clearance schemes. In 1965 the Report of the Committee on Housing in Greater London identified certain areas which required special treatment because of deprivation and stress.

In 1973 the Government acknowledged that the designation of general improvement areas had failed to improve conditions in the older residential areas to the extent which was both possible and desirable and published a White Paper, "Widening the Choice: the Next Steps in Housing" (Cmnd. 5280). This outlined a new policy to give priority to the improvement of areas of stress which local authorities had considered unsuitable as general improvement areas. These were called 'housing action areas'. In addition the Government expressed the view that a municipal monopoly of rented accommodation was unhealthy and proposed a significant expansion of housing association activity. Measures to implement the policy were set out in a second White Paper, "Better Homes, the Next Priorities" (Cmnd. 5399).

These measures were included in the Housing Act 1974 and offered a way of dealing with large areas of vastly substandard housing and of utilising housing associations for the purpose of alleviating some of the worst housing and social conditions which existed. 'Housing action areas', as they were called in the Act, are where: (a) the physical state of the housing accommodation in the area as a whole, and (b) the social conditions in the area are such as to be unsatisfactory and can be effectively dealt with in a period of five years so as to secure (1) the improvement of the housing accommodation in the area as a whole, and (2) the well-being of the persons for the time being residing in the area and (3) the proper and effective management and use of that accommodation.

In contrast to housing action areas, general improvement areas are areas where the majority of the houses are fundamentally sound and their inhabitants generally have confidence both in the area and in themselves. Housing action areas are therefore intended to be not only areas where the social and physical conditions are unsatisfactory but also where there is a lack of confidence in the future

157

THE HOMES AND HOMELESS OF BRITAIN

of the area. In many cases this lack of confidence has been generated by long-term proposals for slum clearance. The provisions for dealing with conditions in housing action areas extend beyond the improvement of the houses and include, for example, changes in the form of tenure of some of the houses, and this might necessitate the local authority using its powers of compulsory purchase in special circumstances. The main objective of designating an area as a housing action area may be to ameliorate conditions pending eventual clearance and redevelopment but in most cases it is to restore confidence in the area and to demonstrate how improvement of conditions can produce a stable future. The achievement of these objectives can lead to the area being designated a general improvement area, for which a higher environmental grant is available, and the houses being improved to a higher standard, which would extend their life.

The main policy objectives of the rehabilitation provisions of the 1974 Act were set out in a Government circular, 160/74 (W.O. 266/74). Local authorities were asked to regard the rehabilitation of existing houses as an integral part of their housing programmes and were reminded that rehabilitation could be carried out by a variety of agencies, e.g. housing associations and housing co-operatives. The Government expressed the view that housing associations should play an important role in housing action areas. In some local authority districts most of the improvement work in housing action areas since 1975 has been carried out by housing associations (Chapter 8 deals with these).

Part viii of the Housing Act 1974 restores local authorities' powers of compulsion with respect to housing improvement, powers which had been repealed by the Housing Act 1969. Also, to try to prevent the spread of decay and deprivation to areas around a housing action area, the 1974 Housing Act enables a local authority to declare areas as 'priority neighbourhoods'. A priority neighbourhood must surround or have a common boundary with a housing action area or a general improvement area. Although grants are available for improvements to houses in a priority neighbourhood there is no grant for environmental work. The declaration of a priority neighbourhood is seen as a holding operation for areas which cannot be dealt with immediately either as a housing action area or as a general improvement area.

There are four types of grant available under the Housing Act 1974:
(a) improvement grants;
(b) intermediate grants (formerly standard grants);
(c) special grants;
(d) repairs grants;
The amount of the grant available to an owner depends on the kind of grant applicable, the location of the dwelling, the work to be done, and the appropriate percentage of the eligible expense. The appropriate percentage was fixed by Section 59 of the Housing Act 1974 as follows:

(a) 75 per cent of the eligible expense where the premises are in a housing action area.
(b) 60 per cent where the premises are in a general improvement area.
(c) 50 per cent where the premises are situated anywhere else.

The eligible expense on which the appropriate percentage grant is calculated is the estimated cost, within certain specified limits, which is approved by the local authority. If applicants satisfy the local authority that additional works are necessary to achieve the required standard, and that these could not have been foreseen, the eligible expense may later be increased. The maximum eligible expense for houses up to two storeys, outside London, was increased in 1977 from £3,200 to £5,000, and in 1980 from £5,000 to £7,500.

To prevent public funds being used to improve or convert houses solely for investment purposes and without the benefit being passed on to the occupiers, the Housing Act 1974 lays down a number of conditions which apply to dwellings after improvement or conversion with a grant. These are:
(a) If the house is, or is to be, owner-occupied, it must be available for the first year and for four years afterwards as the applicant's main residence. This enables a house to be improved with a grant prior to a move, e.g. for retirement, but it prohibits grants being used for second or holiday homes.
(b) If the house is to be available for letting, it must either be let, or available for letting as a residence, or available for occupation by an agricultural worker as a tied dwelling, but not for letting as a holiday home.
(c) If the dwelling is in a general improvement area or in a housing action area or a priority neighbourhood and is let, the local authority must impose further conditions. These are:
  (i) That the dwelling must be let, or available for letting, on a regulated tenancy, or if furnished accommodation, on a contract to which part vi of the Rent Act 1968 applies.
  (ii) That the owner will furnish a certificate to the effect that this condition is being fulfilled.
  (iii) That on the owner's request the tenant will supply the necessary information to enable the owner to comply with (ii) above.
  (iv) That when the works are completed if there is no registered rent for the premises the owner will take steps to have a regulated rent registered by the Rent Officer.
  (v) That any application for a rent to be registered by a Rent Officer will be proceeded with and not withdrawn.
  (vi) That no premium will be required as a condition for granting or renewing or continuing a lease or contract.

These conditions generally last for five years – seven in the case of premises in housing action areas – from the date when the works are satisfactorily completed. Certain dwellings, i.e. parsonages, dwellings on glebe and charitable lands, and dwellings in which a housing association has an interest at the date the grant was approved, are exempted from these conditions.

Improvement grants are available at the discretion of the local authority for the improvement or conversion of properties which are likely to provide satisfactory housing accommodation for a period of at least thirty years. On completion of the works the dwelling must comply with a standard consisting of ten points which include such matters as freedom from damp, natural lighting, ventilation, cooking facilities and drainage. The full standard is specified in Circular 160/74 which is published by the Department of the Environment.

An intermediate grant can be claimed as of right, provided the applicant satisfies the local authority that certain conditions will be met. However, it can only be claimed in respect of one or more of the standard amenities which are not already provided. After completion of the work, the house must be up to a specified standard, e.g. have all the standard amenities, be in good repair, fit for human habitation and likely to have a further life of at least fifteen years.

The standard amenities are specified in schedule 6 to the Housing Act 1974 as a fixed bath or shower, a hot- and cold-water supply at a fixed bath or shower, a washhand basin, a hot- and cold-water supply at a washhand basin, a sink, a hot- and cold-water supply at a sink, and a water-closet.

A fixed bath or shower must be in a bathroom, unless this is not reasonably practicable, but then it must be reasonably practicable to supply it with hot and cold water and the fitting must not be in a bedroom. The water-closet must be inside the dwelling if reasonably practicable, or where the dwelling is part of a larger building be in that building and be readily accessible from the dwelling. In addition to a grant for providing each amenity a grant is payable for any repair which the local authority considers necessary in connection with the provision of the amenity.

In the case of houses in multiple occupation a local authority may give a 'special' grant for the provision of standard amenities in a house even though each letting is not a self-contained dwelling and there is no immediate prospect of the house being converted into self-contained flats or houses. However, a special grant for the provision of a bath can only be given if it is to be in a bathroom.

Grants for repairs were first introduced in the Housing Act 1974. They are to enable dwellings in general improvement areas and housing action areas to be brought into good repair having regard to the age and character of the house and the locality in which it is situated. They are available at the discretion of the local authority.

The Housing Act 1974 allows an occupying tenant to require a local authority to compel the improvement of a dwelling which lacks one or more of the standard amenities, provided it was built before 3 October 1961.

The tenant must apply in writing to the local authority who, if satisfied that the dwelling is capable of improvement to the appropriate standard at a reasonable cost, must exercise their powers of compulsion. However, what constitutes a reasonable cost is not easy to determine and in any particular case may have to be decided by the courts.

Local authorities may make loans to owners to help them finance their part of the improvement work and in the case of compulsory improvement they must be prepared to make a loan provided they can be satisfied it will be repaid. The availability of private finance for works of improvement is also important. In 1979 whilst M£100 was paid out in improvement grants, M£1,226 was paid out in rehabilitation loans from the private sector by building societies, banks and other institutions. M£938 of this amount came from building societies alone. Whilst only a proportion of this money went towards work on the oldest stock, the availability of private funds for rehabilitation of houses is an important support to the improvement grant system.

Since 1949 successive Governments have by legislative and other measures tried to encourage private landlords and local authorities to improve the stock of older dwellings. The encouragement has largely taken the form of financial incentives but these have not given the expected results. With each successive legislative measure the Government has relaxed the conditions which had previously been thought should be attached to the payment of grants from public funds. For example, conditions have been modified and made less onerous in respect of the cost ceilings, the permitted rent of the improved dwellings, the future tenure and the expected further life of the improved dwellings, all with the intention of making the improvement of the older dwellings an attractive proposition, and an alternative to large-scale clearance and redevelopment.

However, the number of improvement grants paid in England and Wales have on the whole been disappointing and have dropped from a peak of 260,364 in 1973 to 64,709 in 1979. Cuts in public expenditure were one cause of the drop between 1973 and 1979. For example, the National Housing Investment programme has been halved in two years from M£2,885 in 1979/80 to M£1,343 for 1981/82 (at 1980 prices). But the cuts in public expenditure were not the only cause of the unsatisfactory progress in dealing with substandard houses. Many owners of houses in the worst physical state have been disinclined to improve them. The social survey carried out in conjunction with the 1976 English House Condition Survey showed that 50 per cent of houses in need of rehabilitation were occupied by one or two person households, and 42 per cent of these householders were aged 60 or over. 47 per cent were either retired or unemployed or in part-time work. Of those in full-time work, 46 per cent had incomes of less than

£4,000 per year (at 1980 prices). 44 per cent of the households had lived in their present accommodation for seventeen years or more.

There was a similar but not so marked trend with owner-occupiers. The 1976 English House Condition Survey found that almost one-third of occupiers of dwellings in need of rehabilitation were retired and between a tenth and one-fifth were unemployed or working part-time. A little over half were in full-time work, but their median income was about 20 per cent lower than that of the working population as a whole. At the time of the survey it was estimated that even with grant aid more than 40 per cent would still have to find a sum equivalent to their annual income to bring their homes up to the full 'ten point standard' of the Housing Act 1974. From these results it becomes clear that many owner-occupiers of substandard dwellings are not in a position to invest in rehabilitation, even with the aid of grants, or are not willing to because of their age or low income. Furthermore, the 1976 social survey found that 54 per cent of the occupiers of all dwellings in need of rehabilitation were satisfied with the state of repair of their houses and 27 per cent of households living in dwellings needing essential repairs thought that no repairs were necessary. It is likely that some of the latter were owner-occupiers who had closed their eyes to defects they could not afford to remedy. As the prices of the older houses have risen and mortgage interest rates have increased many owner-occupiers of these houses have had financial liabilities which have prevented them from being able to pay for major repairs and improvements. In this respect it has to be remembered that if owner-occupied houses fall into such a state of disrepair that they have to be included in slum clearance programmes the local authority has to pay the market value of the houses as though they were not unfit and not just site value. The question arises what to do about substandard houses which the present owners for several reasons are unable or unwilling to repair and improve.

The Dennington Committee in 1965 came to the conclusion that in the interests of the community effective compulsion to repair and improve the better older houses was needed. At the time the Government did not entirely agree but in the Housing Act 1974 local authorities were given a measure of compulsion. However, this does not apply to owner-occupiers.

Since 1949 the Government has adopted a mainly voluntary policy for the rehabilitation of the older housing stock but it has not significantly arrested the rate of deterioration. The 1976 English Housing Condition Survey has shown that poor quality housing is generally occupied either by households who cannot afford rehabilitation without considerable assistance or by certain other groups such as the elderly, who wish to avoid the disturbance associated with extensive works. Also the state of the local housing market may deter investment in rehabilitation either because it is not economic or because owner-occupier households can improve their housing circumstances by moving to a 'better' area rather than improving their present accommodation. With the rapidly increasing number of houses falling into serious disrepair local authorities need to comprehensively examine the housing needs of their areas and decide what steps they need to take in any section of it, for example redevelopment taking into account the demand for owner-occupation, or rehabilitation. In many cases it will call for a mixture of rehabilitation and redevelopment but with the latter the mistakes of the past which left large areas devastated for long periods need to be borne in mind.

In some areas the compulsory improvement of the majority of the housing stock might be necessary in the interests of the community. In such areas a solution would be to give the local authorities the power not only to improve the environment but also to undertake the repair of the external fabric of all the dwellings, but leaving the owners to carry out the internal improvements at a later date according to circumstances, for example on the death of an elderly tenant.

The terms 'general improvement area', 'housing action area' and 'slum clearance area' could be replaced by a single term, 'renovation area'.

The information obtained from the sample House Condition Surveys was helpful to the Government but of little real use to local authorities, who need detailed information about housing conditions in the various sections of their areas, and this can only be obtained by local surveys. In 1948 the Lancaster City Council carried out a comprehensive housing survey which involved the inspection of every house in the city. This is probably the most exhaustive housing survey ever carried out in Britain. The information obtained from the survey was recorded on separate cards for each house and placed in a visible filing system. Different coloured signals clipped on the edge of each card indicated at a glance the most important information about the particular house, for example its state of repair, whether it had a bath and hot-water system, and if it was in multiple occupation. Other information recorded on the cards included such matters as the date and type of construction and the number and sizes of the rooms. Today, when all local authorities have computers, it would not be difficult for them to build up comprehensive records of housing conditions in their areas and thus avoid some of the mistakes made in the past.

A church converted into a house in the 1950s.

Old type of cooking range to be found in millions of working-class houses in Britain in the 1950s.

Between 1949 and 1964 housing improvement was sporadic, i.e. one house here and one there.

The scullery of an 80-year-old house before improvement in the 1950s.

The new scullery with doors leading to new bathroom and inside W.C., provided with the aid of an improvement grant. (1950s)

The solid fuel grate which replaced the old type of cooking range. (Sporadic improvement in the 1950s)

These 8 houses were found to be occupied by 27 families comprising 62 adults and 28 children. The attic rooms had only skylights for light and ventilation. (Late 1950s)

The 8 houses after improvement. Seven houses have each been converted into 2 self-contained maisonnettes with 2 bedrooms. The eighth house has been converted into 3 bedroom maisonnettes. Dormer windows replace the skylights.

163

Row of old cottages apparently beyond repair. Parts of the main walls are bulged and cracked. The rear wall is built into the rock, making the cottages damp.

Housing action area – closer view of the houses after improvement. (1980)

The same row of cottages after repair and improvement.

Rear of council houses built in the early 1930s, before reconditioning in 1972.

The rear of the same council houses after reconditioning.

A once fine house in a well planned and spacious area left to decay and come into multiple occupation without any adaptations. (1960)

The same fine house after renovation by a housing association. (1980)

300 council flats built in 1936 in an inner-city area abandoned and awaiting demolition in 1979.

The same flats transformed by a private developer into modern, low cost, attractive apartments for sale to first time buyers at prices of between £12,950 and £16,950.

167

30 council maisonnettes in a state of gross disrepair and derelict. (1978)

Tall, narrow houses before and after renovation. (1980)

The same maisonnettes after conversion by a private developer into 30 terraced houses for sale.

A housing action area – houses after and in the process of improvement. (1980)

Larger type of house before, in the process of, and after improvement. (1980)

Housing action area – back passage between houses before improvement.

Housing action area – back passage between houses after improvement. (1980)

Detailed information of every house in Lancaster recorded on cards in a visible filing system. (1948)

Chapter 10

SLUM HOMES

Although the term 'slum' is widely used, for example in official publications and by the media, it does not appear in the United Kingdom law on housing. The use of the term usually conjures in the mind a picture of poverty, squalor and bad housing, but poverty and squalor are not necessary characteristics of many of the areas dealt with by slum-clearance procedure at the present time. The use of the term to describe areas of substandard housing derives from the conditions which existed in parts of most of Britain's industrial towns during the 19th century. Slums then were undoubtedly filthy, squalid places which constituted a serious danger to the health of all the inhabitants of the town and not only to those who lived in them. Today slums are houses which are judged by local authorities to be so far defective in respect of certain matters specified in law that, in that condition, they are not reasonably suitable for human occupation. They do not, therefore, have to be dirty, squalid places. Many of them are clean, well furnished homes; a proportion are owned by the occupiers.

The first legislative steps to deal with insanitary dwellings were taken at the beginning of the second half of the 19th century. An Act of Parliament of 1866 (Torrens Act) proceeded on the principle that the responsibility for maintaining houses in proper condition fell on the owners and that houses unfit for human habitation ought not to be used as dwellings but should be closed and demolished and a new house built on the site.

Acts of 1875 and 1879 (Cross's Acts) were based on a different principle, which was that of dealing with whole areas of houses which were so structurally defective and so ill-placed with reference to each other as to require their demolition and reconstruction.

As the result of the work of a Royal Commission appointed in 1884, the Housing of the Working Classes Act 1890 became law. This Act had three purposes: the clearance of unhealthy areas, the closing and if need be the demolition of separate unhealthy dwellings, and the provision by local authorities of new dwellings for the working-classes.

The Housing of the Working Classes Act 1890 remained the principal law for dealing with unsatisfactory working-class housing until after the end of the First World War.

The association between health and the environment has been known since the early days of medicine and in the 19th century its importance was repeatedly stressed in the writings of health pioneers. However, no criteria for assessing unfitness with respect to housing were laid down in the 1890 Act but reliance was placed on the judgement of medical officers of health. The more accurate statistical investigations of the past forty years or so have confirmed the opinion of the early public health workers that there is an association between health and the environment but there are so many other contributory factors, such as occupation, poverty and mental capacity, that medical science cannot give any accurate assessment of the influence of housing on health.

The first attempt to prescribe a fitness standard for housing was made in 1919 by the then Ministry of Health in a "Manual of Unfit Housing", which was circulated for the guidance of members and officials of local authorities. This standard did not have the force of law but was regarded only as a provisional guide. It stated that a fit house should be:-

(1) free from serious dampness;
(2) satisfactorily lighted and ventilated;
(3) properly drained and provided with adequate sanitary convenience, and with a sink and suitable arrangements for disposing of slop water;
(4) in good general repair, and should have:
(5) a satisfactory water supply;
(6) adequate washing accommodation;
(7) adequate facilities for preparing and cooking food; and
(8) a well-ventilated store for food.

These eight matters remain today, with slight modifications, the basis for judging the fitness of houses for human habitation.

Amendments to the law of housing were made from time to time until 1925 when it was consolidated in the Housing Act of that year.

The Housing Act 1930 amended the Housing Act 1925 and among the amendments was the inclusion of criteria for judging the fitness of houses for human occupation. The result was that for the first time there was a statutory basis for claiming that a dwelling was unfit for human habitation. In determining unfitness regard had to be had to the extent that a house, by reason of disrepair or sanitary defects, fell short of local bye-laws for new houses or of the general standard of housing accommodation for the working-classes in the district. The expression 'sanitary defects' was defined as including: lack of air space or ventilation, darkness, dampness, absence of readily accessible water supply or sanitary accommodation or of other conveniences, and inadequate paving or drainage of courts, yards or passages.

The interpretation of what constituted unfitness varied throughout the country and there was uncertainty as to what was meant by the "general standard of housing accommodation for the working-classes in the district". There was pressure for a more objective standard which could be uniformly applied irrespective of housing conditions in the area. In 1936 the law with respect to the repair and clearance of unfit houses was again consolidated to take account of alterations made since 1930.

In 1944 the question of what should constitute unfitness was once again examined by a sub-committee of the then Central Housing Advisory Committee. The recommendations of this sub-committee were included in the Repairs and Rents Act 1954 and in the consolidating Housing Act of 1957. The new criteria closely followed those contained in the Housing Manual of 1919 and dropped the requirement for regard to be had to the general standard of housing accommodation for the working-classes in the district. These criteria proved in practice to be no more certain and no less ambiguous than the previous ones and again there was pressure for more objective criteria which could be applied uniformly throughout the country.

In 1965 another sub-committee of the Central Housing Advisory Committee (the Dennington Committee) was appointed "to consider the practicability of specifying objective criteria for the purposes of slum clearance, rectification of disrepair and other housing powers relating to minimum tolerable standards of housing accommodation; and to make recommendations".

The committee quickly came to the conclusion that it was possible for standards to be expressed more objectively than they were at the time, but that a substantial measure of personal judgement would always be required in deciding what weight should be given to the defects of various kinds. Although some items in the fitness standard could be expressed in more objective terms, e.g. the equipment required for the storage and cooking of food, it was much more difficult to specify the degree of dampness which would justify condemning a house, especially where a combination of defects had to be taken into account.

The problem was first examined by deciding what should be the standard for a satisfactory house which the committee believed ought to be the minimum acceptable. Their standard for a satisfactory house went far beyond the public health concepts on which legislation in the past had been based and leaned towards a socially acceptable standard which took into account the environment in which the house stood. However, the committee realised that because there were so many houses which were below their standard for a satisfactory house there was a need for intermediate standards, and recommended accordingly.

The point at which a house becomes not worth repairing and needs to be replaced is not easy to decide because circumstances differ in different areas of the country. The sub-committee came to the conclusion that it would be unrealistic to substantially alter the grounds on which the decision was taken whether or not a house should be demolished, but recommended the addition of certain matters to be taken into consideration. One of these was the internal arrangements of the dwelling. The Government accepted the recommendation with respect to this matter and in 1969 the law was changed so as to include it in the criteria for deciding unfitness.

Currently the matters to be taken into account when deciding on the fitness of a dwelling for human habitation are contained in Section 4 of the Housing Act 1957, with the amendments made in the Housing Act 1969. They are: repair, stability, freedom from damp, internal arrangement, natural lighting, ventilation, water supply, drainage and sanitary conveniences, facilities for the preparation and cooking of food, and for the disposal of waste water. A house can be judged to be unfit either because of one serious defect or because of an accumulation of defects, no one of which is sufficiently serious to justify condemning the house on that ground alone.

With the hope of obtaining a more uniform interpretation of what constituted unfitness, the Dennington Committee included in its published report explanatory notes for those matters which were thought to need amplification. A condensed version of these notes is given below.

(a) *Repair* – To be satisfactory; any part of the structure must function in the manner in which it was intended. Any disrepair that may exist in the house and its curtilage should not be a threat to the health of, or cause any serious inconvenience to, the occupants. A multiplicity of items may well cause serious inconvenience.

(b) *Stability* – Evidence of instability is only significant if it indicates the probability of further movement which would constitute a threat to the occupants.

(c) *Dampness* – Any dampness should not be so extensive or so pervasive as to be a threat to the health of the occupants.

(d) *Natural lighting* – There should be sufficient natural lighting in all rooms intended for sleeping, sitting and the consumption of meals, and for domestic work to be done without the use of artificial light under good weather conditions.

(e) *Ventilation* – There should be adequate ventilation, to the external air, of all habitable rooms and working kitchens.

(f) *Water supply* – There must be an adequate and wholesome water supply within the house.

(g) *Drainage and sanitary conveniences* – There should be a readily accessible water-closet for the exclusive use of the occupants of the dwelling in a properly lighted and ventilated compartment. The water-closet and bath or shower (if any) should be connected to an efficient disposal system, i.e. a public sewerage system, septic tank or cesspool capable of dealing with the effluent. There should be adequate means for the disposal of water from roof surfaces and yard pavings.

(h) *Facilities for preparation and cooking of food and for the disposal of waste water* – There should be a sink with an impervious surface, located beneath the piped water supply and connected to a suitable disposal system. There should be either a suitable fixed solid fuel or oilfired cooking appliance or provision for the installation of a gas or electric cooker.

(i) *Freedom from internal bad arrangement* – Internal bad arrangement is any feature which prohibits the safe or unhampered passage of the occupants in the dwelling, e.g. narrow, steep or winding staircases, absence of handrails, inadequate landings outside bedrooms, ill-defined changes in floor levels, a bedroom entered only through another bedroom, and a W.C. opening directly into a living-room or a kitchen.

The publication of these explanatory notes was a help towards achieving greater uniformity in the interpretation of housing unfitness but it is not possible to abolish the large element of personal judgement involved, especially in the process of totting up the effect of a number of defects which singly do not constitute unfitness. An owner has the right to challenge a local authority's opinion regarding the unfitness of a house.

Scotland has its own law of housing and therefore its own criteria, which relate to a minimum tolerable standard, not to unfitness, and a points system is used for the totting up process.

The procedure which local authorities must follow in dealing with areas of unfit housing is complex and can take about two years, or even longer, to complete. Under Part III of the Housing Act 1957, if a local authority is satisfied – this is usually by receiving a report from its officers – that the houses in an area are unfit for human habitation and that the most satisfactory method of dealing with the conditions in the area is the demolition of all the buildings in the area, they have a duty to declare the area a 'clearance area' and to define it on a map in such a manner as to exclude from the clearance area any building which is not unfit for human habitation. At the same time the local authority must satisfy themselves that suitable accommodation will be available for persons to be displaced, in advance of demolition, and that the resources of the authority are sufficient to carry out the programme.

After a local authority has declared any area to be a clearance area, it must proceed to secure the clearance of the buildings either by making a clearance order, in which case the owners have to demolish the buildings at their own expense but retain the ownership of the land, or by purchasing the land in the clearance area, if necessary compulsorily, and then securing the demolition of the buildings. Usually local authorities choose the second method and make a compulsory purchase order not only for the land within the clearance area but also for any land surrounded by or adjoining the clearance area which is necessary for securing a cleared area of convenient shape and dimensions for the satisfactory development or use of the cleared site.

A compulsory purchase order has to be in a prescribed form and has to describe, by reference to a map, the land to which it applies. On the map the properties have to be shown coloured differently according to whether they are (a) unfit, which are usually coloured pink on the map, or (b) fit, but included in the compulsory purchase order because they are necessary for a satisfactory development of the area, in which case they are usually coloured grey on the map. The main purpose of this distinction is because the compensation payable is calculated on a different basis.

From the start of slum clearance legislation, the basic financial principle has been that if a house has to be demolished because it is unfit it has no value as a house because it ought not to be let in that condition and therefore no compensation is payable if the land remains in the owner's hands; if the land and buildings on it are acquired by the local authority compensation is at site value only. In calculating the amount of compensation no allowance is made for the fact that the acquisition is compulsory and perhaps against the owner's wishes. Also, if the cleared site is more valuable than the site with the house on it, the owner will not receive this extra value since it is argued that he should not profit from the demolition of the building by the local authority.

From time to time the application of the site-value only principle has been varied to mitigate its severity and to take account of other than strictly economic factors. For example, in 1955, when slum clearance was recommended after its wartime halt, an owner-occupier's supplement was introduced for people who had purchased their homes between 1939 and 1955. This raised the compensation payable for an unfit house to the market value of a fit house. The reason for this was that in the conditions prevailing at the end of the war some people had bought substandard houses for the sake of having a home and without the knowledge and expectation that they may be included in slum-clearance schemes in the near future.

On its introduction the owner-occupier's supplement was regarded as a temporary measure to meet special circumstances but it has now become a permanent factor in the compensation paid to owner-occupiers of unfit houses. Changes in the law now allow for extra compensation to be paid for unfit houses which have been well-maintained and for home loss and for disturbance. Home loss payments, introduced in the Land Compensation Act 1973, are designed to compensate for the upheaval of a forced move from one's home, so far as money can do so. They are paid subject to a minimum residence of five years, and the amount is related to the rateable value of the house. Disturbance payments are related to removal expenses and actual losses sustained, e.g. refixing a cooker or television aerial. Compensation entitlements at the present time are:-

Owner-occupier
1. *Fit house*
   Market value + costs and fees + home loss payment (if appropriate).

2. *Unfit house in successive owner-occupation for more than two years*
   Market value + costs and fees + home loss payment (if appropriate).

3. *Unfit house in successive owner-occupation for less than two years*
   Site value + costs and fees + well-maintained grant (if appropriate) + disturbance payment.

Owner
1. *Fit house*
   Market value as an investment property + costs and fees.

2. *Unfit house*
   Site value + costs and fees + well-maintained grant (if appropriate).

Tenant
1. *Fit house*
   Disturbance payment + home loss payment (if appropriate).

2. *Unfit house*
   Disturbance payment + home loss payment (if appropriate) + well-maintained grant (if appropriate).

In addition to claiming compensation for a house included in a slum-clearance scheme, an owner-occupier of a condemned house may apply to the courts for the discharge or the modification of his outstanding mortgage liability.

During the major part of the 1930s Britain suffered a severe economic depression, yet in 1933 an anti-slum campaign was launched by the Government with a five-year programme to clear 280,000 unfit houses out of an estimated total of 472,000 in England and Wales, i.e. an average of 56,000 per year. At the outbreak of war in 1939 there were still about 173,500 unfit dwellings in England and Wales, but by 1951 about 33,700 of these were no longer in use as dwellings, which left a balance of about 140,000. The number of dwellings which in the interval had deteriorated to such a degree as to become unfit was not known. However, in 1955 local authorities were asked to estimate the number of unfit dwellings in their areas and the returns submitted to the Government showed that there were 847,100 in England and Wales. This turned out not to be a true picture of the size of the problem because in estimating the numbers local authorities had applied different standards and the assessments had been influenced by the general housing conditions in each area. For example

some local authorities submitted only the numbers which they considered they would be able to deal with during the next few years, because in some towns there was still an acute housing shortage.

In 1944 Birmingham City Council acquired a large area, containing about 30,000 substandard houses, for redevelopment, but were unable to demolish them immediately because of the acute housing shortage and adopted a policy of deferring the demolition and of patching the houses up so as to provide tolerable living conditions for a limited period. The Government recognised the wisdom of this step. Now local authorities in general have the power to defer the demolition of unfit houses and may procure the improvement of those included in a housing action area, with the aid of government grants. Housing action areas are discussed in Chapter 9.

Because of the problems experienced in obtaining a reasonably accurate picture of the number of unfit houses in the country as a whole from local authority estimates, in 1967 the Government carried out the first of a series of national house condition surveys. These surveys were conducted on samples of dwellings drawn from the rating lists, with carefully controlled and consistent standards of assessments. The 1967 sample consisted of 6,000 dwellings in England and Wales and the same sample was used in the 1971 survey. The 1976 sample consisted of 9,000 dwellings, plus 430 properties which had been found to be unfit in the 1971 survey. From the 1967 survey it was estimated that in England and Wales there were about 1.8 million unfit dwellings (11 to 12 per cent of the total stock of permanent dwellings). From the 1971 survey it was estimated that the number of unfit dwellings had fallen to about 1.1 million (7 per cent of the housing stock) and from the 1976 survey the estimate was 0.8 million (5 per cent of the housing stock in England and Wales). Another 180,000 to 190,000 dwellings were below the minimum tolerable standard in Scotland.

The number of dwellings demolished in slum-clearance schemes varies from year to year but during the two peak years in the post-1945 period, 1972 and 1973, a total of 133,000 dwellings were cleared in England and Wales, and had this rate of about 60,000 per year been continued the 0.8 million houses which were unfit in 1976 could have been cleared in about fourteen years, that is by 1990-91. However, in Britain the length of childhood is considered to be sixteen years, which means that even at the peak rate of clearance achieved during 1972-73 many children would have had to spend the whole or most of their childhood in unfit dwellings. In the event, this rate of clearance was not maintained, for in 1976 only 48,208 dwellings were demolished in England and Wales and by 1980 the figure had fallen to 30,000, but the switch of resources from clearance and redevelopment to repair and improvement following the first house condition survey resulted in some unfit dwellings being repaired and improved and given an extended life. On the other hand, subsequent house condition surveys have shown that the number of houses needing repairs costing £2,350 or more at 1976 prices (£1,000 at 1971 prices) increased for example, from 636,000 (4% of the housing stock) in 1971 to 911,000 (5% of the housing stock) in 1976.

No programme of repair and improvement can completely prevent the deterioration of the housing stock to a degree where replacement becomes necessary in stages. The whole or most of the present housing stock of Britain will need to be replaced during the next two hundred years or less but at a clearance rate of 60,000 dwellings per year it will take three hundred years to replace the present stock of eighteen million houses, and at the 1980 rate of clearance of 30,000 it will take six hundred years.

For many years Britain has been consuming its housing capital at a faster rate than it is being replaced. It was to a great extent accumulated during the Victorian period by private investment which has not continued for several reasons, e.g. rent control and other restrictions which have contributed to a lack of proper maintenance of much of the housing stock. In addition, the long-term proposals of local authorities for slum clearance have in some areas hastened the decay of housing. Some local authorities, when preparing their longer-term slum-clearance programmes, have included in their proposals houses which although not unfit at the time were expected to become unfit in ten or fifteen years' time. This has resulted in areas of housing becoming blighted, i.e. no repairs to the houses being carried out and a reduced level of services, for example no renewal of sewers, water mains, etc., and finally confidence in the area has faded away and the houses have become unfit because of a lack of interest in their preservation.

From the late 1950s to the beginning of the 1970s there was a drive by the Government to clear all the slums in Britain as soon as possible and various target dates were given for the completion of the task. However, slum clearance has turned out to be a never-ending task, a treadmill operation. In some towns in the drive to clear slums vast areas of land and buildings were devastated and left derelict, with buildings boarded-up for long periods (see Chapter 2). Local opposition to such wholesale clearance and devastation has grown, but the nation is faced with the complex problem of what to do about its large stock of ageing and fast-decaying houses, some of which are owner-occupied, at a time when for several years public investment in housing, in real terms, has been cut to help to try to reduce the rate of inflation.

The measures at present in use to solve the problem are clearly inadequate. Post-1945 Governments, both Conservative and Labour, seem to have failed to comprehend the size and complexity of the replacement problem, they have not used the information available to them for the preparation of plans for the replacement of the housing stock at a fast enough rate, and have not been sufficiently aware of the serious social consequences of these failures.

Since the late 19th century slum clearance and redevelopment have been seen as being almost exclusively local authority functions, with private house building taking place on green field sites. When the legal provisions for the compulsory clearance of unfit houses and redevelopment were first introduced over 90 per cent of dwellings were privately rented. In 1980 over 50 per cent are owner-occupied and the demand for owner-occupation is increasing. Private builders are continually pressing the Government to release more land for house building, but there is a limit, and it has probably been reached, when it would be unwise to use any more agricultural land for urban purposes (see Chapter 3). The alternative is to find ways of utilising private builders to redevelop the older housing areas in our towns and cities, but this would mean examining the cost of cleared sites in comparison with the relatively low cost of virgin land, and finding ways of encouraging private investment in the redevelopment of towns. This could considerably reduce the need for public borrowing for the purpose.

In a Government White Paper, "Better Homes, the Next Priorities", published in 1973, it was stated: "The Government believes that in the majority of cases it is no longer preferable to attempt to solve the problems arising from bad housing by schemes of widespread comprehensive redevelopment." It went on to say: "Large-scale redevelopment frequently diminishes rather than widens the choice available to people in terms of the style of houses, their form of tenure and their price." The White Paper encouraged the idea of gradual renewal instead of large-scale clearance. This allows for groups of the worst houses to be cleared and the sites redeveloped quickly, whilst other houses not in such a bad condition are repaired and given minor improvements pending clearance in the medium term, while sounder houses are repaired and improved to a higher standard and included in general improvement areas, which means that they will then have a probable further life of at least thirty years. The legal provisions for dealing with areas of substandard dwellings in this way are contained in the Housing Act 1974 (see Chapter 9) and in the prevailing circumstances this is better than wholesale clearance, but in the longer term the rate of replacement will need to be increased.

A slum-clearance drive of the late 1960s and early 1970s removed most of the houses which might rightly have been called slums. In 1967 there were 1,836,000 unfit dwellings in England and Wales, and by 1976 the number had fallen to 794,000; therefore, in spite of problems, slum clearance has proved effective in eradicating the worst houses. However, as the clearance programme progressed it proved less and less popular as the proportion of owner-occupied houses in the schemes increased and the standards of the properties involved rose. Also, local authorities had to pay market value for increasing numbers of unfit houses because they were owner-occupied.

The major housing problem in Britain in the 1980s is not that of slums, whatever that term might mean, but the fast rate of decay of the large stock of older houses. Between 1971 and 1976 the number of dwellings in England and Wales in need of repairs estimated to cost more than £4,400 at 1980 prices increased from 636,000 to 911,000. Large-scale slum clearance is not the solution to the present problem. A new concept and a new approach is needed. The Dennington Committee in its report "Our Older Homes, A Call for Action", began by setting a standard for a "satisfactory house". That was fifteen years ago and before the clearance drive of the late 1960s and 1970s. The same beginning would be appropriate for the present problem. What is needed is not an unfitness standard but a standard which reflects the social requirements of houses at the present time. Houses would then be judged either to be satisfactory in all respects or not satisfactory. The term 'slum' no longer accurately describes many houses judged subjectively to be unfit for human habitation.

The Dennington Committee attached great importance to the environment in which houses stand and suggested that a house could not be satisfactory if its environment was not satisfactory and that a standard for a satisfactory house should have regard for the social standards of the day. However, both housing and social conditions vary throughout the country and the decision what to do about unsatisfactory houses would, therefore, need to take into account not only the state of the house but also environmental, economic and local factors. In other words, there should be a return to the provision previously contained in the Housing Act 1936, which required local authorities to have regard to the general standard of housing conditions in the area. Such a provision would permit local authorities to deal with substandard houses in a way that was most appropriate for their peculiar local housing circumstances. They would have a discretion in what to do about the unsatisfactory houses in their area, for example pull them down, carry out temporary repairs and improvements, or bring them up to the standard for a satisfactory house taking into account the general state of housing in the area and the resources available. The introduction of a 'satisfactory' house standard would permit local authorities to take action to prevent houses prematurely falling into a state which would require their demolition.

Because of the increase in owner-occupation during the post-1945 period, it would need to be borne in mind for schemes of clearance that not all households who have to be rehoused desire a public sector tenancy. Many of them, perhaps 20–50 per cent of them, will have been owner-occupiers and will want to purchase another property, perhaps in the same area. Improvement for sale schemes and redevelopment by private builders would help in this respect.

Housing conditions in the inner areas of many towns and cities would need special consideration because of the higher land values and the need to revitalise them. In some cases this might necessitate the clearance of housing which is not grossly substandard and therefore outside the present slum-clearance schemes. On the other hand, the mistakes made in the past when tall blocks of municipal flats were built in these areas and became slums within a few years must be remembered (see Chapter 6).

The adoption of a 'satisfactory' house standard in lieu of an 'unfitness' standard would increase the number of houses regarded as being substandard; for example in England and Wales perhaps from three-quarters of a million to one-and-a-half to two million. To deal with these houses within a reasonable time would increase the demands both for building materials and manpower. However, at the present time Britain has about three million unemployed people and under-used capital equipment. When the cost to the country of keeping such a large pool of labour idle, i.e. on average about £5,000 per person per year, is taken into account, it seems it would be logical to use some of it to alleviate the serious social problems related to bad housing. Some of the unemployed labour could be trained in a relatively short time, perhaps within two years, as general house repairers who would be capable of doing more than one type of work, e.g. bricklaying, plastering and tiling. The co-operation of the trade unions in such a scheme might be necessary but their outright opposition would not be in the interests of the unemployed and the vast number of people at present living in substandard houses.

Unfitness factor – gross disrepair
sufficient by itself to render house unfit. (1963)

Unfitness factors – persistent penetrating dampness
through both roof and walls, and disrepair.

Unfitness factors – no proper facilities for the preparation and cooking of food – and gross disrepair.

Unfitness factors – dampness from leaking roof and disrepair.

Unfitness factors – the height and closeness of adjoining buildings obstruct light and ventilation to the houses.

An unfit rural cottage.

Unfitness factors – houses lack an internal piped water supply and are in gross disrepair.

Unfitness factors – communal W.C.s which are situated in front of houses, and general disrepair.

Rear of unfit rural cottages.

Part of a clearance area in a large city. (1960s)

A street of four-roomed houses in a clearance area. (1980)

Rear of terrace of unfit houses on the fringe of a clearance area. (1960s)

19th century tenement dwellings, one set of dwellings at street level and two-storey dwellings above; included in clearance area late 1950s.

Unfit tenement blocks. (1952)

Former back-to-back houses, improved in the 1920s by making two houses into one, included in clearance area in the 1960s.

A small clearance area of the 1960s.

Slums of the 1930s cleared in the 1960s.

Rear of row of unfit houses. (1955)

Corrugated iron huts used as houses. (1952)

Tenements which were slums before the 1930s still occupied in 1956.

A small court of grossly unfit houses still occupied in the 1950s.

A one-roomed tenement dwelling (1954)

The bathroom in an unfit multiple-occupied house. (1954)

Unfit dwellings patched up by Birmingham City Council in 1945 to provide tolerable living conditions for a limited period.

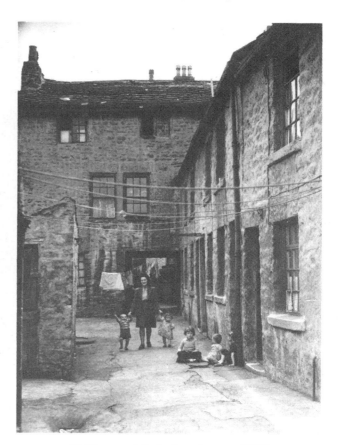

Children and their slum homes. (1955)

The 1980s border-line house – improve or demolish?

The impressionable years. (1958)

Chapter 11

MOBILE HOMES

Until 1939 only a very small proportion of the British people lived in movable dwellings and they were predominantly 'travellers', a heterogeneous group made up of true gypsies, Irish tinkers and others who wanted to be free from the monotony, restrictions and supervision that regular employment entailed. They preferred to be self-employed at work they liked doing, or at least which consumed no more of their time than necessity demanded. Most of them used horse-drawn vans and their camping sites were the roadside and back lanes of the country, which they used without payment.

Modern caravan living in Britain began during World War II in a very small way as people fled from the bombed cities and towns to the relative peace and safety of the rural areas. The demand for residential caravans increased at the end of the war as many demobilised soldiers, sailors and airmen returned to civilian employment in the industrial areas where there was a very acute housing shortage. Times were very difficult, most things were in short supply, and caravans were no exception. Some that were bought for residential occupation were grossly unsuitable for the purpose, yet they provided a shelter and privacy. So did the converted bus bodies, old tram-cars, pantechnicons, glider fuselages and makeshift structures such as adapted hen cabins, which became homes.

Sites on which to park the mobile homes or erect the makeshift structures were very difficult to obtain. Often sites of bombed buildings, commons, roadside verges, quarries and refuse tips were used haphazardly. So desperate was the plight of some of the caravanners that, although normally law-abiding people, they were prepared to resist all attempts to make them move. Conditions on the sites were generally poor and often bad. Many were ill-equipped and lacked such essentials as water supply and toilets. There were no national standards with which the sites had to be made to comply because the size and seriousness of the problem was not known and both central and local government believed caravan living was a passing phase which would be of short duration. For some years, however, the housing shortage seemed to increase and not decrease, and the demand for caravan sites near the cities and towns in need of labour increased, and the unauthorised use of land for the purpose became more common. It then became clear that caravan living was producing serious problems which could not be ignored. It reached a crisis in some areas when the local authorities gave notice to the landowners to clear their land of mobile homes, or take the legal consequences. The caravanners themselves refused to move, pleading that there was nowhere else they could reasonably be expected to go. Some were induced to move only when an alternative site was provided for them by the local authority. A few local authorities began to operate caravan sites themselves and were able to set an example by providing proper facilities, e.g. water supply, toilet blocks, etc. Generally speaking, however, by the end of the first decade after the end of the war no real progress had been made towards improving mobile homes and the sites they occupied. In many parts of the country caravan living was giving rise to very serious problems which could not be solved by harassing the caravanners.

In November 1958 the Minister of Housing and Local Government invited Sir Arton Wilson to conduct an investigation into the nature and extent of the problem arising in connection with caravans used as residential accommodation. The investigation was confined to people who were living in caravans and had no other home. It did not include gypsies and 'travellers', nor did it include converted buses, trams, or horse-drawn vans, etc., but was confined to trailer caravans. It was completed in June 1959. Residential caravanning in Scotland was very limited in scale and was not a problem.

The approximate number of caravans in use as homes in England and Wales in 1959 was 60,000. Most of them had been designed for holiday use only, but a minority had been designed for static use as all-the-year-round homes. They varied in their external dimensions from nine feet to forty-four feet in length and from six feet to ten feet in width. About 27,000 of them were twenty-two feet long and six and a half feet wide, giving an area of about 165 square feet. Approximately another 27,000 were between sixteen feet and twenty feet long with an area of between 100 and 160 square feet. About 2,000 caravans had an area of about 100 square feet or less, but these were mainly occupied by single persons. Something like 4,000 caravans had an area of between 165 and 350 square feet.

Regulations prohibit the towing of a caravan larger than twenty-two feet by seven and a half feet behind a motor vehicle on a public highway. In spite of this restriction, there was a tendency for manufacturers to make more of the larger type of caravan which could only be moved on a transporter.

By 1959 residential caravans were being made in conformity with certain minimum standards relating to materials and construction which the reputable manufacturers had voluntarily agreed to adopt. The framework of the body was usually made from good quality timber and this supported the outer aluminium cladding. The interior walls were of plywood or hardboard with insulating material packed between the inner and outer layers. Provision for ventilation was made by openable roof lights and windows, and some caravans had fixed ventilators as well. The kitchen section contained a bottled gas cooker and a small sink with a tap fed by a hand-operated pump from a built-in cold water tank. In some caravans a hot tap was provided over the sink, the water being heated by the flue of a solid fuel stove. Some of the larger caravans had a separate washbasin and a shower in a small compartment. Toilet accommodation up to 1959 consisted of pail-closets in the van, or in a small structure adjacent to it. On some sites, however, blocks of flush toilets existed. Artificial lighting in about half of the residential caravans in the country was provided by bottled gas and in the other half an electricity supply was available. The sleeping arrangements consisted of berths usually designed to be slid or folded away in the daytime. New caravans were usually sold furnished with wardrobes, cupboards, seating arrangements, floor coverings and curtains, that is, ready for immediate occupation. They were capable of providing tolerable, if limited, accommodation.

Since 1959 there have been considerable improvements in the design and construction of mobile homes, as they are now called. Those manufactured in the last twenty or more years are very different from the canvass-type horse-drawn gypsy van of pre-war days and those made in the immediate post-war years. Some of the larger ones contain a living room, diner-kitchen, bathroom, double-bedroom and an entrance hall, and have an internal area of 350 square feet. The more expensive ones can almost be described as luxurious and are capable, within limits, of providing accommodation up to a middle-class standard. They are well furnished and equipped with central heating and a refrigerator, and a television can be installed without difficulty. Reputable manufacturers claim that they have designed for a lifetime of twenty-five to thirty years, compared with that of conventionally built houses of sixty years. A few mobile home manufacturers have produced prototype models which they claim compare favourably with conventional local authority houses.

However, no matter how well a caravan is designed, constructed and equipped, it will make a very poor home on a bad site. In 1959 the 60,000 residential caravans in use in England and Wales were on 13,000 sites, about 3,000 of which were multiple sites containing altogether 48,000 caravans. The remaining 12,000 caravans were on about 10,000 individual sites. The sites were not evenly distributed throughout the country. The south had many more than the north, but the Midlands also had its fair share. The sites were commonly in two distinctive types of area. One was the sort of area favoured for retirement, for example the south coast of Devon and the Fylde in Lancashire. The other was the semi-rural or rural fringe of an urban area which was experiencing a significant industrial expansion, but without a corresponding increase in the number of houses. Many of the sites had grown without design or planning from a mere casual adjunct to some other business, to become the main business carried on at the site. Some farmers and smallholders found that the use of the land for residential caravans was more profitable than growing crops. Often they were encouraged and helped to expand this side of the business by a caravan dealer with an eye on the market for the sale of new caravans. If planning consent had been obtained for caravan use, then the value of the land was considerably increased. On most sites the layout of the caravans was determined entirely by the convenience and economy in providing the basic services and there was often a total site density of about thirty caravans or more to the acre, which meant that the caravans were ten to fifteen feet apart. However, there were exceptions where the sites had been planned and laid out with care. On these sites there were flower-beds, lawns and shrubs, etc., and the communal and administrative buildings had a pleasant appearance. Of the 3,000 sites in multiple use in 1959, only about 100 could be regarded as being excellent. At the other end of the quality scale, some of the smaller sites consisted of a yard or vacant building plot on which a small number of caravans had been crammed together in surroundings little better than a refuse tip.

The quality of the site is related to the services provided, that is, water supply, sanitation and the provision for refuse disposal. In 1959 about 10,000 of the 60,000 residential caravans were on sites where a piped supply of water was available direct to the van. On all other sites water had to be carried from standpipes and there was no prescribed maximum distance for the positioning of these from the caravans. Communal toilet blocks which contained baths and clothes-washing facilities were available on sites containing a total of about 12,000 caravans. Only on a few sites were there main drainage connections to each caravan, so most of the caravanners had to use W.C.s in communal blocks, often some distance away, or a pail-closet inside their vans. About 20,000 caravan households, or one-third of the total, had only the use of pail-closets. In most of these cases a disposal point for emptying the pail-closets into a drain was available on the site, but on a minority of sites the caravanners had to empty them into a cesspit which had to be emptied from time to time.

Most of the local authorities concerned provided a refuse collection service, either collecting from individual caravans or from central dustbin points.

Shopping facilities were provided on most of the larger sites, even if it was only a converted caravan, but on some there were properly constructed shops, a club bar and recreation room.

The 60,000 caravans in use as homes in England and Wales in 1959 were occupied by 150,000 people or about one in 300 of the total population of the country. No reliable information was available at the time about the number of gypsies and 'travellers' who permanently lived in caravans or similar structures. These 150,000 people were indistinguishable from the rest of the population, apart from the fact that they lived in caravans instead of in houses or flats. They were clearly not predominantly shiftless people, and their incomes and occupations were fairly representative of the community at large, except that perhaps there were very few of the richest or poorest classes. About two-thirds, or 40,000 of the 60,000 households who were living in caravans, consisted of youngish married couples, half of whom had children. The young couples in their twenties with just one baby were very common in the group, and about 15,000 of these 40,000 households had started their married life in a caravan home. Something like 20,000 out of the total caravan population were children under five and another 10,000 were children of school age. Nearly 7,000 of the caravan households consisted of retired couples or elderly single people. Only between 5 and 10 per cent of the households were living in caravans because they entirely preferred that way of life to living in a house or flat. The majority of the households regarded caravan living as a short-term measure to meet their immediate needs.

Fairly soon after the publication of Sir Arton Wilson's report in 1959 the Caravan Sites and Control of Development Act 1960 became law. This Act confers on local authorities powers for controlling caravan sites by means of a licensing system and by Planning Law. The Government's aim was to ensure that all caravan sites were properly equipped and run and that sites were not allowed in the wrong places. However, because site owners might be faced with considerable expense in order to meet the new requirements, the Government envisaged that planning consent would be given on a long-term or permanent basis unless there was some definite reason against this, and that where sites had to be run down or the number of caravans reduced, this would be done in such a way as to reduce hardship.

Section 29 of the Caravan Sites and Control of Development Act 1960 defines what is meant by the term 'caravan'. In brief it is any structure designed or adapted for human habitation which is capable of being moved from one place to another (whether by being towed or being transported on a motor vehicle or trailer) and any motor vehicles so designed or adapted, but the definition does not include railway rolling stock and tents.

To take account of changes in the design, construction and increase in size of caravans which had taken place since 1960, for example the production of twin-unit mobile homes, the definition of 'caravan' was amended by the Caravan Sites Act 1968 so as to include: "a structure designed or adapted, which is composed of not more than two sections separately constructed and designed to be assembled on a site by means of bolts, clamps or other devices and is, when assembled, physically capable of being moved by road from one place to another (whether by being towed, or being transported on a motor vehicle or trailer)". However, a structure designed or adapted for human habitation and which otherwise falls within the definition is excluded if it has a length exceeding sixty feet (18.288 metres) or a width of twenty feet (6.096 metres) or an overall height of living accommodation of ten feet (3.048 metres).

Local authorities were given power to attach conditions to the licences they issue, and to guide them as to what these conditions should be the Government published Model Standards, which most local authorities adopted. The model standards require such things as a hard standing for each caravan, a twenty feet space between caravans, and the gross density must not exceed twenty caravans to the acre. Each caravan standing must be provided with a piped water supply, or alternatively there has to be a water stand-pipe within sixty feet of the standing. For caravans which have a piped supply of water and a water-closet, the caravan standing must be provided with a connection to a foul drainage system, which should be connected to a public sewer or discharge into a properly constructed septic tank or cesspool.

For caravans which do not have their own water-closet, toilet blocks have to be provided with a sufficient number of water-closets for the caravans on the site. The minimum requirements are (a) for men one W.C. and one urinal per fifteen caravans, and (b) for women two W.C.s per fifteen caravans. In addition one shower or bath with hot and cold water must be provided for each sex per twenty caravans. One refuse bin must be provided for each caravan standing and arrangements have to be made for the bins to be emptied regularly.

In March 1965 the Government had a census made in England and Wales of gypsies and other travelling people who were living in caravans, tents and huts, and who made a living by trading and casual work. The census did not include gypsies living in houses, showmen or boat-dwellers and members of the settled caravan community. The gypsy population of England and Wales was found to be approximately 15,000 (3,400 families), scattered throughout the country. About 60 per cent of them had travelled from place to place during the previous year. The travelling had been done predominantly for the purpose of work or trade, and some involuntarily because of site problems. Two out of three families had children under the age of sixteen, and there was a total of 6,000 children. Gypsies and travellers have always regarded unfenced land, the roadside and the back lanes as their place of residence by prescriptive right. In March 1965 about 80 per cent of the gypsies in England and Wales were found camping on farm land, woodlands, commons, roadside verges, quarries or refuse tips. Two-thirds of the families were without access to a mains water supply, 84 per cent did not have access to water-closets. The majority had no sanitary facilities whatever. A common complaint lodged against gypsies is that they leave filth and litter behind when they move. However, this seems to apply more to tinkers and 'travellers' than to the true Romany.

The majority of gypsies and travellers are born into their way of life and have little opportunity to change it because they are always on the move. By and large they are treated with a large measure of contempt by the general public, but on the other hand some of these urban nomads treat the laws and conventions of the urban society with disdain.

The 10 per cent sample census of population made by the Government in 1966 showed that in April that year 63,160 caravans were in use as homes in Great Britain as a whole, and that in England and Wales alone there were 60,140 caravan homes. These were out of totals of 16,274,080 homes in Great Britain, and 14,684,590 in England and Wales. Thus the number of caravan homes in the country did not change very much during the period 1959-66 in spite of an increase in the total number of traditional dwellings during this period. Although the total number of caravan homes did not change the households probably did; as former caravan dwellers moved into conventional dwellings more newly-married couples and retired people, etc., took their places as caravanners.

In the early 1970s concern was expressed about the lack of legal rights of those who live on mobile home sites. In consequence the Mobile Homes Act 1975 became law. Its purpose was to provide a greater degree of security of tenure for mobile home owners by means of written contracts dealing with the terms of occupancy of a pitch. A duty was placed on site owners to offer to enter into a written agreement with each permanent resident. Such an agreement must contain full particulars of the terms and conditions under which the pitch is occupied. The amount of rent has to be specified and this can be reviewed only once per year. Generally the agreement must be for a period of five years, with an option for the resident to extend it for a further three years. There is also provision in the Act to ensure that when a mobile home is sold on the site the vendor receives a fair market price less a fixed percentage discount. The Act has not worked as well as was expected and for many reasons a large proportion of mobile home owners have not availed themselves of the protection it offers.

A Building Research Establishment survey carried out during 1975 found that in England and Wales there were about 67,000 mobile homes on about 9,000 sites. The survey did not include the caravans occupied by gypsies and other 'travellers'. Thus, although in 1975 there were more mobile homes than in 1959, there was a significant drop in the number of sites, which tended to be larger and owned by companies instead of individuals. There were regional differences, with the greatest concentration of mobile homes in the south-east, which had 44 per cent of the total, and only 2 per cent in the northern region of the country.

In 1975 the Government undertook a review of the problems faced by permanent residents in mobile homes. This review found that since 1959 there had been a marked change in the type of household occupying them. As previously stated, in 1959 the great majority were young or youngish married couples, about half of whom had children. In 1975 over half of all residents were over 40, more than a quarter were over 65, and only 28 per cent had children, and 27 per cent of the residents were single people.

The majority of the residents (83%) expressed satisfaction with their home and the site, even though there were marked differences in site conditions. The larger sites tended to be of better quality, some had well laid-out plots and open spaces, well-maintained roads, and social facilities such as a club house. Many of the sites were owned by companies who had considerable interests in mobile home sales. The review found that local authority sites tended to be less spacious and less well looked after than many of the private sites. What the residents liked most about mobile homes was their convenience, easy maintenance and cheapness. Some liked the independent and open air way of life.

20 per cent of mobile home residents move each year, as compared with less than 10 per cent of all households in the country as a whole. A significant proportion of the younger households regard mobile home living as a short-term measure, e.g. as a first home, until they get the chance of a house or flat. Most of the older households choose a mobile home after retirement because it is the kind of life which best meets their circumstances, for example reduced income and a wish to live near the sea or in the country. Very often they have given up a house or flat.

90 per cent of those who live in mobile homes own their home but do not own or lease the land on which it stands. Normally they station their home on the site and occupy a pitch under a contractural licence which is often no more than an oral agreement or permission which can be terminated by the site owner at short notice. In these circumstances (i.e. if there is no written contract) the mobile home owner has less statutory protection than almost any other type of occupier, in spite of the fact that his investment and home would be at stake in the event of a dispute with the site owner. Also, problems of lack of security can arise if the site has only temporary planning permission. It was to deal with these problems that residents of mobile homes were given certain rights under the provisions of the Mobile Homes Act 1975. Those residents who exercise their rights to enter into an agreement with the site owner have a degree of security of tenure of their site, a means by which to challenge increases in pitch fees, and resale rights which greatly enhance the prospects of selling their home at a fair market price. However, these rights are not easy to enforce and probably something like two-thirds of all mobile home owners have no written agreement with the site owner.

In practice very few mobile homes are moved from

one site to another because of high transport and installation costs, the risk of serious damage in transit, and the fact that few site owners will accept a second-hand unit on their sites since part of their business consists of selling new mobile homes.

Security of tenure without some control over charges is of little value but there are problems in devising a fair way of controlling charges. For example, a site operator must not only recover his operating costs, which vary from site to site, but also his capital costs, which vary considerably. During the last few years the cost of developing a caravan site has increased; in 1975-76 it was between £1,700 and £2,000 a pitch and taking about ten to fifteen years to recoup. Running a caravan site can be regarded as a high-risk business which in consequence calls for high returns. A possible solution would be for every agreement for a pitch to contain an implied condition that all charges will be reasonable, and also a provision for arbitration.

Even the best mobile home does not compare structurally with a conventionally built house of similar age, in spite of the fact that it might contain all modern conveniences. For example, although in some mobile homes central heating has been installed, the problems of condensation have not been overcome. The standard of insulation in the better quality models does not reach that required in the Building Regulations, while the standard provided in the cheaper models is often very low. Because the structural standards of a mobile home are lower than those for a conventional home, the mobile home can deteriorate very fast if subjected to harsh use and prolonged severe weather conditions, and the fire risk can be high.

The internal plan arrangements rarely provide the same amount of space as does even the small conventional house. Only the modern twin-units approach this standard.

These disadvantages are reflected in the ex-works prices for mobile homes. The retail price of new caravans designed for use as a home varied in 1970 from £600 to over £2,000. The average down-payment was £300, and the average weekly hire-purchase payment was about £7. In addition there was an average weekly site rent of £1.50 (inclusive of rates). The typical caravan dweller's basic outgoings were therefore about £8.50 per week if he had not payed cash for his home, and about £1.50 if he had. In comparison, in 1970 a post-war three-bedroomed council dwelling in the type of area used by mobile homes was let at a weekly rent of about £5, inclusive of rates. On the other hand, caravan dwellers who rented both van and pitch were paying rents of between £7 and £10 per week.

In the early 1970s when house prices rose much faster than those of mobile homes, retired people in particular saw the advantage of moving into a mobile home and making a substantial capital gain on the sale of their existing houses. Since 1973, however, the gap between the cost of a conventional home and a mobile home has narrowed.

In 1980 the quoted basic retail prices for residential caravans ranged from £4,000 to over £8,000, and for the twin-unit type of mobile home from £15,000 to £20,000. Nearly half of all mobile home residents in 1974-75 reported that they had been required to buy their units either from or through a site owner. There was a substantial difference in the price paid when purchasing under this constraint and when not; in some cases the price was doubled.

Since 1945 a brick and mortar house has been an appreciating asset, with in most cases a long life. The evidence from the Building Research Establishment survey already quoted suggests that a mobile home has a 60 per cent depreciation within seven to eight years, so its capital value is being consumed fairly rapidly. Some of this rapid depreciation is due to site owners encouraging obsolescence in the interests of new mobile home sales, and also to functional absolescence, that is by the changing styles and improved quality of the new models coming on to the market. However, reputable caravan manufacturers give estimated lives for their products of between twenty and thirty years.

Because the mobile home is not a sound long-term capital investment, the methods available for its purchase are more restricted and less favourable than those for a brick and mortar home. Except for the older second-hand models, loans are usually available by hire-purchase agreements. Only about two out of five residents buy their mobile home with the aid of a loan. A loan is rarely made for a period exceeding seven years, but four years is the average period. True interest rates in 1977 averaged about 19 per cent. The higher interest rates and the shorter repayment period usually mean that during the period of the hire-purchase agreement the cost of buying a mobile home is greater than that of buying a traditional home. A study carried out by the Department of the Environment in 1975-76 indicates that it is roughly the cost of buying a traditional home of twice the price. However, once the mobile home has been paid for, and until it has to be replaced, the annual outgoings are less than those for a traditional home because its capital value has been written off.

The median annual repayment associated with mobile homes bought with the aid of a loan during 1974-75 was £440, with 10 per cent of purchasers paying more than £760 and the same proportion paying less than £230. The average level of pitch rents in 1974-75 was £160 per year and the range was between £110 and £270 per year. In 1980 the average pitch rent is about £350 per year. In addition the rates paid for a pitch in 1974-75 ranged from £31 to £66 per year and in 1980 the range is between £70 and £150. In 1974-75 the ratio of annual repayments to the income of the head of household at the time of the purchase was about 18 per cent. If the pitch rental is included, the ratio of total outgoings to income in 1974-75 was about 25 per cent.

If a mobile home owner wishes to sell it he usually does not have to contend with the complex legal procedures connected with the sale of a conventional home and therefore will not have to meet large legal fees, but he is likely to have problems in selling at an acceptable price and in finding a suitable new site because the site owner might want to sell the mobile home on a commission basis and there may be no alternative because the site owner can refuse to accept the new owner as a tenant of the pitch.

Until 1974 the Department of the Environment had not encouraged local authorities to use mobile homes to meet normal housing needs but in that year it suggested that they might be used for meeting urgent housing problems. However, up to 1976 the use of mobile homes by local authorities was small, a total of about 200 units. Most local authorities have taken the view that they are a substandard form of housing and a poor investment.

Generally ownership of a mobile home does not offer the same long-term benefits as does that of a traditionally built one. It is not a secure investment and the occupier has insufficient security of tenure of his pitch. Nevertheless, a small minority of people have a preference for them. Some retired people, especially from industrial towns, value a communal way of life in a rural or semi-rural area. Usually such people will have bought their mobile home outright and will not be concerned about the depreciation of the capital they have invested in it but want a convenient and cheap home to run which will last them for the next twenty years or so. On the other hand, some newly-married couples see a mobile home, even a second-hand one, as a better alternative to living in rooms or with parents until such times as they can acquire a conventional home. Single people also find a mobile home more attractive than living in 'digs' or rooms. The demand for pitches on suitably located and well-run sites exceeds the supply. In 1974-75 it was estimated that there was an unmet demand for mobile home pitches of around 10 to 25 per cent of the total number of pitches then available. The demand varied from county to county but was strong along the south coast, the Cotswolds and South Wales. However, where it is possible, the purchase of a house is in most cases a better option than the purchase of a mobile home because over the longer term it costs less and represents a better investment.

Mobile homes can be produced quickly and at less cost than conventional ones, and the indications are that there will be a continuing demand for them in spite of their relatively short life. The industry is capable of making better types of prefabricated homes, which would comply with standards equivalent to those contained in the Building Regulations, but it is doubtful whether they could be produced at competitive prices. There is a need for a revision of the law so as to give long-term security of tenure of their pitches to mobile home owners, the right of resale on the pitch, and some legal control over charges, but taking into account the cost of developing the site, which can amount at present to about £4,000 per pitch, and the cost of operating the site.

House-boats

House-boats represent only a minute proportion of the country's housing stock – about 15,000 out of a total of 19.8 million dwellings in 1975. They are to be found on rivers, creeks and canals etc., in many parts of the country, but predominantly in the south of England.

Shortly after the end of the war in 1945 the Government sold off unwanted torpedo and air-sea-rescue, etc., craft at low prices. Sometimes this was for as little as £300. They were snatched up by people seeking homes, but the majority of buyers would have preferred a house or flat to a floating home. Most of these wartime boats no longer exist.

The present-day boat-dwellers are largely those with a preference for the special lifestyle which goes with living on a boat. They like living on water and enjoy the communal nature of many aspects of boat life, which leads to a degree of harmony, mutual help and tolerance which is rarely experienced in blocks of flats or streets of houses. People help each other with repairs and improvements on their boats and join together to meet threatened crises, for example in times of expected storms. This gives rise to a supportive community life at each set of moorings. Few boat families want to leave the water and accept the constraints of river life, for example lack of space, difficult and sometimes risky access to their homes, sometimes lack of electricity and a piped water supply.

A few boat-dwellers own their moorings and therefore have a reasonable degree of security. The main risks to this security are the planning proposals of local authorities.

Most moorings, however, are subject to agreements which may provide for a month's notice or for a longer period. Only the law of contract safeguards the rights of the boat-dweller under these agreements because there is no other special legal protection as there is in other forms of tenancy agreements. This leaves landlords free to harass and pressure house-boat occupants, for example by turning off electricity or water or making access to the house-boat difficult.

The number of moorings is growing smaller, and there is little hope of new ones becoming available since navigation authorities make the opening of new ones difficult. House-boat owners who lose their mooring may not only lose their home but may also be faced with the possibility of having to pay to have it towed away and broken up. One reason sometimes put forward to support the closing of a mooring is the bad appearance of the boats due to lack of maintenance and the untidy state of the land near the mooring. On the other hand, the absence of security is not conducive to the spending of large amounts of money on maintenance.

In a country, like Britain, surrounded by the sea there is bound to be a group of people who prefer to live on boats rather than in houses. However, it seems that the group in Britain is a very small one and therefore lacks political muscle. Love of the sea, however, is part of the nation's culture which should be preserved. Legislation is needed to give the small group who choose to live on boats a reasonable degree of security of tenure for the mooring of their homes and reasonable safeguards against harassment by their landlords.

The camping sites of the 'travellers' were often waste lands and refuse tips.

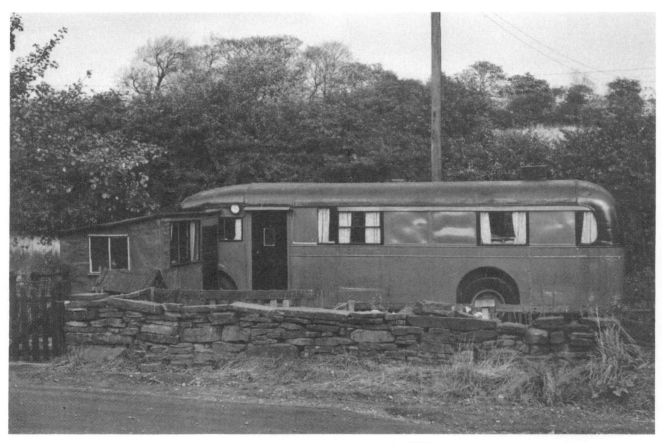

Converted bus used as a home in the 1950s.

Kitchen in caravan. (1955)

A luxury caravan home of the 1950s.

195

Caravan homes became larger and larger and contained a living-room, diner-kitchen, bathroom, and double-bedroom and were re-named "mobile homes".

The interior of a small mobile home of the late 1950s.

The quality of a site is related to the services provided, e.g. piped water supply, drainage and electricity to each home. (1950s)

In the early 1950s some sites were small casual adjuncts to other businesses, e.g. farming and market gardening or garages. Later, under the influence of caravan dealers they often became large unplanned sites.

A mobile home provided with all services and a strip of private garden. (1960)

Mobile homes in an orchard setting. (1960s)

198

An attempt to provide shopping facilities in the early 1950s.

As the sites improved so did the shopping and other facilities.

A twin-unit mobile home which resembles a modern house. (1970)

A row of twin-unit mobile homes on site. (1980)

House-boats moored side by side on the Thames. (1950s)

Former World War II naval craft converted into house-boat. (1950s)

Former sailing barge converted into spacious home.

Family life on a converted barge. (1949)

The lounge on a house-boat. (1960s)

A desire to live on or close to the sea is not uncommon in Britain but only a very small number of people make their homes on boats.

203

Chapter 12

HOMES OF ETHNIC MINORITIES

The first thing immigrants to Britain have to do is to find somewhere to live. If they are rich there are no problems in this respect because they can put up at an hotel until they find more permanent accommodation. If they are students, hostel accommodation may have been arranged, or in any event help is usually available. Most immigrants, however, are neither rich nor students, many are poor, and some are very poor. It is natural for them, therefore, to go where there are relatives or friends, or at least sympathetically disposed fellow-countrymen to help and advise them with the many problems that lie ahead. These problems will be greater if the immigrants do not speak English and in consequence the need to be near compatriats is greater.

White immigrants to Britain are not so obviously foreign as those with coloured skins; also white immigrants can more easily and quickly lose their 'foreignness', and become integrated and absorbed into the general population. For these reasons the housing accommodation they occupy is not easily distinguished from that occupied by the bulk of the population.

Dark-skinned people come to Britain from the West Indies, Africa and Asia, and from all walks of life and for many different reasons, e.g. economic and political. They do not regard themselves as being a homogeneous group but they have one thing in common – they are all newcomers. Having heard a great deal about British democracy and the Welfare State many come expecting to be received with open arms and to be treated immediately as equals, but find that in the minds of many inhabitants of the country they are identified with the lowest social group and that their colour is an important factor in this classification. Many coloured immigrants resent this treatment but perhaps overlook the fact that it is partially because the newcomers do not share the same customs and conventions of the indigenous population. Some want to belong to the larger community and give up some of their distinctive ways of living.

Immigration to Britain is not a post-1945 phenomenon. For example, many protestant immigrants entered the England of Henry VII. So great was the influx into London that the Privy Council compelled foreigners to live in colonies established in Canterbury, Norwich, Sandwich and many other towns. Towards the end of the 19th century there was a big wave of immigraton from eastern Europe. Many of these immigrants were Jews fleeing from oppression in Russia and Rumania, and from Poland primarily for economic reasons.

Before World War II small numbers of coloured people were a familiar sight in most of Britain's large seaports. They arrived without publicity and fuss, and except in the areas where they lived and worked were little noticed by the general public. Information about their numbers and manner of life was small because there were hardly any official statistics about them. These coloured immigrants included Arabs from Aden, Chinese, Indians, Somalis and West Africans. They had been coming to this country as seamen since the last century. Many had left the sea and had started small businesses with money they had saved and regarded Britain as their home. They married, had children and settled in small communities in certain districts of a town, usually in run-down houses near the docks. These communities consisted not only of seamen but also of lodging-housekeepers, cafe owners and shopkeepers. The Chinese established themselves predominantly as laundrymen, and Chinese laundries became common in working-class areas of our major seaports. The Indians worked mainly as pedlars and labourers and in the catering trade. These immigrants were mainly hardworking, thrifty people who kept themselves to themselves but observed the laws of their adopted land and brought up their children in the manner of it.

At the end of the Second World War men from Poland and other Eastern European countries who had fought on the side of the western allies settled in this country. They married or brought over their wives and families and other relatives. At first they settled in small communities in towns where they were able to find employment. Some had been trained in the professions in their own countries but accepted employment as ordinary factory workers as the price for certain freedoms – an important one of them being that of religion. Their first home in this country usually consisted of one or more rooms in the larger run-down Victorian houses, which they shared with compatriots. As they prospered they moved away to other areas of the town and integrated with the general population. Their places in the run-down areas were taken by small groups of migrants from other countries, e.g. Italy.

About the middle of the decade 1950-60 there was a considerable increase in the flow of immigrants from certain Commonwealth countries, mainly from the West Indies, Pakistan and India. An influx on such a scale was a new experience for Britain and she was not prepared for it. These immigrants came purposefully to seek a higher standard of living and to better themselves, either by becoming members of a more prosperous community or by saving capital and returning to their homeland relatively well off, and perhaps with a new skill. Some of the migrants from India and Pakistan were from rural areas and had been pressurised to emigrate by the unsettled political and economic conditions which followed the granting of independence to both India and Pakistan in 1947. At the end of 1958 there were somewhere between 70,00 and 100,000 Indians and Pakistanis in this country. Many of them had no previous experience of the ways of white people and were separated from the natural-born British people by barriers of language, religion and culture. The remaining groups of coloured immigrants totalled about 25,000. Many of the immigrants of this period were men aged between 20 and 45 who were either unmarried or had left their wives and children behind as a temporary measure.

During the early 1960s the number of immigrants to this country continued to increase. According to the 1961 census, 360,000 persons living in this country at that time had been born in three Commonwealth territories, i.e. the West Indies, India and Pakistan. However, this was a very small proportion of the total population of the United Kingdom. In the three years 1960-62 the total net immigration amounted to 388,000 people, about three-quarters of whom had come from the Commonwealth. Since 1967 the balance of migration has had a net outflow. In 1971 it was estimated that coloured Commonwealth immigrants and their families numbered 1.5 million, about 2½ per cent of the total population of Britain. Most of them were living in towns which had 50,000 or more inhabitants.

The first accommodation immigrants find is usually with a relative or fellow-national, often under crowded conditions. This gives them time to find their bearings and to seek the second-stage accommodation, which frequently is in a house in multiple occupation. The 1971 Census Household Composition Tables showed that 21 per cent of households whose chief economic supporter was born in the new Commonwealth lived in a shared dwelling, compared with 4 per cent of all households. The average number of persons per room in the total population was 0.59, the figure for new Commonwealth households was nearly double that: 0.93. Less than 1 per cent of all households did not have the exclusive use of both cooking stove and sink, but 8 per cent of new Commonwealth households were in this position. 18 per cent of all households shared the use of bath, hot water and inside W.C., whereas 33 per cent of West Indian, 35 per cent of Indian and 57 per cent of Pakistani/Bangladeshi households shared these amenities.

Typical houses used by immigrants are the larger Victorian terrace-types which more than half a century ago accommodated middle-class families and their servants, and the small working-class houses built in long terraces and which are now either scheduled for demolition or are approaching the end of their useful life. The large Victorian houses are usually shared by several families or used as lodging-houses for single or unaccompanied men. In the 1960s it was not uncommon to find immigrant families living and sleeping in a single room. In these houses there was likely to be only one W.C. shared by all the families, and if there were more than one, the number was usually grossly inadequate. Cooking and washing facilities had to be shared and the cooking smells pervaded the whole house. In the worst houses no-one was responsible for cleaning staircases and passageways in common use.

In the houses used as lodging-houses for single and unaccompanied men, many of the rooms were turned into dormitories by crowding beds into them. There was evidence that in some of these houses the beds were used in shifts in accordance with the shift system in operation in the local factories. Because of the acute housing shortage in these towns at the time there was little that local Public Health Inspectors could do to alleviate the conditions.

The small working-class terrace houses occupied by ethnic minorities are often dilapidated or substandard. Sometimes they are painted externally in very bright colours which tend to highlight the structural defects and increase the decadent and gloomy appearance of the area.

Amongst the general population of Britain approximately 54 per cent of households are owner-occupiers, 31 per cent rent from a local authority or housing association and 15 per cent rent from private landlords. The percentage figures for West Indian households are 36 per cent, 50 per cent and 14 per cent respectively. Amongst Asian households, 70 per cent are owner-occupiers, only 10 per cent rent from a local authority and 20 per cent rent from private landlords.

Some members of Britain's ethnic minorities have become owner-occupiers out of necessity rather than by choice. On their arrival in Britain the only housing available to them was private rented accommodation in houses in multiple occupation. They realised that for the same weekly payments they could buy a house. Mostly they were forced to buy cheap run-down inner-city property, which happened to be close to areas of ethnic minority settlement, and were thus able to preserve their cultural, religious and social patterns. Owner-occupation amongst ethnic minorities therefore does not indicate their incomes are above average and that they have achieved good standards of housing. In some cases in order to meet the heavy outgoings involved in buying on mortgage, and these can be as high as half the family's income, they have been forced to let off rooms, thereby perpetuating some of the problems of local authorities in relation to the housing of ethnic minorities.

To become an owner-occupier a prospective purchaser may have to borrow a relatively large sum of money at an abnormally high rate of interest because of the type of property he wishes to buy. Building societies are usually reluctant to make loans for the purchase of houses in run-down inner-city areas because of the risks involved, but local authorities are usually more willing to lend for the purchase of this type of property. Where, however, neither a building society nor a local authority is willing to grant a mortgage a prospective purchaser will have to borrow from a bank or from a private individual and pay a higher rate of interest and undertake to repay the capital within a relatively short time. This situation can place a heavy strain on family income.

A P.E.P. study found that about 35 per cent of ethnic minority owner-occupiers had local authority mortgages and about 48 per cent had building society mortgages. For the general population the figures were 13 per cent and 73 per cent respectively.

Ethnic minorities are not debarred from becoming council tenants because they were not born in Britain. In fact, nearly all local authorities of areas where there are ethnic minorities have some of them as tenants. These are families who have moved up the council's waiting list in the normal way, or have been rehoused from slum-clearance areas or were homeless. The available evidence indicates that local authorities as a whole do not bar immigrants from inclusion in their waiting lists for houses. However, for many years the majority of local authorities had a residential qualification for inclusion in their waiting lists. This meant that no offer of accommodation could be made until an applicant had been a resident of the area for a fixed period of time, regardless of housing need. The rule applied to the indigenous population as well as to immigrants, but because the ethnic minorities were often living under the worst of housing conditions the rule was sometimes seen as being racially discriminative. Now that the great majority of ethnic minority adults have been in Britain long enough to satisfy the residence qualification the difficulty has been largely removed. Furthermore, many local authorities have abolished the residential rule.

Some local authorities exclude owner-occupiers from their housing waiting lists. One reason for this is that with house prices rising fast some owner-occupiers stand to make a considerable capital gain if offered the tenancy of a council house. The rule, however, can operate to the disadvantage of ethnic minority households who have bought very substandard property, are on low incomes yet paying off large loans at abnormally high interest rates. This rule also is sometimes regarded as being racially discriminative. As can be expected ethnic minorities are often less aware than the indigenous population of the existence of council housing and those that are aware of it may have difficulties in understanding the procedure for applying for a tenancy of a council house.

Useful work in providing housing accommodation for ethnic minorities is being carried out by housing associations which have been set up largely by voluntary effort in a number of towns where there are serious housing problems. Although the amount of accommodation provided by these associations is small because of their limited resources, they help in other ways, such as by giving advice and sometimes arranging for loans for house purchase.

Overall the proportion of ethnic minority households in private rented accommodation is roughly about the same as for the population as a whole but more of them are in furnished accommodation and in consequence have less security of tenure than if they were living in an unfurnished house or flat. Those living in furnished accommodation are likely to be less aware of their legal rights as tenants than are the indigenous population also living in furnished accommodation.

No matter where they are living – whether in owner-occupied or in council or privately rented accommodation – ethnic minorities can be faced with special difficulties in relation to housing. These difficulties can arise because of differences in culture, conception and language. For example, many Asian families consist of two or three generations, or of two brothers each with their respective families of wife and children. These extended families require large houses and few, if any, local authorities build specifically to meet this need. Also, questions are likely to arise whether or not a house occupied by such an extended family constitutes a house in multiple occupation and therefore requires the provision of extra amenities and perhaps a fire escape, all of which are costly to install. Problems can arise because of conceptual difficulties in relation to a tenancy. The Asian community has a tradition of hospitality to persons from the same area and will provide new arrivals to this country with accommodation without regard to tenancy agreements or to the law, e.g. in relation to overcrowding. Also the British concepts of owner and tenants are sometimes difficult for them to grasp. Any of these difficulties can result in a member of an ethnic minority believing that his problems stem from racial discrimination.

Ethnic minority families sometimes complain of harassment, which on investigation turns out to be difficulties occurring between the families sharing the use of kitchens and bathrooms, etc., but actual harassment by landlords wishing to evict tenants does occur. Other incidents of alleged harassment may arise because of differences between the various communities, e.g. Muslims and Hindus, Sikhs and Pakistanis.

There are many aspects of the work of a local authority which involve face-to-face situations and in the case of members of ethnic minorities communication difficulties can arise because of language. In addition, language difficulties can arise when members of ethnic minorities have to deal with estate agents, landlords, solicitors, etc. Sometimes the frustration resulting from such encounters leads to allegations of racial discrimination when it does not exist.

In most towns where there are ethnic minorities there are also ethnic minority landlords. These have often bought property which has a lease with only a few years left to run or is scheduled for demolition. In any event it is often property for which there is little demand. The ethnic minority purchasers are sometimes aware of the snags, but they buy with the intention of recovering their capital and perhaps making a profit in a relatively short time. Sometimes, however, they are unaware of the full facts. For example, the day-to-day expenses are usually very high because in most of these cases the houses are in multiple occupation and the wear and tear in such property is very high. Most likely the house will be on a short-term mortgage and in consequence the monthly payments will be much higher than average. Many of the ethnic minority landlords are inexperienced in housing management and this leads to difficulties not only with their tenants but also with the officers of the local authority.

An ethnic minority landlord may own several houses. In some cases this type of landlord has a reputation for overcrowding and for charging high rents for very inferior accommodation. On the other hand, ethnic minority landlords perform a necessary function and are entitled to a reasonable payment for their services and on the whole are no better or worse than other landlords of similar property.

Ethnic minorities are disproportionately represented in urban areas containing the older decaying housing. A report by the Department of the Environment ("Census Indications of Urban Deprivation, Working Note No. 8") shows that 70 per cent of the ethnic minorities population is concentrated in 10 per cent of enumeration districts (i.e. districts used for national censuses). In these districts members of ethnic minorities constitute on average just over one-fifth of the total population. Compared with other districts, there are nearly three times as many households living under crowded conditions and over twice as many households lacking the exclusive use of bath, W.C. and other basic amenities. This concentration is partially voluntary in that some members of ethnic minorities prefer to live in these less desirable areas in order to have access to certain amenities which they favour. Most, however, consciously choose an area because of the availability of accommodation and the price of it. With owner-occupiers the pattern of purchase often reflects a compromise between the general housing market conditions and personal ambitions for housing. After a time some ethnic minority households move into areas where there are very few other ethnic minority households and begin to climb the social ladder and to integrate with their neighbours. However, there is a stronger tendency to geographical concentration among Asians than there is among the West Indians. This is partly because there is a greater need for cultural solidarity, arising from the lack of English and the wider cultural differences.

The main argument for the dispersal of minority communities is that their integration can be achieved only by geographical merger with the host population. On the other hand, the value of not breaking up established communities is recognised. A strong community base provides a great deal of support for individual families, especially until they gain sufficient confidence to mix with the host population on terms of equality. When this happens it is common for the more competent and ambitious families to move away to areas where there are better opportunities for integration because most, if not all, their neighbours will have been born in Britain.

The indigenous inhabitants of multi-racial areas are usually the elderly and the less prosperous, and some are socially inadequate. There is therefore a tendency for multi-racial areas to accumulate the less literate and the less socially competent of both the host population and the ethnic minorities. One result of this is that the areas deteriorate at an increasing rate. The blame usually falls upon the ethnic minorities in spite of the fact that these areas were going downhill before the arrival of the newcomers. This wrong apportionment of blame can have wide repercussions. For example, it can be a factor in moulding people's attitudes to race and lead to conduct likely to be interpreted as racially discriminative.

A series of Race Relations Acts (1965, 1968, 1972 and 1976) have attempted, not without some success, to prevent discrimination against ethnic minorities in many aspects of social life, including housing. Section 71 of the Race Relations Act 1976, for example, requires local authorities to make appropriate arrangements to secure that their various functions are carried out with due regard to the need (a) to eliminate unlawful discrimination, and (b) to promote equality of opportunity, and good relations, between persons of racial groups. Discrimination can be direct or indirect. Direct discrimination consists of treating a person, on racial grounds, less favourably than others are or would be treated in the same circumstances. Indirect discrimination consists of applying a requirement or conditions which, whether intentionally or not, adversely affects a particular racial group considerably more than others and cannot be justified on non-racial grounds. However, legal measures alone will not earn for the ethnic minorities the esteem of the host population, for which many seek. There is a need for more mutual understanding if repercussions for the children born in Britain are to be avoided.

Many local authorities have established housing advisory centres to provide the general public with information on local housing opportunities in both public and private sectors and at some of these there are staff who understand the language and the special needs of the ethnic minorities. As a result increasing numbers of ethnic minorities are seeking advice and information there. Well-run information centres are likely to be much more successful in promoting good relations between people of different ethnic groups than is the enforcement of Race Relations legislation.

Race relations are an extremely sensitive matter. So far as housing is concerned many households of ethnic minorities have satisfactorily solved their problems, but some have not and are living in areas of housing stress. As time passes the number of newcomers to this country will grow less and less but there is a need to make provision for the housing needs of the children who have been born in Britain to parents who were immigrants and want or will want to set up their own homes.

Ethnic minorities will benefit most by a general rise in housing standards, but will benefit more quickly if the vast number of substandard houses is dealt with by housing action area procedure without delay (see Chapter 9). In addition there is a need to give ethnic minorities information in their own languages about the often complex legal, financial and administrative procedures involved in many aspects of housing, and to explain such concepts as 'grants' and 'regulated' tenancies, etc.

The Commission for Racial Equality has done considerable work in investigating problems in race relations and has published a great deal of literature on the matter, from which much of the information contained in this chapter has been obtained.

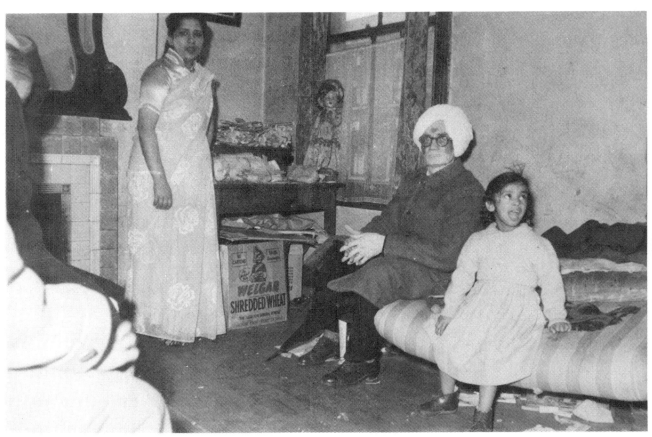

Their first accommodation in Britain is usually with a relative or fellow national, often under crowded conditions.

Sometimes the accommodation had to be adapted to meet the customs of their native land.

In large towns typical houses used by the ethnic minorities are the larger obsolete Victorian terrace-types.

The 1971 Census Household Composition Tables showed that 21 per cent of households whose chief economic supporter was born in the new Commonwealth lived in a shared dwelling.

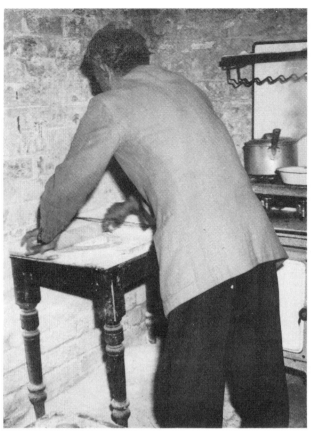

The housekeeper in an all-male household. (1958)

Some members of ethnic minorities buy properties for which there is little or no demand as they have leases with only a few years left to run or are scheduled for demolition.

Paying off a mortgage over a short period often means that the house has to be in multiple occupation.

A street of houses nearly all of which are occupied by ethnic minority households. Such concentrations are usually partially voluntary.

Their natural abilities and aspirations enable some ethnic minority households to climb the social ladder and move into different districts.

213

Some ethnic minority households integrate fairly quickly with the indigenous population and the children born here know only the British way of life.

Chapter 13

HOMES OF THE ELDERLY AND THE PHYSICALLY HANDICAPPED

To live a long time is not in itself a problem because the will to survive is deeply rooted in our nature. However, although to survive a great number of years may be regarded as a triumph the problems of survival generally increase as we grow older.

In Britain the pensionable ages of 65 for men and 60 for women are usually taken as being synonymous with the beginning of old age, i.e. the time when the problems of survival considerably increase. This is not always true. Some people are more or less feeble in their late fifties and others are still young and active at eighty. Nevertheless, for administrative and statistical purposes it is helpful to draw the line at some point on the human age scale so that provision can be made to give help when needed. The proportion of the population above the pensionable ages is rising. In 1900 it was 4.7 per cent, in 1950 it was 10.8 per cent, and in 1980 it is between 16 and 17 per cent, and it has been estimated by the Government Actuary that the number and the proportion of old people will continue to increase until the early 1990s.

People over 65 years of age are not a homogeneous group which suffers from degrees of physical and mental disabilities. The capabilities and needs of the individuals within the pensionable age groups vary enormously. A number of surveys of old people have shown that physical old age does not automatically start at the age of 65. Nevertheless, growing old, no matter at what age it becomes apparent, is accompanied at some stage by varying degrees of physical, mental and social changes which may call for special types of housing accommodation. It is known from research and investigations that many old people are desperately poor, neglected, isolated and lonely, yet there are limits to the resources available for the social services to meet the needs of the elderly.

From 1601 until 1948 the chief provision for housing the elderly poor was the workhouse, which in 1929 was rechristened the Public Assistance Institution. This was where the young and the old, the sick and the infirm, the blind and the lame, the mentally sick and the homeless and the destitute were all given shelter.

In 1601 the custodial institution was seen as the best, and perhaps the only way of dealing on the one hand with destitution and on the other with the protection of society from the moral degradation which follows from idleness and from the embarrassing scene of abject poverty. For a small number of the aged poor, however, charity provided alms-houses, but it was not until the 18th century that voluntary hospitals emerged. They served the middle-classes who subscribed to them, and also because of their charitable aims and their need for research and teaching material some of the poor.

By the mid-19th century, therefore, a few of the sick and infirm poor were cared for by voluntary agencies but the majority found themselves in the workhouses.

These were grim sombre buildings surrounded by high walls like a prison. The entrance to these institutions usually consisted of strong iron gates, kept locked for most of the time, with a porter's lodge just inside. The buildings commonly consisted of large rooms on three floors. The unplastered brick surfaces of the walls were white-washed. Each room contained about ten to fifty iron-framed beds close together, their mattresses usually filled with straw. There was no floor covering, just bare boards which were scrubbed white by the inmates. No furniture was in the rooms except for a few hard chairs. If there was more than one block of rooms they were separated from each other by a small flagged yard in which the inmates were permitted to take an airing. If the institution had a dayroom it was bleak, with hard chairs arranged around the walls. In some workhouses the meals were served in the dayrooms but a common pattern was for them to be served in a central dining hall to which the inmates found their way when summoned by the tolling of a bell situated in a central tower.

The clothing issued to both the male and the female inmates was made from heavy serge or tweed material and was shapeless. Footware consisted of heavy boots for both sexes.

The treatment of the workhouse inmates was based on the principle that they should not experience conditions of life as good as or better than those experienced by the independent lowest paid labourer. This became known as the principle of less eligibility. The idea behind it was that if the able-bodied poor were offered a strict discipline in the workhouse they would be deterred from applying for public assistance and would seek work. If, however, they did enter the workhouse they would find the conditions so harsh that they would very quickly take their discharge and cease to be a burden on the Poor Law. At the time a large proportion of the population lived in such poverty that if conditions in the workhouses had been better more people would have applied for admission to them. The belief was that destitution was due to a person's misconduct or to the irresponsibility of their families. Thus the deterrent discipline of the workhouse was considered to be necessary even for the aged, partly as a penalty for living an improvident or dissolute life and partly as a grave warning to the children and other relations of old people.

By 1839 the average workhouse contained 200 paupers, a mixture of the old, the young, the sick and the able-bodied. In some areas at a later date experiments were made in separating the old from the other inmates, dividing them into classes according to their past behaviour, and treating each class differently. In 1909 a Royal Commission on the Poor Laws reported on a visit to one of the workhouses: "The accommodation for the first and highest class provides for twenty-eight men and twenty-four women. Both the men and the women have two dormitories and two sitting-rooms, the latter having linoleum or a canvas covering on the floor, and being furnished with armchairs, rocking chairs, tables and couches. Meals are served in the sitting-room that appears to be in daily use (the other being reserved for Sundays and receiving friends). As regards food, the inmates get a loaf and a pot of jam for the cupboard (whenever they require them). They are also allowed a cheap and wholesome currant cake to their tea. The inmates may, with the consent of the master, go out any day after the performance of their small duties. Friends, likewise, are admitted on any evening. The qualifications necessary to obtain these privileges are good character, twenty years' residence within the area, freedom from connexion with any crime, and not having previously received relief within the period named."

Some Boards of Guardians made efforts to keep elderly husbands and wives together in their own cubicles or even in special cottages erected in the workhouse grounds. In the country as a whole, however, progress in caring for the aged was extremely slow.

In 1909 the minority report of the Royal Commission complained that of 140,000 elderly persons in Poor Law institutions only a thousand or two in England and Scotland, and none at all in Ireland, were in separate establishments. At the time 45 per cent of people living in workhouses were over 60 years of age. Some of the workhouses were described in the report as being human warehouses, where there was a marked absence of any human interest.

At the outbreak of war in 1914 the situation remained essentially as it was in 1909. Some ablebodied paupers were absorbed into the Armed Services and others into warwork. A number of workhouse hospitals were used as military hospitals, but the workhouse blocks themselves remained the same, both during and after the war.

In 1929 the powers and duties of the Boards of Guardians were transferred to the councils of the counties and county boroughs, and the workhouses were renamed Public Assistance Institutions. Some of them, and parts of others, became general hospitals, which were added to the isolation, tuberculosis, maternity and mental hospitals already managed by local authorities. In the 1930s only a very few local authorities opened residential homes for old people and these were often little different in size and amenities from the former workhouses. At the outbreak of war in 1939 they accounted for less than one-twentieth of the accommodation provided in Public Assistance Institutions. Thus by 1939 the Local Government Act of 1929 had made changes in the administration of the Poor Laws but had not achieved the anticipated reforms in the care of old people. There were still 400 Poor Law institutions which housed 149,000 people, nearly 60,000 of whom were said to be sick.

In 1944 the trustees of the Nuffield Foundation commissioned an investigation into the problem of ageing and the care of old people. In the report of the survey, published in 1947, conditions in some of the Public Assistance Institutions were described. These institutions contained "a motley assembly of the destitute, the great majority were aged, but there were also children, epileptics and feeble minded young, the blind and the sick. The buildings in use were structurally inadequate. They usually had two or three storeys, reached by steep, narrow, stone staircases. Narrow wards – lit by windows that were too few and too high – led one from another, and contained beds, sometimes as many as a hundred, separated from each other by less than two feet. Often the only furniture was a chair for each resident. Dayrooms were large and cheerless. Floors were mainly bare boards, with brick floors in lavatories, bathrooms, kitchens and corridors. In some institutions the rules were harsh, or harshly administered." The Nuffield Survey Committee recommended that all normal old people should be accommodated in small homes rather than in large institutions.

During the 1939-45 war the nation's resolve for a more just and caring society must have included the expectation that the Poor Law would be replaced with something more humane.

In 1947 the Minister of Health, Mr. Aneuran Bevan, when introducing the National Assistance Bill (now the National Assistance Act 1948) stated: "We have decided to make a great departure in the treatment of old people. The workhouse is to go. Although many people have tried to humanise it, it was in many respects a very evil institution. We have determined that the right way to approach this problem is to give the Welfare Authorities, as we shall now describe them, the power to establish separate Homes . . . . It seems to us that the optimum limit for these Homes must be about twenty-five to thirty persons." Also in its 1948-49 annual report the Ministry of Health declared: "The workhouse is doomed."

It is one thing to declare good intentions and to legislate for them, but quite another to fulfil the intentions.

The National Assistance Act 1948 places a duty on

local authorities to provide residential accommodation for persons who by reason of age, infirmity or any other circumstances are in need of care and attention not otherwise available to them. It also requires them to register and inspect homes run by charitable organisations and private individuals. In 1948 there were about 400 Public Assistance Institutions in England and Wales which provided accommodation for 130,000 poor persons. Shortly after the National Assistance Act became operative, 100 of these institutions were classified as hospitals and transferred to the National Health Service. A further 200 were used jointly by the National Health Service and local authorities, largely for housing the elderly, chronically sick and other old people who needed a great deal of care and attention. The remaining 100 institutions were used for residential accommodation. The result was that out of the 130,000 persons in Public Assistance Institutions in 1948, only 42,000 remained in residential accommodation in 1949. This means that 60 per cent of the inmates of workhouses in 1948 were really sick people. One of the first effects of the National Assistance Act 1948 was the separation of old people who were ill and needed hospital care from those who were only in need of care and attention. The separation of the sick from the well was not an easy task.

The policy of the Government in 1948 was based largely on the recommendations of the Nuffield Committee's Report, i.e. homes with thirty to thirty-five beds, predominantly in single rooms, and with the standards of comfort of residential hotels. However, in the early post-war years the demand for new housing and factories was so great that the building of new homes had to be postponed and the emphasis placed on the conversion of existing buildings. The immediate post-1948 programmes therefore concentrated on the improvement of the workhouses and the acquisition and conversion of other buildings, e.g. large houses and former mansions.

The amount and type of improvements to the former workhouses varied throughout the country but the general pattern was to install modern methods of sanitation and heating, to plaster the brick walls and to cover the old floor boards with plastic tiles or composition flooring. The rooms were painted in cheerful, bright colours and pictures were hung on the walls. Comfortable furnishings were provided, including a combined wardrobe and dressing-table for each bed, and labour-saving devices such as heated food trolleys were provided. In some institutions potted plants were placed on the window sills. Outwardly, however, the buildings remained workhouses.

Many of the other buildings which were acquired and adapted at this time had originally been private mansions owned by millionaires or other very rich or important people. Some were gracefully designed, others ostentatiously displayed the wealth of their former owners. Nearly all stood in their own grounds, which often consisted of well-kept lawns, flower-beds and shrubberies. A few had a tennis court or a bowl-ing green. Unfortunately, the large houses which were suitable for conversion into old people's homes were mainly situated outside urban areas. Only a few were near the heart of a town. The result was that often the old people had little incentive to go out and their friends and relations had difficulties in travelling to see them. After conversion some of these homes remained almost luxurious, and all were a vast improvement on the workhouses.

In the early stages it was not an easy task to decide which of the workhouse inmates should be transferred to the new homes. It was thought that some of the old people might have difficulty in adjusting to the relatively luxurious new environment. Compared with the population of the workhouses, in the first few years after 1948 the residents of the new homes were on the whole of a higher social class. It would seem that local authorities were guided in their choice by the social class rather than by the physical needs of the old people.

By 1954-55 the building situation had eased and the Government decided to review the situation with regard to the provision of accommodation for old people. It suggested to local authorities that in view of the increasing proportion of very old and infirm residents, with the consequent need for more staff, it might be reasonable to build homes with up to about sixty beds. By 1975 most, if not all, the former workhouses were no longer in use for accommodating old people. By 1978 local authorities had provided about 2,500 residential homes, either by adaptation or new building. These accommodated about 120,000 people, or 2 per cent of the population over 65 years of age.

The majority of local authority homes are new, purpose-built, and have accommodation for between thirty and seventy elderly people. They differ in the standards of accommodation and the facilities they provide. The best old people's homes have about fifty beds, mostly in single rooms, and accommodate both men and women. There is a large dining-room and more than one lounge and a sheltered garden area. The furnishings are usually modern and colourful. However, all the homes are not up to this standard. Some still have dormitories, lack sufficient lounge space and have poor staff accommodation. Also, in some of the modern homes the atmosphere is too clinical and impersonal for a home. Residents pay for their care according to their means and all have an amount of money for their personal use.

In 1944 over 6,000 old people in Britain lived in homes managed by twenty-six different religious organisations and roughly another 3,000 lived in homes managed by 120 different charitable organisations of a secular nature. About 6,000 out of the 9,000 lived in homes with no more than thirty to forty beds. The Nuffield Committee in 1947 reported favourably on these homes. Some were opened originally to serve the needs of the very poor of the industrial towns, others were opened as adjuncts to groups of alms-houses, some for the elderly members of a particular religion or profession, and some as quasi-residential hotels for retired middle-class people. A number of these voluntary homes had been opened specifically to meet the needs of particular kinds of disabled persons, e.g. the blind, the deaf or the epileptic. In 1980 in England and Wales there were about 800 homes run by voluntary organisations which provided residential accommodation for the elderly.

In addition to the homes managed by local authorities and voluntary organisations there are those which are run by private individuals for profit. Both voluntary and private homes have to be registered with the local authority. In January 1960 there were 1,106 private homes for the elderly registered in England and Wales, with accommodation for 11,643 persons. 24 per cent had five or fewer beds, and a further 38 per cent had between six and ten beds. Only ten per cent had more than twenty beds. The number of private homes has grown since then and in 1980 there were about 1,700 in England and Wales. They vary widely in their amenities, furnishings, staffing and management. Many of the voluntary and private homes are used by local authorities on an agency basis, which means that some of the residents are supported by local authorities. In 1980 the voluntary and private homes provided accommodation for about 56,000 elderly people.

The majority of elderly people wish to remain independent for as long as possible and do not want to go into a home, and experts agree that it is better, whenever possible, to keep people in their own homes. However, if elderly people continue to live alone a time will probably come when they need some assistance in order to maintain the independence they value so much. They will need not only the support of the domiciliary health and social care services, but also suitable premises. Reduced mobility and increasing frailty call for accommodation which is adequate for coping with these conditions, but in Britain the elderly are often found to be living in the worst housing of any group. A higher percentage of the elderly than the general adult population lives in accommodation built before 1919 and this is often poorly maintained and situated in run-down inner-city areas. A third of all elderly people live alone, but the proportion is much higher for women, especially for those aged 75 and over.

In 1977, in England and Wales, there were 237,000 housing units for the elderly with a warden service, and 228,000 without a warden service, equivalent altogether to sixty-six housing units per 1,000 people aged 65 or over. A survey in England conducted by the Office of Population Censuses and Surveys in 1976 indicated that 8 per cent of those aged 65 or over lived in such accommodation. In Scotland there were 13,000 such dwellings, of which 7,000 had a warden service. These units provided accommodation for 21,000 people.

There is therefore a need for more self-contained bungalows and flats and also for more accommodation midway between the self-contained dwelling and the residential home. The essence of good housing for old people is that it should be easy to run, heat and clean, and internally arranged so as to reduce the risk of accident and injury to the inhabitants. It should be conveniently situated, for example near shops, etc., afford independence and privacy for the occupants and yet provide opportunities for social intercourse and regular human contact.

For subsidy purposes the Government recognises two categories of old people's housing. These are self-contained dwellings designed to the Parker Morris standard and grouped flatlets with warden's supervision. If they are to qualify for the special subsidy, the self-contained dwellings must have handrails, a heating installation which can maintain a temperature of 21 °C throughout the dwelling when the outside temperature is −1 °C, and a refrigerator or ventilated cool cupboard. Self-contained dwellings built in groups can also be provided with certain communal facilities such as a common room with a kitchen, and an emergency alarm system.

Groups of flatlets must have a self-contained warden's dwelling, an emergency alarm system by means of which tenants can communicate with the warden, a common room with provision for light refreshments and cloakroom accommodation, a laundry room and storage facilities. The communal accommodation has to be accessible from the flatlets by an enclosed and heated circulation space. In blocks of flats for old people lifts have to be provided if there are more than two storeys, instead of three storeys as is the case in family housing. Guest accommodation and a warden's office are optional extras.

It has been accepted that in order to avoid an institutional atmosphere, groups of flatlets should not exceed thirty dwellings. Also, one warden on a full-time basis can look after a block of about thirty dwellings, with temporary help for days off and holidays. The duties of a warden normally involve visiting tenants each day, responding to the bells or communication system which connects the warden with each dwelling, and in some cases helping with shopping and contacting the necessary services, for example the doctor, nurse, etc., when necessary.

The warden's accommodation is generally a self-contained house or flat which is large enough for a married couple. Most wardens are women, but married couples or men are sometimes appointed. They may be people with nursing experience, but what is more important is a practical and patient disposition and an understanding of the wishes of old people for privacy and independence. A number of services for elderly people in their own homes are provided by statutory and voluntary bodies to help them live there for as long as possible. These include the advice and help of social workers, domestic help, a chiropody service, laundry and a meals service.

Housing for old people is also provided by housing associations and other voluntary bodies. It includes accommodation similar to that provided by local authorities, but some of these bodies, for example the Abbeyfield Societies, also provide accommodation by converting larger older-type houses into bedsitting rooms in which the occupiers can have their own furniture and personal belongings. In this type of accommodation there is usually a communal dining-room, the provision of main meals and the friendly attention of a resident housekeeper.

Alms-houses were one of the earliest types of special accommodation provided for old people. Many of these are of outstanding architectural beauty and some are good examples of the vernacular domestic architecture from the 12th century to the present day. Many were designed by famous architects such as Sir Christopher Wren, and some contain furniture by great designers and other articles of great beauty.

Some trustees of alms-house foundations have funds from the endowments which enable them to give further assistance, for example free fuel, in addition to providing free accommodation. In most of these cases the original endowment was sufficient to enable a small pension to be paid to the occupants of the houses but the diminution in the value of money over the years now renders this impossible. On the other hand, the universal availability of retirement pensions in Britain has reduced the need for financial assistance from the trust funds.

There does not appear to be a complete record of all the alms-houses in Britain but from the information which the National Association of Alms-houses has available it is estimated that in England alone there are about 2,500 sets of alms-houses, with accommodation for about 35,000 people.

The experiences of about a thousand years have shown that the ideal form of housing for the elderly who are largely able to care for themselves is a house or flat for which they have no worries about paying rent and rates and for repairs, and from which they will not be evicted except for disorderly conduct, where they may have around them pieces of furniture and family belongings which they cherish.

The state has done more in providing suitable accommodation for old people since 1945 than in any other period of British history. The workhouse, once the last refuge for the elderly poor, has been replaced by local authority homes which accommodate about 2 per cent of the population over 65 years of age. Also, since the late 1950s local authorities have provided an increasing number of small dwellings and sheltered housing for the elderly, and housing associations and other voluntary bodies have provided increasing amounts of accommodation specially suited for old people. Rent rebates and allowances and rate rebates have helped many old people to continue living more or less independent lives in their own homes.

In 1980 about 17 per cent of the population of Britain is over retirement age, compared with 15 per cent in 1961. It has been estimated that although they will remain at about nine and a half million up to the end of the present century, the balance between the younger and more active element will change considerably. The number of those 75 and over, for instance, will increase by 21 per cent between 1979 and the end of the century, while those between the age of retirement and 75 will decrease by 11 per cent during the same period. There is at present a need for

accommodation midway between the residential home and the geriatric hospital ward, and this is likely to increase in the near future. In the past organisations have been great innovators in the social field and they should be encouraged to provide and staff this kind of accommodation. Also, because the amount of money available from public funds for the social services in general is limited, if the care of the elderly is to be improved, or even maintained at its present level, more voluntary labour will be needed. Occasional disasters and the experiences of war have revealed the large reservoir of voluntary labour that is available to meet certain social needs but if it is choked by organised labour demanding that all forms of labour must be paid it will dry up and then the needy will suffer.

The physically handicapped

Estimates made by several people indicate that between 3 and 6 per cent of the population of Britain suffers from some degree of physical disability which is likely to handicap them. Many are young people.

The most common, but not the only, causes are: osteo and rheumatoid arthritis, multiple sclerosis, hemiplegia and various neurological disorders. The range of disability stretches from the ambulant who have restricted movement in their limbs to the paralysed who are dependent upon a wheelchair for mobility and the help of the family and the community services for all their daily activities. The physically handicapped therefore have a variety of housing needs which differ from person to person, but basically these needs can be met by two types of housing: the mobility house and the wheelchair house. The mobility house is an ordinary house which is modified to make it more convenient for the handicapped person to move about and live in. The wheelchair house is also an ordinary house which has been designed or adapted so that there is more space for the movement of a wheelchair and additional amenities so that the handicapped person can be as independent as possible.

Before 1970 local authorities had permissive powers to provide special housing accommodation for the disabled, either by building or adaptation, but very few special units were provided. In most cases the physically disabled who were housed by local authorities were offered houses which had not been adapted or houses built for old people which were not entirely suitable. In many instances the local authorities seemed to be unaware of the special needs of the handicapped. On the other hand, some voluntary organisations made big efforts to fill the gap either by new building or by adapting existing houses at their own expense.

The Chronically Sick and Disabled Persons Act 1970, as subsequently amended by the Housing Act 1974, the Housing Rents and Subsidies Act 1975 and the Housing Act 1980, now makes it mandatory for local authorities to identify disabled people and amongst other things to provide special housing for them, or alternatively make grants available towards the cost of adapting accommodation for their use.

Many old people are desperately poor and feel neglected. (1958)

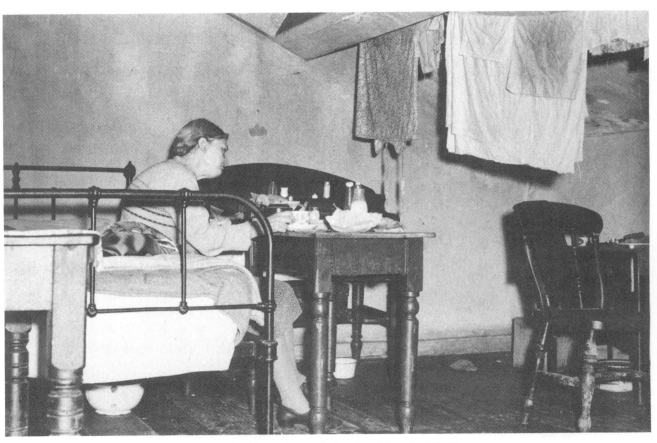

Some old people are isolated and lonely. (1958)

An 87-year-old man, living alone, who preferred independence and had no wish to go into a Home. (1959)

The grim entrance to a former workhouse part of which in 1948 became a hostel for old people. (1953)

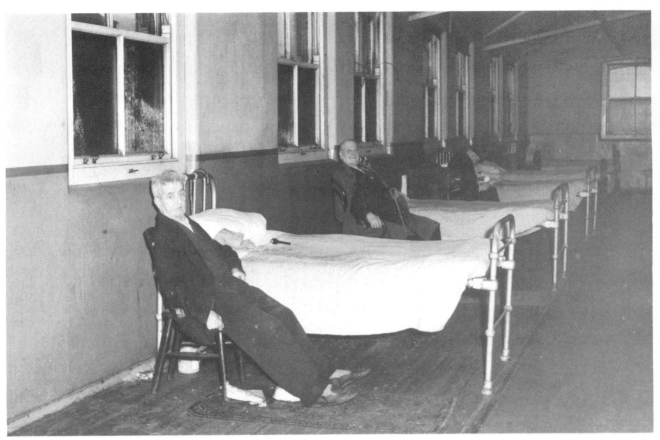

Ward in former workhouse in use as a hostel for old people until 1954.

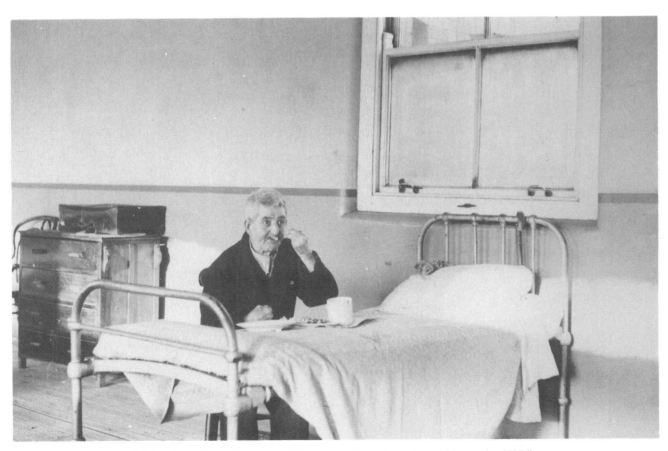

Dining facilities in former workhouse used as a hostel for old people. (1954)

Local authority accommodation for the elderly, early 1950s.

Former infectious disease hospital converted into a hostel for old people. (1951)

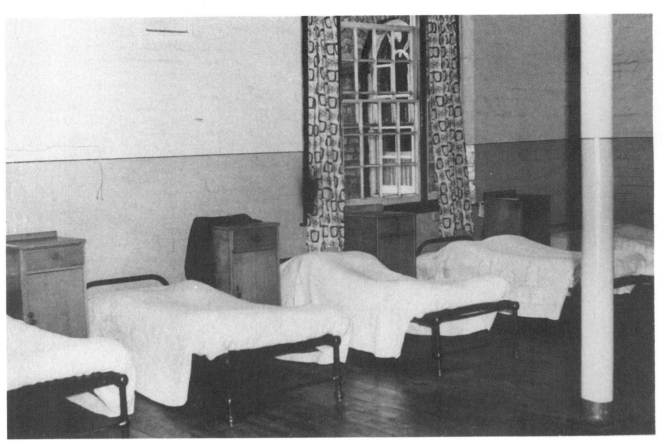

Dormitory in old peoples' hostel (former workhouse) after improvement. (1951)

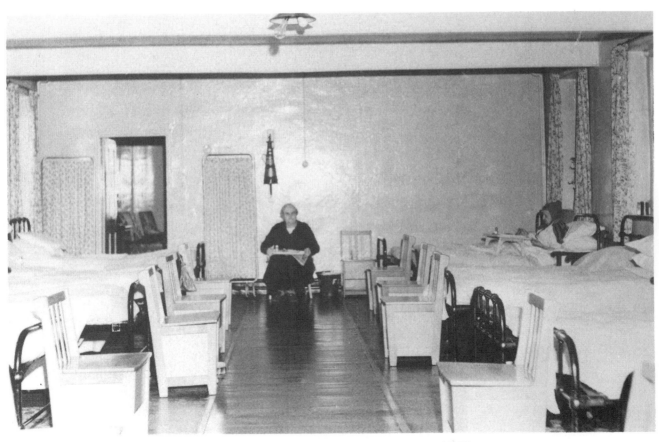

Ward in former workhouse after improvement. (1953)

224

Dining-room in former workhouse after conversion into hostel for old people. (1954)

Lounge in former workhouse after conversion into hostel for old people. (1954)

The real break with the workhouse concept came in the late 1950s. A mansion after conversion by a local authority to a home for old people.

The preparation of afternoon tea in the kitchen of the former mansion.

226

The dining-room in the converted mansion.

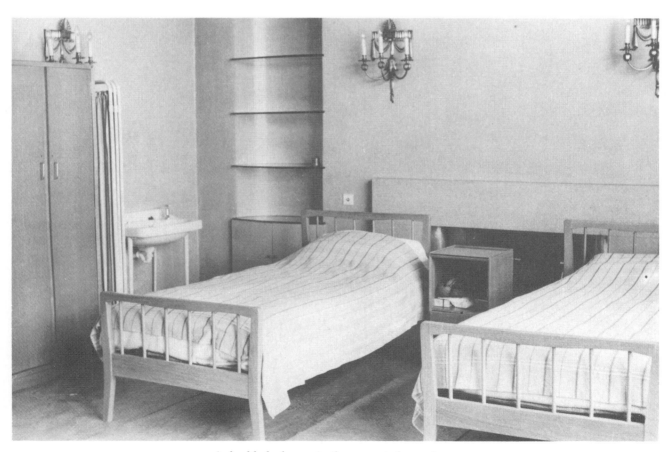

A double bedroom in the converted mansion.

227

A local authority purpose-built home for the elderly. (Late 1950s)

A later purpose-built local authority home for the elderly. (1960s)

228

The matron chats with the residents in the lounge of a Salvation Army home for the elderly.

A dining-room in a Salvation Army home for the elderly.

229

A bedroom in a Salvation Army home for the elderly.

A single bedroom in a Salvation Army home for the elderly.

230

Bungalows built for old people by a local authority during the inter-war years. Only a few were built by local authorities in this period.

Local authority bungalows for old people set around a beautiful garden.

Post-1945 local authority bungalows for old people. Situated on a large housing estate but with a secluded garden with a shelter.

Block of old people's flatlets built by local authority in the 1950s. Each flatlet consists of bed-sitting-room and kitchenette. W.C.s and bathrooms are shared. There is a resident warden.

The bed-sitting-room in one of the flatlets.

The kitchenette in one of the flatlets.

233

Block of old people's flatlets built by local authority in the 1960s. All flats have their own cooking facilities and there is a laundry, common room and resident warden.

The entrance hall to a house converted into flatlets for old people by a local charity. (1956)

The kitchen in one of the flatlets. The 90-year-old lady doing her own cooking. (1956)

234

Alms-houses built more than 100 years ago in the open country now surrounded by urban development. (1960s)

Living-room in flatlet provided by a local charity. (1950s)

Local authority bungalow designed specially for handicapped people. Note wide entrance and garage for small car.

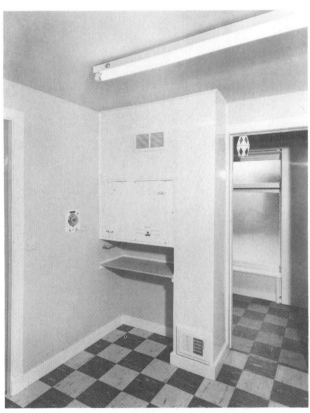

Bungalow for handicapped people – hall showing thermostat and other controls for heating etc. at a suitable height.

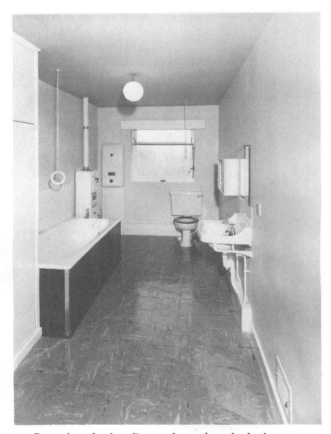

Bungalow for handicapped people – the bathroom.

Bungalow for handicapped people – the kitchen.

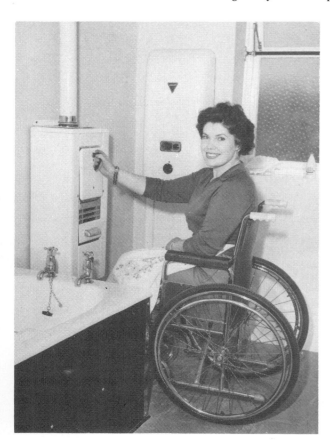

A bathroom adapted for the handicapped.

A stairlift for which a local authority can make a grant.

Chapter 14

HOMES FOR CHILDREN IN COMMUNITY CARE

To be rejected or abandoned by one's natural parents or to be deprived of one or both parents can be a devastating experience for a child, especially a young child, and can have serious repercussions for the rest of his or her life. Also, grossly inadequate care by parents can have disastrous consequences for the child and perhaps, in later years, for the community. When a child is deprived of proper care and support most communities act in some way to deal with the matter and usually find substitute parents and homes. In Britain it is largely, but not entirely, the local authority which takes on the task of the substitute parents. There are also many voluntary organisations engaged in this work.

Before 1948 children in the care of local authorities were regarded as poor persons, i.e. as paupers in need of relief. The statute which enabled this relief to be given was the Poor Law Act 1930, which was a consolidation of earlier Poor Law legislation. The language of the 1930 Act reflected the thinking and the spirit of the earlier Poor Law. The Act was administered, under the general direction and control of the Minister of Health, by county and county borough councils who normally acted through their public assistance committees. The only obligation placed on the authorities in respect of the children, other than giving them relief, was to set them to work, or to put them out as apprentices. No general duties as regards ensuring proper care and education were specifically laid upon the authorities by the law. If they wished, however, they could, and nearly all did, provide for the children by maintaining them in institutions described as 'schools'. They could:

(a) Establish 'separate schools' for the relief and management of the children to be received therein.

(b) Send children to 'schools' which were supported wholly or partially by voluntary subscriptions and certified by the Minister as being fit for the reception of children, and pay the reasonable expenses of maintenance, clothing and education.

(c) Send deaf and dumb or blind children to special 'schools' suitable for their reception, whether certified or not.

Although the Poor Law Act did not specifically authorise the boarding out of children, most local authorities considered it implied that boarding out was one of the recognised methods of providing for the care of destitute children and by the late 1930s they were making an increasing use of this method. The number of children boarded out by public assistance authorities was approximately 5,700 in 1939 and 4,900 in 1946.

At the end of World War II approximately 33,000 children were in the care of public assistance authorities. About 5,000 had become homeless as a result of the war, i.e. they were orphans or had been abandoned by their parents (see Chapter 1). Over 6,000 of the children were in public assistance institutions (former workhouses), nearly 17,000 were in children's homes, including grouped cottage homes, over 5,000 had been placed in homes run by voluntary organisations, and nearly 5,000 were boarded out. Another 33,500 children were in the care of voluntary organisations and accommodated in 886 homes of various types run by these organisations, which were certified as suitable by Government inspectors. There were also other children's homes which, for several reasons – for example, they did not depend on public subscriptions or take in Poor Law children – were not subject to public control. The number of these homes and the number of children they accommodated were not known.

So far as the public assistance authorities were concerned, there was no uniform pattern of administration in the country. Sometimes the institutions or homes were administered by local Guardians' Committees which had been established under the earlier Poor Law and had continued to function after Boards of Guardians had been abolished. The members of these committees were often imbued with the general ideas and spirit of the earlier Poor Law. In some areas the public assistance committee, the committee statutorily and primarily responsible for the administration of the Poor Law, took full responsibility for the care of the children thrust upon them. In other areas the duty was entrusted to the education committee. In the latter case the standard of child care was rarely any higher than in the others.

The accommodation provided by public assistance authorities for deprived children fell into five categories: public assistance institutions (former workhouses), in which the children were cared for in a part of a building which was used for the care of destitute and often senile adults; large institutions or barrack-like buildings, physically separated from the institutions for the adults; single homes, smaller in size than the institutions but larger than a family group home; grouped cottage homes; and scattered homes.

By 1945 only a few of the public assistance institutions had been structurally altered to make them suitable for child care. The majority remained in essence 'workhouses', with their bleak stone stairways and corridors, the same baths and lavatories installed for the adult paupers, and their long wards with bare boards. In most of the institutions the provision for play and occupation was very inadequate and only a few were provided with gardens in which the children could play.

The large institutional homes had mainly been built during the last century to house 50 to 200, or even more, children on institutional lines, but the buildings were physically separated from the workhouse. The children slept in large dormitories and the living quarters were usually large bare rooms similarly furnished and equipped to workhouses.

The single homes were often converted private dwellings, sometimes set in fairly extensive grounds with kitchen gardens in which the boys helped to grow some of the food. The converted homes usually had a more homely appearance than the purpose-built ones, but some had not been properly maintained and had fallen into a serious state of disrepair. Many were ill-equipped for child care.

The grouped cottage homes mainly built at the beginning of the present century were without doubt an improvement on the other types of buildings in use for Poor Law care of children. Nevertheless, the appearance of the cottages still lacked homeliness and they were often set in grounds which were forbidding with large main gates of an institutional type, immediately inside which was a 'lodge' which was used as an enquiry office or check point.

Some of the larger grouped cottage homes had their own schools and churches in the grounds so that the children in care of the local authority were isolated from other children. This often left the home child with a serious inferiority complex.

The scattered homes were small houses, usually one in a row of similar houses, occupied by families, and the arrangements provided something approximating to the family household rather than an institution.

In 1945 voluntary organisations from whom information could be obtained had a total of about 33,500 children in their care. These organisations varied widely in size, funds and capacity. At one end of the scale there were the large societies, for example, each caring for thousands of children in homes established all over the country; and at the other end were the small villa homes for about ten local children, managed by a local committee and financed as a local charity. A large number of these organisations, both great and small, owed their inspiration to the religious denomination to which they belonged. Some societies provided homes for a particular type of child, e.g. the legitimate, the illegitimate, children of fathers in certain occupations (e.g. seamen's orphanages), the crippled, blind or mentally retarded.

In the main, the homes run by the voluntary organisations expressed the sincere and general desire of their founders to care for orphans and other deprived children at a time when the nation regarded them as paupers and a burden on society. In some instances the level of child care provided by the voluntary organisations was well above that provided by the local authorities, or ever conceived by them.

There were other organisations with a very narrow and limited view of child care. If they possessed sufficient funds to be independent of outside donations, their homes were not subject to Government inspection. In such cases it was possible for the children to be shut away from any outside contact or help for the whole of their childhood, with the result that when they were old enough they were sent out into the world so institutionalised as to be unprepared for ordinary life. These organisations professed different religious faiths.

The type of home provided by the voluntary bodies varied as widely as did the organisations themselves. A large proportion were institutional homes of the barrack variety. Some had imposing facades to impress the passers-by with the standard of charity and philanthropy of the particular organisation, but the standard of accommodation provided behind the facade was often little different from that provided in public assistance institutions, and the rooms were bare and comfortless.

There were, however, voluntary organisations which were conscious of the requirements for proper child care. Some of these had built groups of cottage homes of a high standard, which provided excellent substitute homes and were well managed by good house-mothers. The children in these homes lived in a good family-like and relatively secure atmosphere.

The general situation prior to 1948 was that the level of care of deprived children varied greatly. In most of the homes and institutions the deprived child was not recognised as an individual with his own personality, his own life to live, and his own contribution to offer. Still more important he was a prisoner of the unfortunate circumstances in which he found himself through no fault of his own, and with no-one to whom he could turn who was vitally interested in him and cared for him as an individual.

In March 1945 the Government appointed a committee (the Curtis Committee) to enquire into the methods existing for the care of children who, because of the loss of parents or through any other cause whatever, were deprived of a normal home life with their parents or relatives, and to consider what further measures were necessary to ensure that these children were brought up under the conditions best calculated to compensate them for the lack of parental care. The report of this committee was published in 1946, and new legislation – The Children's Act – followed in 1948. The report was a lengthy one and dealt with most aspects of the care of deprived children. So far as the type of home was concerned, the committee said that the need of the deprived child was for a home or a good substitute home which would supply:–

(i) Affection and personal interest, understanding of his defect, care for his future, respect for his personality and regard for his self esteem.

(ii) Stability, the feeling that he could expect to remain with those who would continue to care for him until he went out into the world to stand on his own feet.

(iii) Opportunity to make the best of his ability and aptitudes, whatever they may be, in the same way as such opportunity is made available to the child in the normal home.

(iv) A share in the common life of a small group of people in a homely environment.

The Children's Act 1948 changed the legal concept of child care and required each local authority, i.e. county, county borough and London Borough councils, and in Scotland the council of a large burgh, to appoint a children's committee and a children's officer to be responsible for the care and upbringing of children in the authority's care. Since 1948 there have been changes both in the law and in the services which administer it. In 1968 the children's departments of local authorities, created under the Act of 1948, were absorbed in the general social services departments of local authorities, and in 1974, when local government was reorganised, the social work of local authorities was concentrated in the hands of county councils. In Northern Ireland, the Children and Young Persons Act (N.I.) 1950 gave the welfare authorities of each county and county borough the duty of caring for homeless and neglected children. Arrangements for their care follow the same principles as in the rest of Britain.

The main legislative provisions relating to child care in England and Wales now are the Children's Acts of 1948 and 1958 and the Children and Young Persons Acts of 1933, 1963 and 1969. Central responsibility for the administration of these Acts, which relate both to children deprived of normal home life and to juvenile offenders, was for many years with the Home Office. Since 1970, in order that the child care services can be better co-ordinated with the other social services, the central responsibility for them has been with the Department of Health and Social Services.

A child may be received into the care of a local authority in England and Wales under Section 1 of the Children's Act 1948 if he is abandoned or lost, if he has no parents or guardian, or if his parents or guardian are prevented by some specific reason from caring for him. The procedure is on a voluntary basis, so the child can be removed from the care of the local authority at the discretion of his parents or guardian, and in any case the local authority has a duty to ensure, wherever appropriate, that the child is returned home. However, the Children's Act 1975 places some limits on parental discretion when the child has been in care for more than six months. In these cases the parents have to give twenty-eight days' notice of their intention to remove the child from care.

Under certain conditions specified in Section 2 of the Children's Act 1948 and in Section 57 of the Children's Act 1975 the social services committee of a local authority may pass a resolution in respect of a child already in care, in order to assume parental rights. At any one time about 20 per cent of the children in care under the provisions of the 1948 Act are likely to be subject to such resolutions. If the child's natural parents object to such a resolution being made it automatically lapses. The local authority can, however, apply to a juvenile court, and after hearing both sides to the case the court will decide whether or not the resolution should lapse. The parents have a right of appeal against the decision of the juvenile court. In cases in which the local authority assumes parental rights, normally the child remains in its care until he reaches eighteen years of age.

In addition to the children who come into care under the provisions of the 1948 Act the social service departments of local authorities have to receive into care children committed by the courts under the Children and Young Persons' Acts of 1933, 1963 and 1969. The main reasons why children are committed into care under these Acts are that they themselves committed an offence, they are in need of care, protection and control, or they or another child of the same family have been victims of an offence, or are in the same household as a person convicted of a serious offence such as manslaughter, cruelty and so on. Furthermore, certain powers exist under matrimonial and other legislation for the committal into care of children involved in wardship proceedings and children whose parents have been engaged in divorce proceedings and where the issue of custody has not been resolved.

Children who are committed by the courts to the care of a local authority cannot be taken home whenever the parents wish. The local authority is given parental rights over the child by the court order and unless this is revoked the child remains in care until he reaches eighteen years of age.

Because of the changes that have taken place since 1948 both in the law and the reasons why children are taken into care it is not possible to make accurate comparisons between the numbers of children in care in 1948 and in 1980. For example, the 1971 census revealed that there were 3,200 children in places of detention in Britain, that is in detention centres, borstals, remand centres, prisons and special hospitals. However, in 1971 approved school orders were abolished, so children under nineteen in approved schools and those in remand homes and detention centres, etc., were put in the care of local authorities.

In 1978 there were 100,700 children in the care of local authorities in England and Wales, a big increase over the number in the care of the public assistance authorities in 1948. However, the turnover is much greater now than it was in 1948 because care is not confined now to orphans and the very poor. For example, although 52,680 children were received into the care of local authorities in England and Wales during 1974, the vast majority were short-term cases, e.g. because of the illness or confinement of the mother.

Whether sent into care by the courts or their parents, all children are likely to suffer because they have been forced to leave their home, no matter how squalid it might be, and from the separation from their parents, siblings and familiar surroundings. The separation is likely to be no less alarming when it is expected to be for a short term.

The type of care available to children must vary according to their needs but the aim should be to find substitute homes as near as possible to what might be regarded as normal. Only if the children taken into care experience a sense of security and understanding will they be able to cope with the shock of being taken into care. Since 1948 a great deal has been learnt about the psychological needs of children, and this has led to the abandonment of the large institution as a receptacle for all children in an area taken into care, and to a policy favouring the boarding out of children in ordinary homes, where possible. In 1947 the Curtis Committee strongly urged that this should be the first choice in finding substitute homes and local authorities now have a duty to place children in foster-homes unless this is not practicable or desirable in the child's best interest. Therefore, since 1948 the emphasis has been on the boarding out of children with foster-parents rather than segregating them in institutions. The foster-parents receive an allowance to cover the cost of maintenance. If a foster-home cannot be found for a child, or the child is not suitable for boarding out, then there is no alternative but to place him in a children's home provided by the local authority or a voluntary organisation.

Most if not all the local authority institutional-type children's homes have been closed and local authorities now run small family group homes instead. These usually cater for about twelve children, boys and girls, of various ages. They are run by a house-mother, with some daytime assistance. Often the house-mother is a married woman whose husband goes out to work but acts as a father to the children in the evenings and at weekends. The home is usually a converted older house, a large council house on an estate or even a purpose-built house on an estate. The children do not wear a distinctive uniform, which was a hallmark of the Poor Law, and attend the schools, churches and clubs of the neighbourhood. In cases where fostering would entail splitting up a family the children can be kept together in one of these homes.

In recent years the wisdom of fostering has been questioned on the grounds that the atmosphere in a home with other children in care can be less emotionally demanding. Practice varies in different parts of the country but some authorities now favour larger homes which accommodate fifteen to twenty children.

When a child has been taken into the care of a local authority because of serious domestic discord, efforts are made by the local authority to bring the family together again and, if necessary, to rehabilitate it. Some former grouped children's cottage homes have been adapted as units of family accommodation and are used for this purpose.

Local authority social services departments co-operate closely with voluntary organisations concerned with the welfare of deprived children. They can place children in homes run by voluntary organisations and make contributions to their costs, and they have duties with respect to the inspection of voluntary homes. Voluntary effort has been prominent in the development of services for deprived children since the 19th century. Organisations such as Dr. Barnardo's, the National Children's Society and the Catholic Rescue Society have pioneered methods of child care and still play an important part in caring for deprived children. In 1976 voluntary homes in Britain had about 12,000 places for them.

About 37,000, or 36 per cent, of the children in the care of public and voluntary bodies in 1978 were accommodated in residential homes or schools of one kind or another. It takes in total a staff of about 20,000 to look after that number of children but the standard of residential care varies considerably from home to home. In 1971, for every three children in homes or approved schools one was in hospital for the psychiatrically ill or mentally subnormal, one in hospital for the physically ill and more than one in a residential school for the handicapped. In Scotland there were about 17,000 children in care or under supervision. A third of them were living at home under the supervision of a social worker, nearly half of the remainder were living with foster-parents, relatives or friends and the rest were in residential care.

Since 1948 there have been big changes in the law and in the methods for dealing with children who are in need of community care. The status of these children has been changed from that of paupers to that of children requiring sympathy and understanding care. The grounds on which children can be received into community care have been widened and the methods of care made sensitive to the psychological as well as the physical needs of the children and also made to compensate as far as possible for the loss of certain essentials of childhood. During the last thirty years or so a great deal of knowlege about the emotional needs of children has been gained from the experience of local authorities and voluntary bodies concerned with deprived children. Much has also been learned about the difficulties within families and the ways in which families can be helped to cope with these. Poverty, bad housing conditions and the threat of homelessness are still important factors why children have to be taken into the care of the community. Local authorities now have a duty under the Children's and Young Person's Act 1963 to try to prevent and forestall the suffering of children through neglect in their own homes. Also, there have been steps in recent years to deal with young offenders as deprived children. The arguments in favour of this move are based on the assumption that the child is the product of his home and not a totally responsible individual and in consequence punishment is an inappropriate response to his behaviour. Not everybody is prepared to accept that this is a valid assumption and many think it may be a reason for the increase in crime amongst young people during the last few years.

Child care legislation has moved a long way from the Poor Law and is now extensive and complex, but like all the public services the level of care must depend to some degree on the resources available.

Poor Law children's home built late 19th century within the curtilage of workhouse. Used as children's home until about 1960.

Play room in local authority children's home (former workhouse), 1957.

Dining-room in local authority children's home (former workhouse). 1957

The gates to the entrance of a local authority grouped cottage home. (1950)

One of the grouped cottage homes. (1950)

Dining-room in a former Poor Law children's home after improvement in the early 1950s.

Dormitory in local authority children's home after improvement in the 1950s.

Exterior of post-1945 local authority children's home. The exterior design is indistinguishable from other houses on the estate.

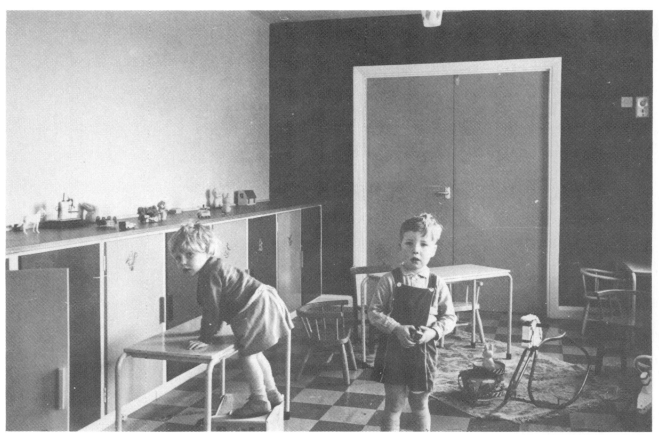

Play room in post-1945 local authority children's home.

Kitchen in post-1945 local authority children's home.

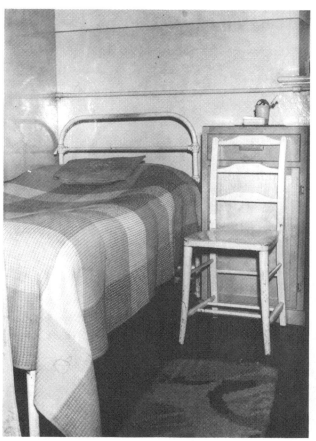

The rear of the post-1945 local authority children's home built on a new housing estate.

A cubicle for a senior girl in a school for deaf children.

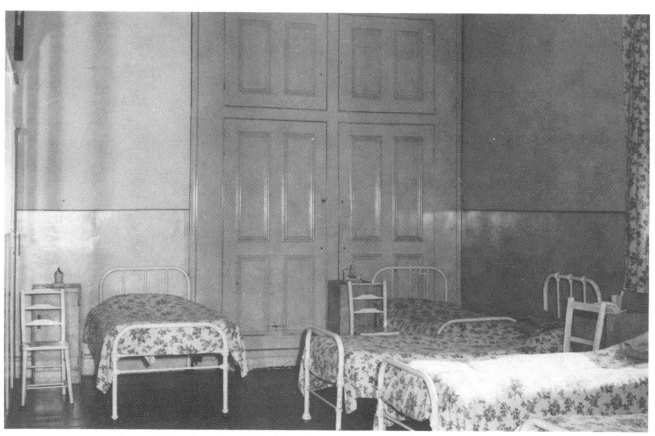

A dormitory in a school for deaf children run by a religious charity.

A Dr. Barnardo's home for ten children.

A Dr. Barnardo's home for twenty children.

250

A Dr. Barnardo's home for thirty-three children.

A Dr. Barnardo's post-1945 grouped cottage home.

A bedroom in a Dr. Barnardo's post-1945 cottage home.

The play room in a Dr. Barnardo's post-1945 cottage home.

Chapter 15

THE HOMELESS

It is difficult to find a practical definition of homelessness. There has been a suggestion by a charitable organisation that anyone who is inadequately housed, for example living in accommodation which is substandard because it lacks certain basic amenities such as a bath and hot-water service, is in fact homeless because such accommodation cannot be regarded as a real home. On this basis the inhabitants of several million dwellings in Britain, many of whom are owner-occupiers, would be regarded as homeless. It has also been said that the truly homeless in Britain are those who go to social security offices, local authority housing departments and voluntary organisations to seek shelter in temporary accommodation. Furthermore, there has been a suggestion that the real homeless are to be found only amongst those who sleep rough. An inference to be drawn from the last two suggestions is that a home need only be a place to sleep, but very few people would accept this concept of it. For accommodation to be regarded as a home the occupants must at least have the legal right to use it not only at night for sleeping, but also in the day-time for the usual activities of eating and the preparation and cooking of food and for personal washing, etc. In this chapter, therefore, people who do not have this minimum standard of accommodation, for example the residents of common lodging-houses, certain hostels and night shelters, etc., besides those that sleep rough, are regarded as being homeless.

However, there is a legal definition in Section 1 of the Housing (Homeless Persons) Act 1977 of two broad groups of people who local authorities are to regard as being homeless. These are:

1. People who have no legal access to accommodation of any kind because:
   (a) they have been evicted from rented accommodation through the courts,
   (b) a building society or other mortgagee has repossessed the property they were buying on a mortgage,
   (c) they have been turned out by friends or relatives with whom they have been staying,
   (d) they have been turned out of lodgings, a lodging-house or hostel or discharged from prison or hospital or any other institution,
   (e) they have lost their tied-accommodation by losing their job,
   (f) they are unlawful squatters.
2. People who have accommodation but are unable to use it because:
   (a) they have been illegally evicted,
   (b) they risk violence or threats of violence if they return to their home,
   (c) they have a mobile home, caravan or houseboat but nowhere to site it or moor it.

Before 1939 homelessness was not such a complex problem as it is today. In most towns both furnished and unfurnished rooms were available at relatively low rents because letting rooms was much more common, especially in the larger obsolete houses which existed in fairly big numbers in the inner areas of the larger towns, and sharing a house was more acceptable to the lower-paid worker than it is today. People evicted were usually able to find a room or rooms without a great deal of difficulty. There were also numerous lodging-houses throughout the country where for a small sum, perhaps about 4d, it was possible to obtain a bed for the night and facilities for cooking one's own food and for having a wash or even a bath. The term 'homeless' applied only to those people who slept rough or were accommodated in the casual wards attached to the workhouses.

The casual wards were usually very grim buildings containing cells, like a prison. The casual paupers, as the people who frequented these places were officially called, were generally regarded as being vagrants and wastrels who were little better than criminals. In the evening when a person was admitted to a casual ward he was given a meal, usually consisting of a pint of tea, a thick slice of bread, a pat of margarine and a lump of cheese. After the meal he would have a bath and be loaned a night shirt, or dress in the case of females, and then he would be locked up for the night in a cell. His clothes would be disinfected by steam during the night and returned to him in the morning. Families were divided, the adult males went to the male casual ward and the females to the female casual ward, whilst the children were placed in separate accommodation in the institution. For one day's compulsory work, which usually consisted of breaking a fixed quantity of stone or sawing wood, or in the case of females cleaning or laundry work, the casual pauper would receive a bed for two nights and food during his stay. On the morning of the third day he was freed to again seek work and a place to live, or, if unsuccessful, to travel, with his family if any, to the next casual ward. He was not allowed to leave his family behind in case he abandoned them and they became a charge on the rates of the area.

During the economic depression of the 1930s some of the people who used the casual wards were unemployed who in sheer desperation had left their homes to travel from place to place seeking work. On the night of 27 May 1932, when the economic depression was about at its worst, 16,911 people spent the night in casual wards in England and Wales. On the night of 1 September 1939, when everyone living in Britain was registered as part of the preparation for war and the employment situation had improved at least partially because of rearmament, there were only 7,227 people accommodated in casual wards in England and Wales.

In the 1939-45 war all men and women capable of work were on some form of National Service, either voluntarily or by conscription, so the casual wards slowly fell into disuse. The cells which had witnessed so much misery in times of peace, in war became silent and blanketed with dust.

Homelessness in times of war takes on a new perspective as homes are destroyed and people flee in anticipation of disaster. In these circumstances it is no longer regarded as a near crime or the result of fecklessness, but a condition requiring sympathetic understanding and the maximum of public help. In the immediate post-1945 period when all the social services were being extended it was natural, therefore, that the provisions for helping the homeless should be reviewed. In 1948 the National Assistance Act of that year made provision for the creation of the National Assistance Board. Section 17(1) of this Act laid upon the National Assistance Board the duty "to make provision whereby persons without a settled way of living may be influenced to lead more settled lives" and to "provide and maintain centres to be known as reception centres for the temporary board and lodging of such persons". Under Section 34 of the Ministry of Social Security Act 1966 responsibility for providing and maintaining reception centres passed to the Supplementary Benefits Commission on behalf of the Minister of Social Security, and the National Assistance Board was abolished.

'Persons without a settled way of living' was a new description for persons previously known as 'casuals', 'vagrants' or 'wayfarers', and 'reception centres' was a new term for the 'casual wards' of the former workhouses where the 'casual paupers' were accommodated before 1948. An important change made by the 1948 Act was to transfer executive responsibility from local authorities to the central Government, and influencing people to become settled into the community became a statutory duty.

Because of the many calls on the nation's resources in 1948 it was not possible to provide new buildings and the necessary equipment quickly, and the National Assistance Board had to make use of the existing casual wards, which were often attached to former workhouses and hospitals. Immediately prior to the transfer of the responsibility for caring for those leading an unsettled way of life from local authorities to the National Assistance Board there were about 290 casual wards in England and Wales but many of them were little used. For example, in July 1948 the number of persons accommodated nightly was on average only 1,384 and it was therefore decided that more than half the casual wards were not needed as reception centres and only 134 were retained. In Scotland in July 1948 there were eighty-one establishments, which on average accommodated seventy persons nightly.

This reduction in the number of reception centres was seen by the Board as a necessity to enable it to carry out the national policy of giving the maximum help towards the rehabilitation of those who led an unsettled way of life. Most of the former casual wards were like prisons, with their rows of cells which made them unsuitable for the task of encouraging the acceptance of training for resettlement. As a first step towards resettlement it was necessary to induce persons using the centres to stay there whilst employment was found for them, or whilst efforts were made to get them to accept a more settled way of life. This called for the replacement of the cells with dormitories and the provision of common rooms for recreation and in which residential care could be given. Also, provision was made for medical attention to be available if necessary. A resettlement programme also called for separate accommodation for the persons being 'resettled' so that the residents, as distinct from the casuals, could become accustomed to better surroundings and the behaviour expected from them in society. There were high hopes that with all the services available in the welfare state the need for reception centres would considerably diminish.

In 1948 the responsibility for providing temporary accommodation for homeless families as distinct from single people was placed on the larger local authorities, i.e. county councils and county borough councils. The latter were abolished in 1974 when local government was reorganised. In the early years after the end of the 1939-45 war homelessness was not expected to develop into a serious problem because the nation's social services had been considerably extended. What has happened since 1948 is examined in the remainder of this chapter under two principal headings – the single homeless and homeless families.

The single homeless
From 1948 until its demise in 1966 the National Assistance Board from time to time arranged censuses of persons using reception centres. During 1964 and 1965 concern was expressed by certain organisations and individuals about the apparently increasing problem of people who were rootless and drifters in society and in particular about those who slept rough or frequented lodging-houses and shelters. It was not a new problem but the public were becoming more sensitive to it. The National Assistance Board, which was due to carry out one of its surveys among users of

reception centres towards the end of 1965, agreed to extend the scope of this survey and obtain factual information about the scale of homelessness in the country. The difficulty of defining homelessness has already been discussed. For practical purposes, therefore, the survey was planned to cover all accommodation and places where experience suggested that unsettled persons could be found. This meant the survey had to cover the following people:

(i) persons sleeping rough,
(ii) persons using reception centres,
(iii) persons using lodging-houses, hostels and shelters,
(iv) persons seeking financial help from the National Assistance Board's offices when they were without accommodation.

Gypsies were excluded from the survey because although they lead unsettled lives they move around in their own accommodation in family groups.

The people sleeping rough were counted on one night, 6-7 December. This part of the survey covered about 2,800 sites spread throughout England, Wales and Scotland out of a list of about 3,000 sites compiled from information supplied by social workers, voluntary organisations, the police and British Transport police as well as from information from the local offices of the National Assistance Board. It was the first nationwide count of its kind. That winter night nearly a thousand people (965 persons), mostly men, were found sleeping out. It was impracticable to visit the remainder of the 3,000 listed sites because some were too isolated, others were used only very infrequently and some were no longer in existence, for example buildings which had been demolished. It was not claimed that every person sleeping out that night was counted so the figure of 965 was regarded as an indication of the size of the problem rather than an exact number.

The sites surveyed differed greatly in extent, for example from whole streets of derelict houses to single huts in gardens or at road works. On the majority of sites people were found in groups and only 282 persons out of the total of 965 found sleeping rough that night were alone. Sixty-three was the largest number of people on any one site. Derelict buildings were the most favoured sites, no doubt because they offered reasonable shelter from the weather, and afforded opportunities for lighting fires for warmth and a considerably reduced risk of disturbance by the police. Also, until demolition commenced they provided a base to which to return each night and even in the daytime if the weather was bad.

23 per cent of those sleeping rough were found in derelict buildings and another 22 per cent were found on railway property, i.e. in stations, sidings and coaches in sidings. The warmth to be found in brickworks attracted 9 per cent of those sleeping out. Buildings which were unoccupied but not derelict were used by $7\frac{1}{2}$ per cent, whilst just over 5 per cent spent the night with little or no shelter in streets or squares. Farm buildings were the obvious choice in rural areas, and 4 per cent were found there. Public

shelters, public lavatories, building sites and huts in gardens and at road works, etc., were each used by 3 per cent of those sleeping rough. Church premises, i.e. porches, crypts and burial grounds, and all-night cafes accommodated about 2 per cent. The remainder were found in bus shelters, under bridges, on the banks of rivers and canals, and in tents, school boiler-houses and in old cars and vans.

In addition to the people sleeping rough, there were 1,232 people accommodated in reception centres spread throughout the country, most of whom could be regarded as being homeless. This shows little change since July 1948, when on average 1,384 people were accommodated nightly in the former casual wards, but a big reduction from the 7,227 accommodated on 1 September 1939. The count of people in lodging-houses, hostels and night shelters was made on the night of 27-28 October 1965. On that night 29,475 people occupied beds in 567 lodging-houses or similar establishments scattered throughout the country.

In the last quarter of 1965 there were therefore about 32,000 homeless single people in Britain out of a total population of about fifty-five million. Since then the number must have increased considerably as in 1972 the Department of Health and Social Security issued a circular (37/72) to local authorities in which attention was drawn to the rapid increase in single homelessness and the authorities were asked to experiment with a variety of small units of accommodation in their areas. The circular also stressed the need for supportive social work. The number of homeless single people in Britain in 1980 is not known.

The single homeless do not originate from one social class nor can they be placed in a single category, except that they are homeless. Of the 920 men found sleeping rough on 6 December 1965, about 40 per cent said they were working and another 27 per cent, although not working, had an income. Only 14 per cent of the men were aged under 30, and 68 per cent were over 60.

A survey carried out in 1972 of single homeless people living in hostels and lodging-houses found that 50 per cent of the men of working age were in employment and that 33 per cent of all residents had been staying in the same hostel, etc., for at least two years and could not therefore be regarded as migrants. The survey also found that 47 per cent of the residents had been living in some sort of hostel or lodging-house for at least ten years but half of them said they would prefer to be living elsewhere, e.g. in a bed-sit or a flat, where they would have greater privacy and independence.

The picture from the 1972 survey of the single homeless who live in lodging-houses and hostels does not vary a great deal from that obtained from the 1965 National Assistance Board survey of similar establishments. For example, in the 1965 survey 40 per cent of the men under 60 were unemployed against 50 per cent of the men of working age in 1972. 59 per cent of the men in the 1965 survey had been living in lodging-houses for five years or more whilst 47 per cent in 1972 had been living in hostels or lodging-houses for at least ten years.

On the night of 6-7 December 1965 when the National Assistance Board carried out its count of reception centre users, 14 per cent of the men were aged under 30, 53 per cent were aged between 40 and 60, and almost 14 per cent were aged over 60. About 80 per cent of the men were unemployed and most of those in employment had unskilled occupations as labourers, kitchen porters or casual workers. Some men had been placed in employment while at the centre, and would remain there until they were ready to settle down in other accommodation. 21 per cent of the men were judged by interviewing officers to be either physically or mentally handicapped, or both. However, a Government-commissioned survey in 1972 of the people who used the Camberwell reception centre in London found that 85 per cent of the casuals and 94 per cent of the residents there either had a physical disability or had at some time required psychiatric help, and that 19 per cent of the 400 men were elderly and in need of accommodation where proper care and assistance would be given.

Some of the men who use reception centres are verminous when they arrive and a few are so filthy that their underwear has to be destroyed. Some are alcoholics. These groups account for perhaps 20 per cent of reception centre users and create special problems for their staffs. A few of the reception centre users are seeking work and in the meanwhile have nowhere to live and have to resort to the centres or sleep rough.

The number of women who lead unsettled lives is relatively small. Of the forty-five found sleeping rough in the 1965 survey ten were over 50 years of age. Five women were working, and twelve who were not working said they had an income. About 500 (29 per cent) of the women using lodging-houses, etc., were under 40 years of age; 600 (32 per cent) were between 40 and 60; and about 700 to 800 (39 per cent) were aged 60 or over. Over half the women had been living in lodging-houses for two years or more; about 750 (over 40 per cent) had been doing so for five years or more. About another 750 had been living in them for less than two years. Rather more than half the women were unemployed and about 32 per cent had been continually employed for six months or more. There are few reception centres which accommodate women and it seemed at the time of the 1965 survey that for the majority of women a stay in a centre was for a short period, a once-in-their-lives experience. The women in the reception centres tended to be younger than the men. During the census period in 1965 on average thirty women were accommodated in the centres each night. 39 per cent were under 30 and only 22 per cent were 50 or more. 36 per cent of the women were in work and about 25 per cent were thought to be unemployable because of their physical or mental condition or because of age.

Any investigation into the causes of homelessness has to rely largely on information given by the people themselves. Unfortunately few homeless people are willing to disclose their true life stories, although many are willing to talk freely to explain their predicament. The reasons they offer, sincerely or otherwise, are often a long way from the truth but frequently there is an awareness of failure. Some of the single homeless have histories which they wish to forget or hide. An individual may decide to sever his or her connections with society and become anonymous to escape documentation and questioning which is likely to resurrect some hurtful or shameful incident. Many wish that their pasts could be cremated but as this is not possible they have buried them and do not wish them to be exhumed. The best information available on the causes of single homelessness is still that obtained from the 1965 National Assistance Board's survey, even though it is dated.

Disintegration of the family because of the death of a parent or because of the drifting away of children or the break-up of a marriage was a factor which was commonly given for being homeless. For example, amongst those sleeping rough on the night of 6-7 December 1965 were a significant number of middle-aged men who went to pieces after the death of their mother, with whom they had lived. 60 per cent of the men sleeping rough that night had either no living relatives or had lost touch with any they had. Chronic alcoholism was a significant factor, so was mental abnormality or illness. About 30 per cent said they slept rough because they were enuretics, alcoholics or drug addicts. Rarely, however, do these problems exist singly. Incontinence, for example, might follow an alcoholic bout. On the other hand, it might be due to age or to some physical defect and the person might be a life enuretic.

The main reason given by those living in lodging-houses and hostels, etc., in the 1965 survey was a breakdown in relationships. About 33 per cent said they had started living in lodging-houses after they had left home because of a disagreement with, or through the death of, a wife, parent or some other relative. About 8 per cent had never experienced a normal home life because all, or most, of their childhood had been spent in a public assistance, Poor Law or similar institution. These people had become completely institutionalised. About 19 per cent were living in lodging-houses and hostels because they had been evicted from their previous accommodation and felt more secure in a lodging-house from the possibility of another eviction.

From the 1965 National Assistance Board's survey it would seem that reception centre users can to a large extent be divided into those who have suffered a breakdown in their personal lives before they leave home and those who without such a breakdown leave their homes to seek work and for various reasons drift into an unsettled existence. Drink was given as the cause of their homelessness by 14.8 per cent of the men using reception centres on 7 December 1965, and most of these were middle-aged. Being turned out by their family or relatives, or the death of a wife, parent or other relative was given as the cause by another 28 per cent. The sad story of never having a proper family relationship because they had been brought up by foster-parents or in workhouses or other institutions was given by 8 per cent. Although 60 per cent of the men had at some time been in prison, only 8 per cent gave it as a reason for leading an unsettled way of life. Another 8 per cent gave discharge from the Army as a reason for their homeless state.

Social isolation was an important cause of homelessness among women in 1965. 40 per cent of the women interviewed in lodging-houses and hostels had no living relative or had lost touch with any they had. Age and unemployment were also common factors and 10 per cent of the homeless women were physically handicapped.

In spite of the reasons for their homeless state given by the people themselves it would be misleading to place the single homeless in categories according to a single cause, because like all human beings they have many-sided characters and more than one problem. Some are old, others young; some employed, others unemployable. A proportion are physically or mentally ill. Many have criminal records, others (a very small proportion) have contracted out of the acquisitive society. There are alcoholics, drug addicts, enuretics and homosexuals amongst them. A proportion would welcome help but some seek anonymity.

One of the most serious aspects of single homelessness since 1965 has been the number of young people who travel each year to London with high expectations of fulfilling their dreams of a well-paid job, a flat of their own and a social life among the bright lights. Often they have made no plans but walked out with little money after quarrelling with their parents. What money they have is gone after paying for a night or two in a cheap hotel and for food. In these circumstances London becomes a frightening and an inhospitable place. Alone, they begin to sleep rough. A few find their way to reception centres, others to the night shelters run by voluntary organisations, where advice can be offered but not always accepted. Another aspect of single homelessness which has developed during the last three or four years is the movement of refugees from the serious shrinkage in the economic activity of the north and the midlands, to the south, with the hope that they might find employment. A high proportion of the refugees are skilled workers who have left their homes and families behind to seek work. Many of them prefer to sleep rough rather than suffer the indignities that go with a bed in a reception centre or in a hostel run by a charitable organisation or in a lodging-house where the bedding is likely to be filthy and perhaps verminous.

Some of the factors which have contributed to the increase in the number of the single homeless during the last few years are: (1) slum clearance and redevelopment which in many towns has led to the demise or a big reduction in the number of lodging-houses and a large drop in the number of houses where rooms are let off; (2) increased rents for accommodation available at short notice; (3) an increase in unemployment.

The accommodation legally available and most likely to be within the means of the single homeless is: common lodging-houses, hostels, cheap hotels, night shelters and reception centres.

A common lodging-house in England and Wales is defined in the Public Health Act 1936 as "A house (other than a public assistance institution) provided for the purpose of accommodating by night poor persons, not being members of the same family, who resort thereto and are allowed to occupy one common room for the purpose of sleeping or eating, and includes, where only part of a house is so used, the part so used". In Scotland it is defined in the Public Health (Scotland) Act 1897 as "A house, or part thereof, where lodgers are housed at an amount not exceeding 4d a night, or such other sums as shall be fixed under the provisions of the Act for each person, whether the amount be payable nightly or weekly or for any period not longer than a fortnight, and shall include any place where immigrants are lodged and all boarding-houses for seamen irrespective of the rate charged for lodging or boarding".

Every keeper of a common lodging-house has to be registered with the local authority and the authority has the power to fix the maximum number of persons who may sleep on the premises on any night and can lay down conditions in bye-laws regarding lighting, ventilation and the cleanliness, etc., of the lodging-houses in its area.

Because of the vast social changes which have taken place since 1945 and the difficulty of deciding which premises fall strictly within the definition of a common lodging-house, e.g. what is a poor person?, the law relating to their control has largely fallen into disuse. The number on the registers of local authorities at the present time therefore does not give an accurate indication of how many there are. During the 1930s there were somewhere between 20,000 and 50,000 registered common lodging-houses in England and Wales alone but by 1965 the number in the whole of Britain had fallen to 251.

Common lodging-houses vary a great deal in the numbers of people they can accommodate. The 1965 National Assistance Board survey found that the majority of them (about 80 per cent) provided accommodation for men only, that 8 per cent provided accommodation only for women and the remaining 12 per cent for both sexes. The largest can accommodate several hundred people at any one time and the smallest have less than twenty beds. Most of the smaller registered common lodging-houses, i.e. those catering for twenty people or less, are run by private owners on a commercial basis, but these are fast disappearing as the owners die or retire. The larger registered common lodging-houses are run mainly by local authorities, the Salvation Army, the Church Army and other voluntary organisations. The common lodging-houses exclusively for women are generally smaller than those for men.

In 1965 about half of the common lodging-houses

provided beds only in dormitories, and in less than 10 per cent were the beds all in separate rooms or cubicles. The remainder provided beds both in separate rooms and in dormitories. The condition of the sleeping accommodation, whether dormitories or cubicles, varies from lodging-house to lodging-house, as does the state of the beds.

Local authority bye-laws usually fix the maximum number of beds which can be placed in any room on the basis of forty square feet of floor space per person but it is not uncommon for the standard to be disregarded, especially where bunk beds are used. In the large dormitories there may be as many as a hundred or more beds, sometimes symetrically arranged like parking spaces in a covered car park or cattle pens in a lairage. Even in the better run establishments it is the usual practice to change the bed linen only once per week, so more than one person may sleep between the same sheets during that time, giving rise to a serious risk of the transmission of vermin and contagious diseases. Enuretics create special problems in this respect and if known will not be admitted to many lodging-houses. In some lodging-houses the bedding is not only very dirty but insufficient so that in cold weather the lodgers sleep in most of their clothes or pile coats, etc., on top of the beds. Alcoholics can cause serious nuisances not only by fighting but also by urinating on floors, especially of passages and staircase landings. The W.C.s and washhand basins provided for the lodgers are often insufficient in number and in a bad state.

In the larger lodging-houses efforts are usually made to enforce certain necessary rules, and because of the type of clientele staff cannot afford to be too gentle. On the other hand, in those run by voluntary organisations, such as those of the Salvation Army, the staff want to help towards rehabilitation and to give advice.

In the smaller lodging-houses, especially those run by a family, discipline is less strict because efforts are often made to create a homely atmosphere, even if this means a less hygienic one. If a lodger is ill the keeper's wife will often try to nurse him. However, in spite of this apparent intimacy there is a tradition amongst the private lodging-house keepers that a person's history is his own affair and they are proud of the fact that they keep no records of their lodgers other than those strictly required by law. This old type of common lodging-house keeper is rapidly becoming extinct.

A small proportion of lodging-houses, perhaps 25 per cent, provide no meals but they do provide facilities to enable the lodgers to cook their own food. In some of the older lodging-houses these facilities consist of a large solid-fuel cooking range in a big kitchen-cum-living room which makes a warm general-purposes room for the lodgers. However, because of the steep rise in the cost of solid fuel during the last few years this type of facility is becoming less and less available. In others there is a small kitchen, which may be a cellar, containing a small grate which provides a means for cooking and heating the room.

The common lodging-houses for women differ in many respects from those for men. They are usually more homely and maintained to a higher standard.

In a minority of lodging-houses an inclusive charge is made for bed and breakfast, whilst in others, although the nightly charge is for a bed only, there are canteens where meals can be purchased.

The charges per night for a bed have changed over the years and vary from place to place. In 1956 the nightly charge varied from 5p to 28p, and in 1965 it varied between 10p and 40p. By 1977-78 the average charge had risen to £1.50.

Most of what are called 'hostels' are really registered or unregistered common lodging-houses. Those run by religious organisations, such as the Salvation Army and the Church Army, are usually registered with the local authority and conform to its requirements; many of the others fall well below these standards, partially because they are not registered as common lodging-houses. Whether an establishment is called a hostel or a lodging-house usually makes no difference to the standard of accommodation and facilities it provides.

In addition to the lodging-houses and hostels there are the night shelters run by religious and other voluntary organisations. These are to be found predominantly in the large towns, e.g. Birmingham, Liverpool, London and Manchester. They are characterised by the basic level of the amenities they are able to offer but they do provide a shelter and food without charge and are often preferred to the reception centres by those in extreme poverty. The facilities provided in them vary, for example from a space on the floor with a blanket for cover to a bed in a room shared by five or six other homeless people. The buildings themselves vary from former mansions in decaying parts of a town to disused factories and church crypts.

There are twenty-three Government reception and resettlement centres in Britain, of which eight are in London. The others are spread over the country but are fairly close to heavily populated areas such as Liverpool and Manchester. They provide in total about 2,500 beds but three-fifths of these are in London, where the need is greatest. The cost of running these centres is about £5 million per year. Some of the centres are former workhouses, the others have various histories, for example one was a wartime miners' hostel and another was a wartime anti-aircraft gun site.

The purpose of the reception centres is to provide temporary board and lodgings for persons without a settled way of life and to try to influence them to lead a more settled life. The cells which were a feature of the old Poor Law casual wards have been replaced by dormitories, some small, some large – large enough in a minority of cases to hold about 150 beds. Because of the mixed clientele the precaution has been taken of covering the mattresses with a waterproof material. The dormitories are denuded of all unnecessary furniture so that they can be readily cleaned. The previous Poor Law requirement of a compulsory bath and the steam sterilising of each person's clothing has been replaced by a demand to take a shower and submit clothing to be examined for vermin. The old system of sterilising clothing with steam was less embarrassing both for the homeless person and the staff than the present one, and an individual cell ensured privacy and more peace than is obtainable in a dormitory.

Conditions in the reception centres are far from ideal and some people may regard them as being appalling. However, although they could be improved it is difficult to find alternative ways of dealing with those single homeless people who are the derelicts of society.

Homeless families

Besides homeless single people there are also homeless families. Nationally, statistics in relation to homeless families were compiled by the Department of Health and Social Security until 1974 but the task was then taken over by the Department of the Environment. In 1976, according to the DOE over 50,000 families became homeless in England alone and this meant that family homelessness had doubled over the previous five years. In 1979 the figure fell to 40,400 and local authorities accepted responsibility for providing accommodation for 28,500 of these families.

Marital breakdown, landlord/tenant disputes and bad management of the family's affairs are common causes of family homelessness, but these are not problems confined to those who become homeless. What distinguishes the families who become homeless is their inability to overcome the difficulties because of their economic or social vulnerability. Two-thirds of the families in accommodation provided by local authorities for homeless families at the end of 1965 gave eviction from previous accommodation as the cause of their homelessness, but with so many legal safeguards for tenants and other legal occupiers eviction is not easy to achieve. The reasons given for eviction were varied, but rent or mortgage payment arrears were the most common. In 1979 the main reasons given for family homelessness were: because relatives or friends were no longer able or willing to accommodate them (40 per cent); because of a court order or because they were unable to pay rent or mortgage, etc. (20 per cent); marital dispute (17 per cent); because they had to leave unprotected accommodation (7 per cent); loss of service tenancy (5 per cent); eviction from illegal letting (2 per cent); other, e.g. because of fire, flood or storm, or movement to new area (9 per cent).

In the large towns the majority of the homeless come from furnished accommodation and they are predominantly young families in the early stages of bringing up their children. The incomes of these families are often well below average.

The demolition of older housing and a reduction in the supply of furnished and unfurnished privately rented accommodation have contributed to homelessness amongst families. Another contributory factor is the steep rise in rents for accommodation available at short notice. Single-parent families often have

complex problems and one of the main ones is obtaining suitably priced accommodation. A report of the National Council for One-Parent Families states that in 1975 there were 650,000 lone parents looking after a million children. In November 1974 about 40 per cent of them were claiming supplementary benefit, which means they were on the poverty line. This no doubt is a contributory factor in the increase in homeless amongst them.

Until 1977 when a family had nowhere to live and the local housing departments could not offer it accommodation the legal responsibility for providing temporary accommodation for the homeless family fell on the social services departments of the larger local authorities, i.e. county councils, and until local government was recognised in 1974 also county borough councils. When this duty was placed on these authorities in 1948 instead of on the housing authority, it was apparently not anticipated that the problem would become as big and as complex as it has become today. With ambitious house-building programmes, rent control and a wide range of social services available it was probably thought that all that was necessary was a small amount of temporary accommodation to meet the needs of urgent cases. In other words it was seen as a welfare and not a housing function.

In 1948 the resources were not available for the building of specially designed accommodation for homeless families and in consequence local authorities had to make do with whatever buildings they had. In most cases this meant using former workhouses, parts of old hospitals, former children's homes, Army barracks and even disused police stations, etc. In all cases some modification was necessary. For example, former workhouse and hospital wards had to be divided into separate units each with its own sink and cooking facilities, but usually W.C.s and baths had to be shared by two or more families. In some areas the demand by homeless families for temporary accommodation was far greater than was expected and then the only privacy available to them was in the bedrooms because dining-rooms and cooking facilities had to be shared.

In 1966 a Government circular (MHLG 20/66 Homeless Families) recommended to local authorities that their primary aim should be to keep families together. It discouraged the use of shared accommodation and asked local authorities to try to make their temporary accommodation self-contained. However, the Government recognised certain problems, including the types of temporary accommodation then available, and gave guidance on minimum standards.

Firstly, it recognised that emergency centres providing immediate 'overnight' shelter for families might have to be communal, with fairly basic furnishings. Secondly, short-term reception centres, mainly in cities, should be used only for short periods. Conditions would be basic, but the accommodation should be flexible enough to allow privacy for parents and older children. Thirdly, the main type of temporary accommodation, i.e. family units, should have standards nearer to those of ordinary housing. Self-contained should be the ideal. If hostels and older houses were used they should not have more than nine families. Fourthly, guidance was given on the standards of rehabilitation units for families in need of social work support and help to learn to manage their affairs before moving into ordinary housing. In 1974 the Government reaffirmed much of what it had said in 1966 but in addition it advised local authorities to use short-life properties, i.e. dwellings awaiting either rehabilitation or demolition.

In spite of the preparations made by local authorities for helping the homeless families in some areas, especially London and other big cities, the demand for emergency accommodation exceeded the amount available. In consequence, many local authorities were forced to put some homeless families into bed and breakfast accommodation in cheap hotels at the expense of the ratepayers. The national cost of housing homeless families in this way has been estimated at somewhere between M£4 and M£6 per year. The conditions in many of these cheap hotels in the big cities leave much to be desired but very few hotels are prepared to take in families off the street and especially at very short notice. The alternative is for the children to be taken into the care of the local authority; the number of those that were because of homelessness almost doubled during 1965-70.

During 1967-68 squatting began to develop as a quasi-political campaign to focus public attention on the plight of the homeless, and to force local authorities, especially in the big cities, and in London in particular, to allow homeless families to use the great number of publicly owned houses which were lying empty. In some cases there were streets and even areas of housing capable of providing at least a reasonable shelter, which had been purchased by the local authority well ahead of proposed redevelopment and which had been lying empty for a number of years.

At first the progress of the squatting movement was slow and responsible. Official squatting groups were formed and these entered into legal agreements with local authorities, by which, in return for rent-free use of the empty houses, the squatters undertook to carry out essential repairs, to pay rates and for electricity and gas, and to vacate the premises when demolition or rehabilitation work was about to begin. This type of squatting attracted a great deal of public sympathy. By 1973, however, some of the squatting, especially in London, seemed to be motivated towards creating a confrontation with authority rather than having predominantly the purpose of obtaining shelter for homeless people. On occasion, with this type of squatting homes were entered when the legal occupiers were absent. Also there were isolated cases of squatters moving into newly decorated homes that had already been allocated to families on the council's waiting lists. In addition, there were reports of wanton damage to dwellings, drug taking and sex orgies in some of the squats. This behaviour turned public opinion against the squatters, and there were demands for changes in the law to prevent illegal squatting and to facilitate repossession when it did occur. In 1974 the Law Commission published an interim report in which it recommended that squatting should be made a criminal offence instead of a matter for civil law. However, there has been opposition to this suggestion.

In 1975-76 it was estimated that there were 30,000 squatters in England and Wales and that 25,000 of them were in London. Nearly all were in publicly owned property.

Since 1948 family homelessness has been on the increase and over the years it became obvious to the Government that the social services departments of local authorities did not have the resources, in the form of proper accommodation, to deal satisfactorily with the problem and that it was predominantly a housing problem. In consequence the Housing (Homeless Persons) Act 1977 became law in England and Wales on 1 December 1977 and in Scotland on 1 April 1978. Under this Act local housing authorities have a duty to assist people who are "homeless or threatened with homelessness".

The definition of 'homelessness' in the Act has been given earlier in this chapter. The Act requires local authorities to offer housing to homeless people only if they have priority of need as defined in the Act. Those homeless people who do not fall into the 'priority need' categories are entitled only to advice and assistance from the local authority to enable them to obtain accommodation independently. Furthermore, even if a person is in priority need the council need not offer accommodation if they are satisfied that he is intentionally homeless, e.g. because of a deliberate act or a deliberate failure to act, and that he was fully aware when he acted or failed to act of all relevant facts, for example the possibility of obtaining help, particularly financial help from social security, housing department or building society. However, neither 'battered women' nor pregnant women are to be considered as intentionally homeless nor are those people who are incapable of managing their affairs on account of old age or mental illness. The local authority can also inquire whether or not a homeless person has a local connection in the area. This is to prevent people from deciding they would like to move to a more desirable area of the country and simply presenting themselves as homeless in that area and demanding housing there.

Homelessness in Britain has not, over the years, decreased as it was anticipated it would do in the early post-war years. The homeless, whether single people or families, include a disproportionate number of people classifiable as personally inadequate, socially incompetent, recalcitrant tenants and problem families but with many the pattern of their behaviour is the result of homelessness rather than the cause. They are all in need of help and a failure to give it could have serious consequences for society. For break up of some of the families and the scattering of the children, some of whom would become delinquents with children of their own also becoming delinquents, and lead to an increase in the number of children who have to be taken into care. In the long run society gains by giving the necessary support to homeless families, provided the support given does not encourage complete family irresponsibility.

For the single homeless various types of smaller hostels are required to cater for different categories of homeless people, e.g. those seeking work, the mentally and the physically disabled, and the old. In the end, however, there remains the problem of conflicting demands on limited resources.

A home under a tarpaulin tent. (1956)

The inside of the tarpaulin tent.

Rows of cells in a public assistance institution (former workhouse) used for accommodating the homeless. This particular accommodation fell into disuse during the 1939-45 war.

A homeless itinerant.

The front of a former workhouse. The single-storey building on the right contained the cells for accommodating casual paupers. After 1948 the cells were improved to accommodate the homeless and this part of the institution became a reception centre.

263

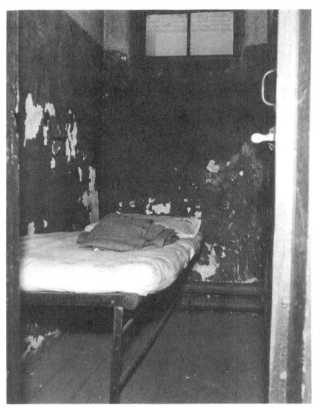

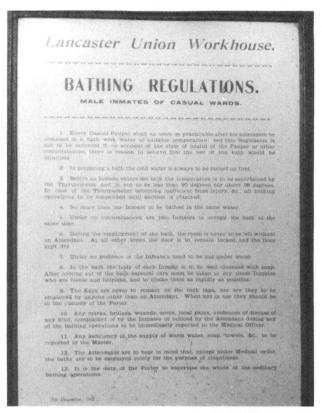

Inside one of the cells after nearly twenty years of disuse.
(1958)

Instructions for bathing casual paupers which were in operation at the end of the 1939-45 war.

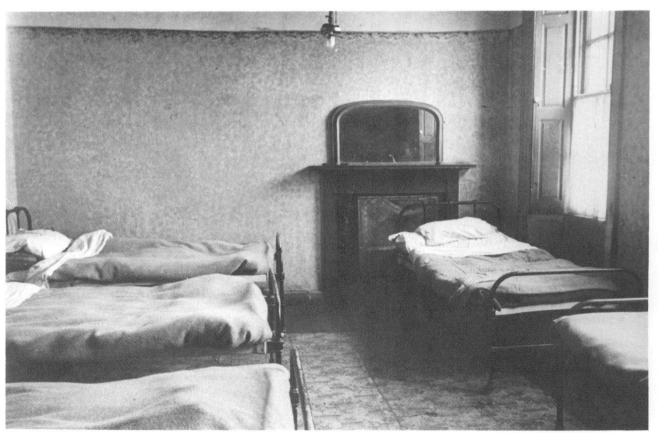

A dormitory in a higher class common lodging-house, described as a hotel.

The inside of a cell in a reception centre (1958). The occupants were no longer locked up for the night. Some, like this man, were travelling from place to place seeking work.

Cells in a reception centre (former workhouse) for the homeless and itinerant poor. (1955)

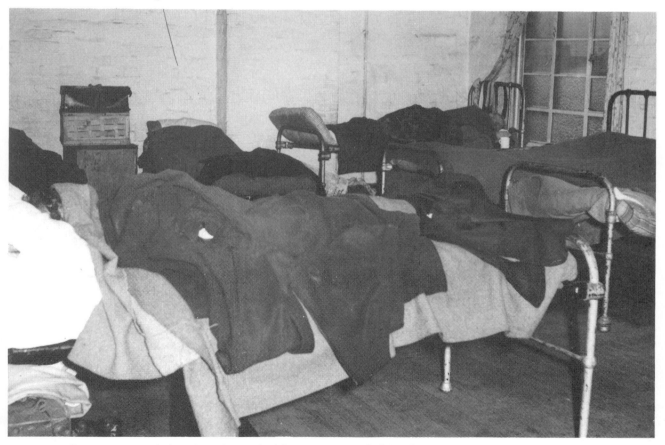

A dormitory in a privately run common lodging-house. (1960s)

A lodging-house signboard.

A small privately run common lodging-house.
(Transport house)

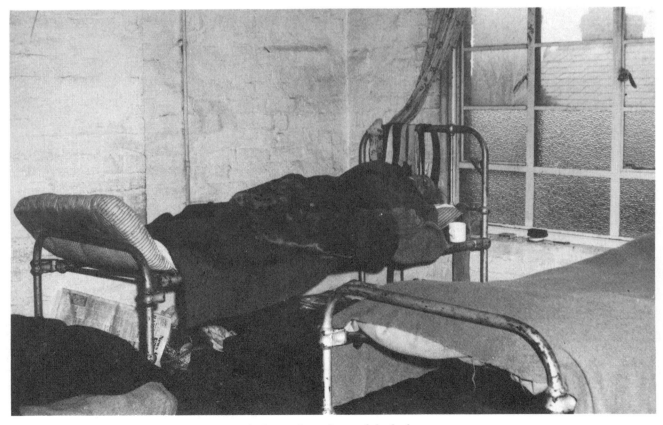

A closer view of one of the beds.

266

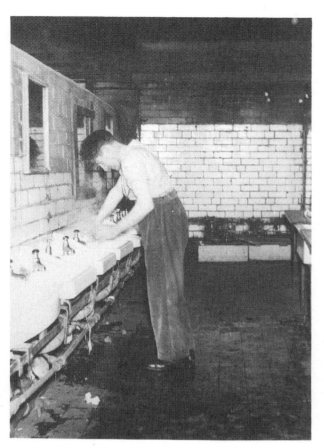

The ablutions in a large common lodging-house.

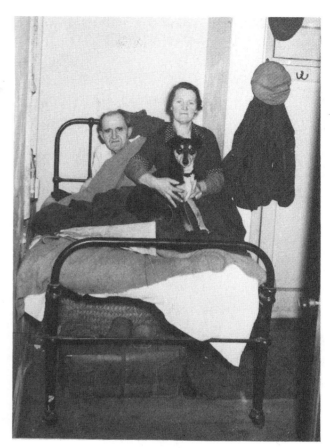

The keeper of a common lodging-house acts as a nurse.

The cooking range in a large common lodging-house. (1960s)

Time for a talk.

A rarity – a sitting-room in a mens' common lodging-house. (1960s)

The cooking range in a common lodging-house for women.

The dining-room in a common lodging-house for women.

A few religious and charitable organisations provide hostels for the homeless.

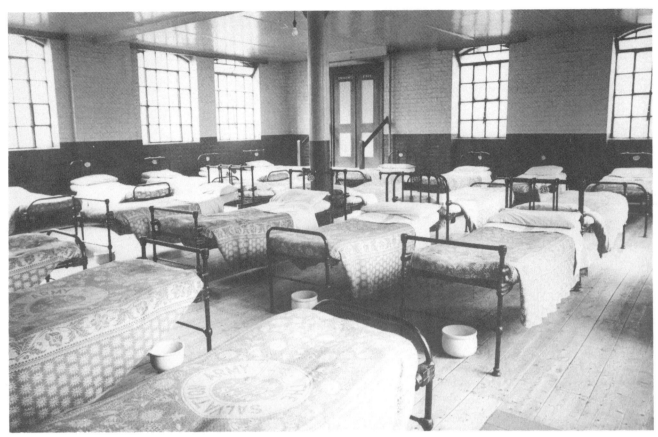

A dormitory in a Salvation Army hostel. Each bed is numbered.

A dormitory in a hostel provided by another charitable organisation.

The dayroom in a common lodging-house for women. (1960s)

A cubicle in a charity hostel.

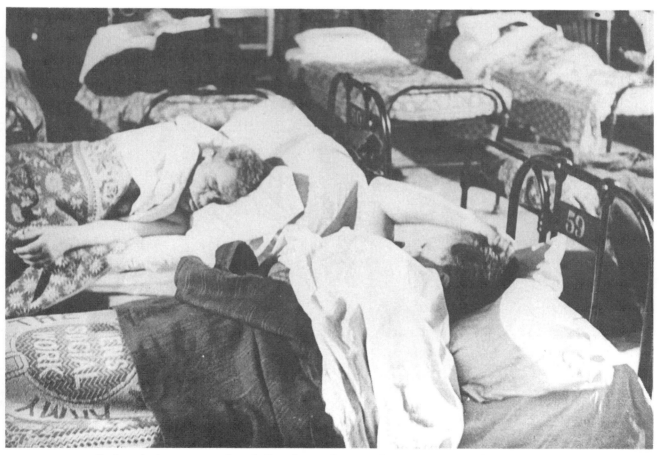

Early to bed may mean sleep before the snoring, coughing, groaning, and screaming begins.

271

The dayroom in a charity hostel.

Companionship at the table.

272

Nearing the end of the road.

A free night shelter run by a voluntary organisation.

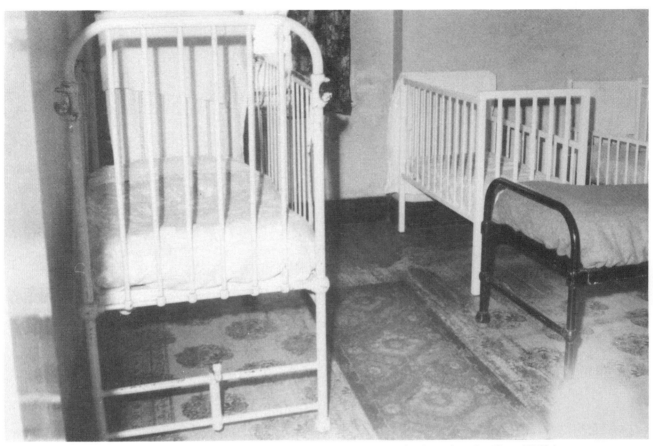

Bedroom for mother and children in local authority unit for homeless families. (1960s)

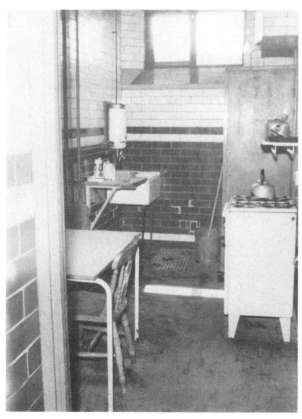

Cell in former police station converted into kitchen in a unit for homeless families. (1956)

Another living room in basic accommodation provided for homeless families. (1956)

Inside the night shelter.

Former Poor Law children's home used for accommodating homeless families. (1960s)

BIBLIOGRAPHY

Listed below are the published sources most often used in the preparation of *The Homes and Homeless of Post-War Britain*.

Bonham-Carter, Victor, *The English Village,* 1955
Bournville Village Trust, *Bournville Village Trust,* 1900-1955
Calvocoressi, Peter, *The British Experience* 1945-75
Cullingworth, J. B., *Housing in Transition*
Donnison, D. V., *The Government of Housing,* 1966
Jones, Emrys, *Towns and Cities,* 1970
Merseyside Socialist Research Group, *Merseyside in Crisis*
Smith, Mary E. N., *Guide to Housing,* 1977
Swift, Stewart and Shaw, Frederick, *Housing Administration* 1958
Townsend, Peter, *Family Life of Old People,* 1957
H.M.S.O., *History of The Second World War. Studies in the Social Services,* 1954
H.M.S.O., *Homeless Single Persons,* 1966
H.M.S.O., *Housing Manuals* of 1944, 1949, 1952
H.M.S.O., *Manual of Unfit Housing,* 1919
H.M.S.O., *Our Older Homes; a Call for Action,* 1966
H.M.S.O., *Report of the Care of Children Committee,* 1946
H.M.S.O., *Rural Housing— Report of Rural Housing Sub-Committee of Central Housing Advisory Committee,* 1944

ACKNOWLEDGEMENTS

The Author expresses his thanks to the following for supplying certain specific information:

Bournville Village Trust, The Commission for Racial Equality, The Federation of Alms Houses, Merseyside Improved Housing Association, Nationwide Building Society, and Uni-Lever Merseyside Ltd. Port Sunlight Estate. The Author also acknowledges the help given from the following who supplied photographs and gave permission for their reproduction in the book.

Barratt Urban Renewal (Northern) Ltd. (page 167, page 168 T.L. and Bottom); Birmingham City Council, (page 185 B.L., page 232 T.); Bournville Village Trust, (pages 144, 145, 146, 147, 148, 149, 150, 151 B); British Travel and Holiday Association, (page 26 T); Central Lancashire Development Corporation, (page 131B, page 132, page 133); Central Office of Information, (page 41 T, page 234 T); City of Sheffield Architects Department, (page 30, page 114); Concrete Ltd., (page 117 B); Cwmbran Development Corporation, (page 124 B, page 126 T.R.); Dr. Barnardo's Homes, (page 250, page 251, page 252); Greater London Council, (page 9 T, page 117 T.L.); John Laing and Son Ltd., (page 111 T); Liverpool City Council, (page 99 T, page 100, page 103 T); Milton Keynes Development Corporation, (page 128 B, page 129, page 130, page 131 T); National Trust, (page 128 B, page 129, page 130, page 131 T); Norfolk Reed Thatchers, (page 54 B); North West Gas Board, (page 165); Radio Times Hulton Picture Library, (page 8, page 11 T, page 185 T.L., page 202 B, page 211 B); Salvation Army, (page 229, page 230, page 269 B, page 270 T); Scottish Special Housing Association, (page 152, page 153); Stannah Lifts, (page 237 B.R.); Waites Ltd. Builders, (page 84 T.R., page 121 T); Warrington and Runcorn Development Corporation, (page 126 T.L. and B., page 127, page 128 T); George Wimpey & Co. Ltd., (page 81, page 82 B, page 84 T.L., page 88 B, page 109 T, page 113 B).

INDEX